*Sy* **◢** *1dicate* Women

The publisher and the University of California Press
Foundation gratefully acknowledge the generous support
of the Richard and Harriett Gold Endowment Fund in
Arts and Humanities.

# Syndicate Women

*Gender and Networks in Chicago Organized Crime*

CHRIS M. SMITH

University of California Press

University of California Press, one of the most distinguished university presses in the United States, enriches lives around the world by advancing scholarship in the humanities, social sciences, and natural sciences. Its activities are supported by the UC Press Foundation and by philanthropic contributions from individuals and institutions. For more information, visit www.ucpress.edu.

University of California Press
Oakland, California

Library of Congress Cataloging-in-Publication Data

Names: Smith, Chris M., author.
Title: Syndicate women : gender and networks in Chicago organized crime / Chris M. Smith.
Description: Oakland, California : University of California Press, [2019] | Includes bibliographical references and index. |
Identifiers: LCCN 2018057020 (print) | LCCN 2018059706 (ebook) | ISBN 9780520972001 (e-book) | ISBN 9780520300750 (cloth : alk. paper) | ISBN 9780520300767 (pbk : alk. paper)
Subjects: LCSH: Organized crime—Illinois—Chicago—20th century. | Female offenders—Illinois—Chicago—20th century.
Classification: LCC HV6795.C4 (ebook) | LCC HV6795.C4 S65 2019 (print) | DDC 364.106082/0977311—dc23
LC record available at https://lccn.loc.gov/2018057020

Manufactured in the United States of America

28  27  26  25  24  23  22  21  20  19
10  9  8  7  6  5  4  3  2  1

*For Sis*

Heroines of the booze mobs, the gun-molls of a cock-eyed era labeled prohibition, some day may emerge as a composite, legendary figure in literary form worthy of becoming a prominent part of American folklore. This epic gun-moll will be the modern Maid Marian of rollicking songs in which her man, the hero, will be an amazing character, pictured as pirate, gorilla, and great lover, rolled into one. The story will tell how the hero's machine guns mowed down enemies like blades of wheat before a sickle until, one day, he was "taken for a ride." At this point the gun-moll will take the spotlight in a finale of tears, wailing before an officious but future person labeled law.

JOSEPH U. DUGAN, "Gang Women of Dry Era Bid for Spurious Fame," *Chicago Daily Tribune,* December 31, 1933, G3.

# Contents

# Illustrations

TABLES

# Acknowledgments

Writing a book does not take a village. It takes a social network—especially a social network of durable professional and personal ties. First and foremost, I thank Andy Papachristos for his incredible mentorship, investment, training, creativity, sense of humor, and support. We bond over being first-generation college students, cool finds in the archives, naming computers, and fun academic writing. Social ties predict outcomes, and Andy made the process from research assistant to dissertation to book fun, engaging, fruitful, and inspiring. The first time I met Andy, I was working in the graduate computer lab during my first few weeks of graduate school. He asked me why I was not enrolled in his social networks graduate course. I told him that I didn't know what social networks were. That was over a decade ago.

Don Tomaskovic-Devey has a high degree of mentorship ties to some of my favorite sociologists. I am fortunate that Don shared his relational resources, friendship, and mentorship with me. Theoretical orientations for books do not usually come directly from your mentor, but I also get to thank Don for his work on relational inequality and pushing me to engage these hard, theoretical questions even days before my deadlines. Bob Zussman thinks creatively and relationally. He convinced me that there was something in this research topic when I could not see it, and he continued to help me to see it. Jen Fronc's period expertise, historian's voice, and writing inspired me to not neglect the historical narrative. It has been a pleasure and an inspiration to work with these four intellectual giants.

I thought publishing a book was going to be difficult, but my experience with the University of California Press has only been supportive. Maura Roessner was on board within six days of my sending the proposal and sample chapters. Maura's enthusiasm for the project and our meetings kept me motivated. I had the most encouraging and detailed set of reviews from

Vanessa Panfil and Carlo Morselli. Whenever I felt stuck, I returned to their comments to remind me what the book was about and how to make it better. Lindsey Halsell's detailed copyediting and encouraging commentary got me through the last few weeks of preparing the manuscript. Thank you, Sabrina Robleh and Madison Wetzell, for keeping the project organized.

University of Massachusetts Amherst Sociology is a dense section of my social network full of amazing people. I owe many thanks to Beth Berry, Roland Chilton, David Cort, Christin Glodek, Rob Faulkner, Naomi Gerstel, Sanjiv Gupta, Sandy Hunsicker, Janice Irvine, James Kitts, Jen Lundquist, Karen Mason, Joya Misra, Wenona Rymond-Richmond, Laurel Smith-Doerr, Millie Thayer, Barbara Tomaskovic-Devey, Maureen Warner, Wendy Wilde, and Jon Wynn. UMass Sociology became increasing multiplex through friendships with fellow graduate students. Thank you, Dustin Avent-Holt, Irene Boeckmann, Laura Heston, Missy Hodges, Ken-Hou Lin, Elisa Martinez, Sarah Miller, Tim Sacco, Mary Scherer, Eiko Strader, Mahala Stewart, Shawn Trivette, and Ryan Turner. Melinda Miceli was my broker to UMass, and I thank her for my introduction to sociology at the University of Wisconsin-Eau Claire, mentoring me through graduate school applications and encouraging me to apply to UMass, and for friendship throughout the years.

The Sociology Department at the University of California, Davis, contributed to the intellectual fine-tuning of this book and provided me with letters of support, mentorship, manuscript workshops, and general good cheer. Many thanks to Sondra Byrd, Sheline Calvert, Angela Carter, Courtney Caviness, Orly Clerge, Max Craig, Bob Faris, Ryan Finnigan, Jess Gold, Ryken Grattet, Erin Hamilton, Jacob Hibel, Jonathan Jordan, Jared Joseph, Jacque Leaver, Val Ludovina, Bill McCarthy, David McCourt, Stephanie Mudge, Rachel Nickens, David Orzechowicz, Caitlin Patler, Zach Psick, Kim Shauman, Vicki Smith, and Matt Thompson. Bill McCarthy read the manuscript in its entirety and gave me the exact level of feedback that I needed just before the final summer of writing. Ryken Grattet wrote multiple letters of support and encouraged my writer's voice. Bill and Ryken pushed me to think more critically about co-offending and legal ambiguity, and their research inspired large portions of my revisions. I received excellent research assistance from UC Davis undergraduates Cierra Bordwine, Liann Tucker, Johanna Vega, and Lauren Wong. My engaging students from the spring 2018 Gender & Crime seminar showed me how accessible and exciting this work was for the undergraduate classroom.

My broader intellectual community includes Nicky Fox, Katherine Irwin, Rory Kramer, Andrea Leverentz, Sam Mitrani, Carlo Morselli, Jonathan

Obert, Vanessa Panfil, Brianna Remster, Tim Thomas, Garen Wintemute, Katie Young, and Marjorie Zatz, who all have talked with me about this project, Chicago history, gender and crime, and book publishing over the years. Your work and our conversations continue to inspire me.

I received assistance from archivists and research coordinators at the Chicago Crime Commission, Chicago History Museum, and the National Archives Great Lakes Region—special thanks to Scott Forsythe and Matt Jacobs for their assistance in the archives. This research received support from the National Science Foundation under grant number 1302778, the National Institute of Justice, Office of Justice Programs, US Department of Justice under Award number 2013-IJ-CX-0013, the University of Massachusetts Amherst Graduate School, and the University of Massachusetts Amherst Department of Sociology. I received a publication assistance grant from the University of California, Davis Office of Research and the College of Letters and Sciences.

Personal ties brought balance, smiles, and support during the long writing process. Thank you, Soha Achi, the Alegria family, Jess Barrickman, Melissa Beaufoy, Eric Burri, Tesa Z. Helge, Yumi Henneberry, the Hill family, the Jensen family, Kristle and Jon Kendrick, Amanda Lincoln, Anne Magratten, Jen Maietta, Jason Moore, David O., Amanda and Kem Saichaie, Andy Sewell, Katie Trujillo, Zulema Valdez, Rachel Weber, and Nicole Wilson. I am grateful for writing retreats and Sociology Writes with friends Katherine Eriksson, Ryan Finnigan, Nicky Fox, Erin Hamilton, Caitlin Patler, Whitney Pirtle, and Jeff Sacha. My siblings, Amber and Matt Smith, have been with me on this journey since they were too young to remember. Much of what I do is for them. Sharla Alegria brings joy, adventure, strong social theory, statistical reassurance, and brilliance to our home every day. Thank you, Sharla, for our wonderfully multiplex social tie.

# 1. Gender and Organized Crime

For nearly fifty years Vic Shaw, a woman of Chicago's underworld, sold sex, booze, and narcotics. Over the course of her career Shaw rose to her prime as Chicago's charming and beautiful "vice queen" in the early 1900s, during which time she coordinated her illicit activities with Chicago's organized crime network and married a mobster. Not long after she reached her prime, Shaw fell to the status of Chicago's "faded queen," operating her brothels, drug dens, and speakeasies in isolation from organized crime and facing regular raids by law enforcement.[1] Shaw's public persona and biography are uncommonly detailed for those women of Chicago historically involved in organized crime. Yet her rise and fall paralleled the broader pattern of women's early entrepreneurship and embeddedness in Progressive Era Chicago organized crime (1900–1919) and their near exclusion from organized crime during Prohibition (1920–1933).

As Vic Shaw told it, she arrived in Chicago as a young teenager around the time of the 1893 World's Columbian Exposition.[2] Her real name was Emma Fitzgerald, and she had run away from her parents' home in Nova Scotia. Her first job in Chicago was as a burlesque dancer. One night after her performance, a handsome socialite named Ebie, whose parents were Chicago millionaires, ran away with Shaw to Michigan. There, he convinced Shaw that they had gotten married.[3] Ebie's family lawyer caught up with the young couple, who were posing as newlyweds, and informed them that they were, in fact, not legally married, and that Ebie had committed a crime, as Shaw was a minor. Upon their return to Chicago, the lawyer arranged a large payout to Shaw in exchange for her leaving Ebie and his family alone.[4]

Shaw suddenly had more money than she knew what to do with, and her friends from burlesque advised her to invest in a brothel, which she did. She bought a brothel on South Dearborn Street and another on the former

Armour Avenue in the late 1890s. In the beginning Shaw was not a great entrepreneur, as she was, in her words, "more interested in men than the business," but by the turn of the twentieth century she was operating two successful luxury brothels in Chicago's red-light district.[5] She had little competition in the luxury brothel market. Shaw benefited from strong legal and political protection, arranged through her corrupt friends and organized crime associates, Aldermen Michael Kenna and John Coughlin. According to members of Chicago's underworld, Shaw was their "queen" as her photograph from 1910 in figure 1 portrays.[6] Although she entered the high-end brothel business because of her experience and personal connections in Chicago's red-light district and the start-up capital she had received from Ebie's lawyer, it was her connections to men of Chicago's organized crime network that kept Shaw in business.

When Vic Shaw was around seventy years old, reporter Norma Lee Browning interviewed her, preserving Shaw's reflections on her fifty-plus-year career in Chicago's underworld.[7] The *Chicago Tribune* published Browning's interview with Shaw in a three-part series in 1949, just a few years before Shaw's death.[8] Browning was a brilliant reporter at a time when few women did investigative journalism, and her published interview with Shaw is a unique archival treasure.[9] During their meeting, Shaw confessed her one regret in life: "'Listen, chicken,' she [Shaw] says philosophically, 'I wouldn't trade places with anybody. If I had it to do over again, I'd live every day just the same except for one thing. The only regret I have is giving up a good man like Charlie . . . to marry Roy Jones.'"[10] Charlie was one of Shaw's lovers, a hotelman who had bought Shaw her brownstone at 2906 Prairie Avenue, where she ran a brothel during Prohibition and spent her later years running a hotel for transients.[11] When Shaw expressed regret over losing Charlie, she was referring to having eloped to New York City in 1907 with Roy Jones, a fellow Chicago red-light district saloon owner and brothel keeper.[12] Roy Jones was the second of Shaw's four husbands, and they were married for about seven years.[13] Most likely they met in Chicago's red-light districts, where they both ran organized crime–protected businesses. The archives do not reveal why Shaw chose Roy over Charlie.

Roy Jones became a well-established figure in organized crime during the Progressive Era in Chicago through his gambling dens, saloons, brothels, and sex-trafficking rings.[14] In 1912 Jones and other prominent pimps and madams were arrested, along with more than two hundred prostitutes and clients, during a raid on the red-light district.[15] Vic Shaw's Dearborn Street brothel was the raid's first target. There, the raiders found ten prostitutes

FIGURE 1. Vic Shaw, resort keeper associated with the Nat Moore case, in Chicago, Illinois, 1910. *Source:* DN-0055519, *Chicago Daily News* negatives collection, Chicago History Museum.

and loaded them into a patrol wagon.[16] Shaw was nowhere to be found and avoided arrest. She was not the only illicit business owner to be lucky that night.[17] According to one account, the city's "vice lords" were immediately released on bail when they arrived at the station for booking.[18] The implication in this account is that they had organized crime connections that gave them immunity from formal criminal charges.

Chicago organized crime offered Roy Jones opportunities in the illicit economy during both the Progressive and Prohibition eras but eventually left Vic Shaw behind. A stark difference between Shaw's and Jones's organized crime careers was that during their marriage, Jones's organized crime associations continued to grow as he developed new relationships and expanded his businesses, whereas Shaw's organized crime relationships dissolved. She continued to draw protection benefits from organized crime, but these benefits came through Jones rather than through her own illicit businesses and direct connections to other men of organized crime.[19] By 1914, around the time of Jones and Shaw's divorce, Chicago's underworld heralded Roy Jones as one of its "vice kings"—a moniker implying that he had usurped Shaw's status as underworld royalty.[20] In fact, within a year after the divorce, reporters were referring to Shaw as Chicago's "faded queen."[21]

Following their split, Shaw's businesses suffered and she lacked organized crime's protection, while Jones's businesses continued to thrive. Shaw opened a more discreet brothel on Michigan Avenue and expanded her business into narcotics distribution. She was unable to connect her new business to the protection market coordinated by organized crime. She faced regular raids by police and morals inspectors (inspectors from Chicago's Morals Court, which specialized in prostitution cases and other violations of morality).[22] During a 1914 raid on her resort led by Morals Inspector William Dannenberg, Shaw was so enraged at the continued attacks on her businesses that she refused to leave her bed when inspectors entered her room. Instead of yielding, she waved around a revolver and threatened to shoot Dannenberg if he tried to get her. The morals inspectors simply laughed at her.[23] Meanwhile, one of Jones's apartments was cased, wiretapped, and raided in 1914 because of allegations that he was running a national sex-trafficking ring from that location.[24] Investigators arrested the three men and one woman they found in the apartment, but Jones was not present and escaped arrest.[25] Even with "voluminous records obtained by the stenographers," the state was unable to prosecute Roy Jones or the other defendants.[26] These two examples illustrate Shaw's and Jones's diverging paths in Chicago's underworld after their divorce. Jones maintained connections to organized crime that provided legal immunity even when morals inspection raids escalated in Chicago, but Shaw did not.

The prohibition on the production, transportation, and sale of intoxicating beverages in the United States from 1920 to 1933 dramatically altered organized crime in Chicago, to the benefit of men and, as I show in the following chapters, the near exclusion of women. Only six years after their divorce, Shaw, consistent with her entrepreneurial spirit, attempted to capitalize on the evolving illicit economy. Following the introduction of Prohibition, Shaw moved her own business enterprises into bootlegging by exploiting her brothels' underground passages to move and store booze.[27] But even with her prime location in the central city, her operations were isolated from organized crime. Shaw encountered renewed police raids and faced charges of violating Prohibition laws.[28] Her declining status as organized crime's faded queen became evident when she was the victim of a $32,000 jewelry heist in 1921 and when she was fined $500 for violating Prohibition in 1928.[29] Roy Jones persisted in organized crime during Prohibition, but he was less active and less connected as a nearly retired "vice king." Jones moved to the northern suburbs of Chicago around 1923 to run the Green Parrot roadhouse for organized crime, where he appears to have continued escaping arrest and prosecution.[30]

The gap between Roy Jones's and Vic Shaw's organized crime experiences had emerged in the later years of the Progressive Era. Prohibition exacerbated their differences when Chicago organized crime mostly excluded women. Shaw's access to women who could work in prostitution did not change, her involvement in illicit economies did not change, and her prime real estate locations in red-light districts did not change. Rather, as I show in this book, her relationships to the men of organized crime who were embedded in the restructured criminal organization changed. This restructuring dramatically altered women's participation and position in Chicago's organized crime syndicate. As the title of this book implies, and as I detail in the upcoming chapters, Chicago organized crime was referred to as a "syndicate" during the Progressive Era and was later called "the Syndicate" during Prohibition.

## SYNDICATE WOMEN

The wives, girlfriends, relatives, and women entrepreneurs of Chicago's gangster era are an often forgotten and hidden part of the history of organized crime. Vic Shaw's and Roy Jones's reputations in organized crime have not withstood the test of time as have those of "Big" Jim Colosimo, Johnny "the Fox" Torrio, Al Capone, George "Bugs" Moran, and Jack "Machine Gun" McGurn. The men of Chicago organized crime are remembered for their fashion, glamour, wealth, and violence, immortalized in celluloid and pulp fiction by the public and Hollywood's fascination with gangster-era Chicago. Hollywood screenplays might portray a beautiful woman on a gangster's arm in the role of mistress or "gun moll," but she was destined to be the wailing widow by the end of his tale.[31]

Unlike the popular versions of this history, this book is based on years of archival research conducted in Chicago and online. I did not uncover hidden gems on gangster-era Chicago. I accessed the same archives and documents that dozens of fiction and nonfiction writers and historians have used before me, but my approach to the archives was unique. Using the tools of social network analysis and spatial analysis, I set out to plot the web of Chicago's organized crime network and to map the illicit economy locations across the city of Chicago. I accessed thousands of pages of archival documents to find mentions of people, relationships, and addresses that were alleged to be part of the Chicago underworld. I organized all of these mentions into a database designed for the analyses presented in this book. Unlike the "gumshoes" of early 1900s Chicago, my sleuthing work in the archives relied on keyword searches, document scanners, relational spreadsheets, and closed criminal cases.

Rather than upholding the popular narrative of glamorous mobsters and their violent rivalries, this research shows that organized crime was mainly a day-to-day grind of informal, illicit, and behind-the-scenes work, in which glamor-less brewers, drivers, bouncers, saloon waitstaff, brothel madams, prostitutes, and couriers were the source of organized crime's income-generating schemes and illicit activities.[32] Infamous men—such as Colosimo, Torrio, Capone, Moran, and McGurn—and their criminal relationships shaped large sections of the organized crime network. Their criminal establishments were part of the geography of the illicit economy. However, these powerful mobsters and their positions in Chicago contrast with the ordinary men and women of organized crime around them. Women's erasure from organized crime history has created a blind spot for the dramatic organizational change around gender and power that occurred in the early 1900s—a blind spot that, once illuminated by research, proves to be insightful for understanding the social processes through which the powerful consolidate their power, the powerless fall further into the margins, and women lose their already precarious foothold in criminal economies.

My analytical approach in *Syndicate Women* allowed me to trace Vic Shaw's and Roy Jones's connections through the same organized crime network and revealed how illicit markets, the criminal landscape of Chicago, and the structure of organized crime changed in ways that included men while increasingly excluding women. As I detail throughout the book, Progressive Era organized crime was a small, loosely clustered, nonhierarchical, decentralized group of politicians, police officers, collectors, and illicit business owners. During this period organized crime was territorial, focusing on geographically concentrated red-light districts of gambling dens, brothels, and saloons to coordinate the collection of protection and bribery fees and the corruption of legitimate offices. Entrepreneurial women such as Vic Shaw connected to organized crime's protection market through the location of their or their husbands' brothels. Even though women were part of the organized crime network, their involvement in Progressive Era organized crime was marginal. No women became central figures in organized crime, and all of the women of organized crime were dependent on their relationships to men in organized crime. However, the importance of brothels to organized crime's protection market, as well as women's ownership and management of many of Chicago's brothels in the geographically concentrated red-light districts, were keys to women's inclusion in organized crime during the Progressive Era.

During Prohibition, organized crime in Chicago tripled in size, became a more centralized organization with a powerful core of bosses, spread geographically into neighboring villages, and surged in profits and influence. Organized crime's markets became less territorial and less specialized. Gambling dens and brothels remained important establishments for organized crime because they generated even greater profits thanks to the sale of bootleg booze. Beyond gambling and prostitution, organized crime diversified its income-generating portfolio to include bootlegging, labor racketeering, political corruption, and racetracks, in addition to investment in legitimate businesses. A major consequence of organized crime's restructuring during Prohibition was that an individual business's physical location was less critical for connecting to organized crime. Roy Jones ran an organized crime roadhouse, but it was located in a northern suburb of Chicago. Even as he retired from his prominence in organized crime, he persisted in organized crime during Prohibition. Vic Shaw continued to run brothels and expanded into bootlegging near the city center, but she was no longer connected to the organized crime network. She operated in isolation from the protection market and faced burglaries and raids. Jones's and Shaw's experiences were typical of men's and women's diverging paths during Prohibition, when women were increasingly excluded from organized crime. Connections to the restructured criminal organization required relationships to crime bosses or their associates, rather than running a business in a particular territory—a relationship-forming process that began with, and reproduced, greater gender inequality in organized crime.

I uncovered an intriguing puzzle while conducting this research: women composed a substantial part of Chicago's organized crime during the Progressive Era, but during Prohibition, when criminal opportunities increased for men and women across the United States, women were mostly excluded from organized crime. Women's entrepreneurial spirit and economic need did not change in this twenty-year period; rather, the structural barriers of access and prosperity developed in ways that were compounded by status, preferences, organizational restructuring, and as a consequence, gender. Conventional theories of gender and crime are limited in explaining such a dramatic, rapid shift in a criminal organization's gender composition. This book attempts to solve this puzzle by leveraging broader relational and market theories, historical data, and criminal networks. A relational theoretical approach requires a slight departure from examining gender differences as strictly categorical ones between women and men. It does so by foregrounding and interrogating how gender interacts with the social processes generating or limiting relationships, producing unequal outcomes for men and women. Relational approaches do not replace theories of categorical difference, but rather accommodate them by prioritizing processes over outcomes. In doing this, I hope to provide a theoretical and empirical model for advancing research on inequality in crime.

## GENDER INEQUALITY IN CRIME

Gender inequality in crime and criminal organizations is the location of one of the largest gender gaps persisting in the twenty-first century, especially when compared to the dramatic shrinking of gender gaps during the twentieth century in employment, wages, educational attainment, and political participation.[33] Official US statistics show that 73 percent of all arrests in 2016 were men; in 2018, men accounted for 93 percent of the state and federal prison population.[34] Criminologists have referred to the gender gap in crime as "universal" or "a criminological truism" because it has been so persistent over time and exists for most types of crime, especially violent crime.[35] Other scholars have argued that the gender gap in crime is largely a phenomenon of the past two hundred years. Legal scholars Malcolm Feeley and Deborah Little's research on the gender gap in crime examined 226 years of British court data from 1687 to 1912. They found that it was not until the 1800s that the gender gap in convictions began to increase toward its present-day rates.[36] Feeley and Little argue that the dramatic gender gap in crime is largely a product of historical and cultural shifts in ideals about womanhood.

The gender gap is especially prominent in violent criminal organizations. According to members of some criminal groups, such as mafias, a defining feature of organized crime is a complete absence and distrust of women.[37] However, women are at the very least instrumental in criminal organizations that center on family and kin.[38] Historical research has revealed that criminal organizations offered work to poor, often immigrant women at the turn of the twentieth century in New York. For example, historical criminologist Alan Block identified more than three hundred women in New York's organized crime rings involved in prostitution, theft, drug dealing, and managing brothels and gambling dens.[39] Historian Rona Holub's research uncovered an organized crime ring in New York City led by "Queen of Fences" Fredericka "Marm" Mandelbaum, who syndicated a network of men and women thieves and amassed approximately $1 million from stolen goods in the 1880s.[40] Research on contemporary cases of Italian mafia–style organizations shows a range of women's involvement, from silent complicity to assisting incarcerated husbands to assuming leadership positions.[41] These women in historical and contemporary organized crime are not just exceptions to some masculine organizational rule or the subjects of dismissible anecdotes. Instead, they provide a glimpse into the ways that gender is both a resource and a limitation for women in criminal economies. Gender is a resource when implicit assumptions and stereotypes about women being nonthreatening and noncriminal permit women in organized crime to operate under the radar, to gain others' trust, or to access their mob husbands' information and instructions. Gender is a limitation when women navigate patriarchy and stratification in criminal economies and face perceptions that they are criminally incompetent and incapable of violence.

Explanations for gender inequality in crime face the dilemma of needing to explain the gap in men's and women's offending while still providing theoretical room to understand how and why women offend.[42] This dilemma requires a theory that mostly explains difference but is flexible enough to explain instances of similarity. For example, theories of masculinity or gender socialization in which men leverage crime (especially violent crime) for hypermasculine accomplishment can explain why men commit more crime than women if crime is a resource for "doing gender."[43] However, the implicit assumption in this theory of difference is that women who offend are gender deviants.[44] Yet women offenders are seldom gender deviants. Research shows that gender very much shapes the ways in which women offend, such as enacting a feminine sexual desire to lure targets for robbery, relying on law enforcement's assumptions of women as innocent when drug dealing, and being stuck in subordinate and normative gendered roles in criminal schemes.[45] In these examples, the accomplishments of femininity in crime challenge gender socialization or crime as masculine theories of difference. Crime events vary so much by context and situation that labeling crime as either masculine or feminine is not a particularly useful distinction, even when attempting to explain the gender gap in offending.

Theories that focus on relationships provide more flexibility to how gender inequality arises and are insightful for thinking about the gender gap in offending. Learning theories of crime, starting with Edwin Sutherland's 1947 differential association theory, stress how people learn and adopt criminal values, attitudes, behaviors, and techniques from their friends and associates over time.[46] Similar to how they adopt conventional behaviors or values, people must first learn how to commit criminal acts and to embrace criminal values through meaningful social relationships in the context of social groups. Learning theories of crime that prioritize social relationships and social groups are less deterministic than gender socialization theories and can accommodate gender differences in offending. For example, one of the strongest and most persistent predictors of juvenile delinquency is having delinquent friends, and gender is a salient component of peer influence.[47] Some research shows that girls are more susceptible to peers' influence on their own violence.[48] Related research consistently finds that women's entrée into offending is often through their romantic associations with men.[49] In these examples, the gender composition of peer influence explains instances of girls' and women's offending without assumptions of gender deviance.

Peer influence theories build on learning theories to show that groups matter above and beyond individuals and their attributes. Research shows that the gender composition of peer groups influences pro-social and nondelinquent behaviors. For example, female-dominated peer groups are less likely to engage in delinquency, street gangs that have a balance of boys and girls are less involved in violence than street gangs with a majority of boys, more mixed gender friendships in schools decrease school bullying, and loving dating relationships have a deterrent effect on youth delinquency for girls and boys.[50] In these examples, mixed-gender social groups experience different learning processes, content, and contexts that orient adolescents away from delinquency—again showing how learning theories and peer influence theories explain gender differences in delinquency while providing enough flexibility to understand girls' delinquency.[51]

Relational theories are also useful for understanding processes that perpetuate other categorical inequalities in offending. Race, class, and gender are attributes of various categorical groups overrepresented and underrepresented in crime and delinquency, but these attributes alone are not a direct explanation for involvement in crime and delinquency. In contrast to the underrepresentation of women in crime, racial and ethnic groups marginalized by legitimate organizations and labor markets are overrepresented in underground economies and criminal organizations.[52] Attributes such as race, class, and gender shape social groups through homophily, a social process whereby people with similar attributes or from similar backgrounds are attracted to each other.[53] Learning theories and peer influence theories situate crime and delinquency as a product of social groups. More attention is needed to social groups and relationships of those both overrepresented and underrepresented in crime. Relational dynamics of homophily, preferences, availability, exclusion, trust, geographic proximity, criminalization, and risk generate criminal groups and criminal organizations that tend to be more similar rather than diverse along categories of race, class, and gender.[54]

## ADVANCING RELATIONAL APPROACHES TO INEQUALITY AND CRIME

Moving in this direction, criminology needs to explicate the relational conditions perpetuating inequality in crime. Gender—as well as other categories of inclusion and exclusion—comes into play at the macro, meso, and micro levels. Relational approaches are theoretically flexible enough to explain difference and similarity across these levels because they focus on processes informed by socially constructed, yet sticky and durable, categories such as gender. Previous explanations for the gender gap in crime are compatible with a focus on social relationships, because the processes producing gender inequality occur within social relationships or shape social relationships. The difference is that relational approaches identify specific actors, network structures, and locations of action and inaction.

Relational approaches to inequality in crime benefit greatly from social network analysis. Social network analysis is a growing field that combines theory and method. It centers social relationships among sets of actors and analyzes how patterns of relationships affect various outcomes.[55] Social network researchers gather, compare, and analyze multiple network properties at the individual, group, and system levels to describe organizational types; structural changes over time; and patterns of behavior, influence, and interaction. Historians, criminologists, and other social scientists have been plowing forward with the tools and theories of social network analysis, but the same has not held true for scholarship on gender inequality. Social network scholarship tends to be weak on gendered and intersectional analyses, but there is much theoretical potential in work on gendered relationships.[56]

Co-offending provides a strong example for advancing the relational approach I advocate. Social networks are the starting location of inequality in criminal contexts. At least half of all crimes are committed as group offenses, which means that at least half of all crimes begin with some sort of partnering, collaborating, or recruiting.[57] Crime settings and opportunities are volatile and ephemeral, and criminal information has to be hoarded within a trustworthy social network or offenders risk detection, punishment, or betrayal.[58] Co-offending is a cooperative process in which social networks of potential co-offenders pool their differing levels of criminal knowledge, skill, and information to improve their success in crime.[59] Potential co-offenders often assess each other's knowledge, skills, desperation, and reputation and select those who are available, most similar to themselves, and most willing to align with their needs.[60] The co-offending selection process tends to favor individuals who have criminal experience or knowledge, and this favoring produces inequality when co-offenders recruit only from their small, trustworthy social networks.

Gender is a powerful category of inclusion and exclusion in co-offending; men mostly co-offend with men, whereas women mostly co-offend with men rather than women.[61] Men tend to access crime through their family, peers, and mentors, almost all of whom are other men.[62] Women's entrée to offending is often through their associations with their husbands and romantic partners.[63] These patterns show that inequality in co-offending is not a simple process of gender homophily, since women tend not to co-offend with other women; rather, gender inequality in co-offending comes from a selection process that privileges masculinity and men's criminal competence within small, insular social networks. In criminal markets, men are the preferred, structurally available, and advantageous co-offenders.

Trust within social networks is at the core of understanding how relationships perpetuate inequality in crime. Different arrangements and absences of people with criminal information mean that some social networks are flush with criminal opportunities while others are deficient. Even if social networks had equal co-offending opportunities, trust interferes with any potential equity in the referral and selection process because co-offenders must privilege secrecy over efficiency to avoid prosecution.[64] Trust is an informal property of social networks that shapes selection processes, but the research on crime, trust, and gender has had mixed findings. Some research has found that men of the underworld unabashedly admit that they think women cannot be trusted and categorically exclude women from illicit economies and criminal organizations.[65] Men's accounting for women's exclusion relays stereotypes of women as weak, gossips, or opportunistic gold diggers.[66] In contrast, other scholars have found that criminally involved men consider women, especially their wives, to be the most trustworthy people in their lives.[67]

Relational approaches to understanding the gender gap in crime reveal the processes through which informality and biases mostly exclude, but occasionally include, women in crime. These informal processes are intertwined with more formalized gender-stratified market conditions. Research on criminal markets shows that women have greater criminal opportunities when markets are open to criminal entrepreneurs, flat (i.e., nonhierarchical), and decentralized, rather than closed to outside entrepreneurs, hierarchal, and centralized. This is especially the case in drug markets.[68] Sociologist Patricia Adler described drug dealing and smuggling in the 1970s in the US Southwest as a market of free enterprise, entrepreneurialism, disorganization, short-term deals, and high turnover.[69] Adler found that women could participate as high-level dealers in this type of market with the knowledge and connections gained from their dealer boyfriends and ex-husbands.[70] In contrast, public health scholar Lisa Maher found that the drug markets in New York City were vertical hierarchies with strict tiers between employers and employees.[71] In this market, women, with one exception, were completely absent from the boss and management tiers of the hierarchy; only a very small number of women worked in the lowest levels of street dealing, and then only on a temporary basis.[72] Instead, women found work in the peripheral sex market, a market so intrinsically connected to the drug market that, as the drug economy grew, the profits for sex work decreased and violence against sex workers increased.[73] Beyond drug markets, research on Chinese human smugglers finds the same pattern of women's increased participation in flatter organizations. Chinese human smuggling operations are sporadic and completely decentralized, relying on a long chain of one-on-one interactions between individuals who fill only a single role in the smuggling process.[74] Women fill some of these roles, and women's presence alleviates some families' concerns for safety while negotiating the smuggling of women and children.[75] The market perspectives across these three studies all emphasize access or barriers to criminal organizations that determine relationships between women and men.

Social capital provides the theoretical foundation of this research. Growing and dissolving relationships are essential to a social capital framework of understanding how gender differences develop in criminal organizations. Social capital is the resources that can be accessed through relationships.[76] Resources accessed through social capital can include access to information such as a job opening, recommendations such as a promotion or a letter, and trust such as vouching for someone's credibility. In criminal organizations, among the resources available in these relationships are inclusion and protection. When women and men have different access to relationships containing resources, gender inequality results.[77]

Returning to the opening case with these relational and market perspectives, Vic Shaw's initial success in organized crime in Chicago during the Progressive Era likely occurred for two reasons. First, she accessed start-up financial capital from the scandal with Ebie. Most men and women of Chicago's underworld never made the amount of cash that Vic Shaw received from Ebie's family, and Shaw might have returned to burlesque dancing without this opportunity for investment. The flat, nonhierarchical organized crime network coordinating the protection market in Chicago's red-light districts accommodated entrepreneurs with financial capital even when they were women. The second reason Shaw likely had initial success in Chicago organized crime was her social capital with organized crime men. Social capital resources can be trust, inclusion, and opportunities to generate more financial capital. During the early years of the twentieth century, the resource contained in Vic Shaw's relationships was access to the legal protection she gained through her relationships with men in organized crime.

One of the two factors that helps explain Shaw's initial success in Chicago organized crime during the Progressive Era also helps explain her downfall during Prohibition. Her social capital in organized crime dissolved. Shaw still had financial capital. She had properties, income, jewels, and employees, but the resources of protection, patronage, and trust embedded in the organized crime network were no longer available to her. She became Chicago underworld's faded queen. I argue in the coming chapters that the processes that pushed Shaw out of organized crime were rooted in the organized crime network's broader structural changes that increasingly excluded women during Prohibition.

This puzzle of syndicate women composing a substantial part of organized crime before Prohibition compared to their near exclusion during that period requires use of relational theories, historical data, and understanding of criminal networks. I document how women's criminal locations in brothels and booze actually increased between the Progressive Era and Prohibition, but this growth occurred outside of organized crime. Gender was a salient category generating unequal relationships in organized crime during the Progressive Era, but the salience of gender as a mechanism of exclusion changed within organized crime's structure and interests during Prohibition.

Bringing relational and market perspectives together shows that the relational rules of the game for women in criminal organizations occur in an unregulated and unequal opportunity network wherein their relationships to men are even more consequential for women's access to organizational resources. Why and how these violent and masculine institutions are so successful at excluding women are sociological questions meaningful to understanding broader relational processes. These patterns from a hundred years ago suggest that men will continue to dominate criminal organizations and criminal economies so long as those who broker criminal relationships continue to see women as not criminally useful in the moment or the long term. The process of forming a criminal relationship requires someone who is trustworthy, experienced, compliant, strong, or whatever characteristic is needed for the criminal task at hand. Occasionally women possess the preferred characteristics: a sexy entrapper, a successful brothel owner, a desperate addict, or an unassuming markswoman. A structural analysis of relationships within a criminal organization moves beyond traditional gender roles and characteristics to understand the gendered processes of social capital producing and limiting criminal opportunities for offending women.

## TERMINOLOGY AND ORGANIZATION OF THE BOOK

The terminology of prostitution or sex work has shifted in the past hundred years, which calls for a brief note on word usage in this book. The Progressive Era was a period in which open discussion and publication of issues related to sexuality were taboo.[78] The word "vice" largely described the selling of sex or other violations of sexual morality. The words "resort," "den," "house of ill fame," and "disorderly house" described places where sex was sold. As I show in chapter 3, state laws and city ordinances included the word "prostitution" but more commonly used veiled language such as "houses of ill fame" or "disorderly houses." Inherent in this terminology is the moralizing of sexuality and stigmatizing of prostitution. This historical terminology is also inconsistent with the more contemporary, but still historically accurate, conceptualization of prostitution as a form of criminalized gendered work.[79] Moving forward, I opt for the term "sex work" when not directly quoting historical sources. This term is useful because it reinforces the inequality women experienced in formal and illicit labor markets and serves as a reminder of women's limited economic alternatives.[80] It is also more inclusive than the term "prostitution" and in some instances may be a more accurate description of what was happening behind Chicago's closed doors.

The organization of the book is as follows. Chapter 2 provides the nuts and bolts behind the evidence and analysis that are the foundation for the arguments in this book. First, the chapter orients readers to the ambitious archival research and database creation required for this project. Second, it explains the analytic and conceptual moves made to measure Chicago's organized crime network. I present network visualizations and a descriptive structural analysis showing how organized crime and its gender composition changed from the Progressive Era to Prohibition. Third, I introduce the geographic data on brothel and alcohol establishments to map the spread of Chicago's illicit economies. Finally, chapter 2 discusses data limitations and what they mean for the analysis presented in the book. Chapter 2 is the most technical chapter of the book, establishing the transparency of the research and showcasing the methodological contributions of this project.

Chapter 3 provides a historical overview of the legal and geographic conditions that permitted organized crime to develop and thrive in Chicago at the turn of the twentieth century. Urban growth, Progressive Era politics, fluctuating regulations, and law enforcement discretion made sex work an increasingly risky business during this period. This risky business generated incredible profits and provided alternative working conditions for men and women within Chicago's spatially concentrated red-light districts at a time when women were part of the ownership and management of 39 percent of Chicago's brothels. Organized crime developed a territorial protection market in the red-light districts in which politicians, law enforcement, and both men and women owners of illicit entertainment businesses coordinated a loose and profitable syndication of protection payments, collections, and extortion in the face of increasing regulation.

Chapter 4 zooms in on the Progressive Era's organized crime network and details the decentralized nature of organized crime. Women made up 18 percent of the organized crime network and had moderate successes in the small, flat, nonhierarchical, decentralized structure when organized crime was predominantly a territorial protection market. Women connected to organized crime through the locations of their illicit businesses even after the Progressive Era activists succeeded in formally closing the red-light districts. This chapter extends previous conceptualizations of organized crime by situating women of the sex economy as relevant actors in the Chicago organized crime network and establishes the importance of decentralized organizations and brokerage to women's involvement in criminal organizations.

Chapter 5 details how the 1920 prohibition on the production, transportation, and sale of intoxicating beverages was an exogenous legal shock to illicit markets and especially opportune for Chicago's preexisting organized crime network. Prohibition ushered in new income-generating opportunities for many Chicago residents from all walks of life, including women and families outside of organized crime. However, domestic bootlegging contrasted with organized crime's industrial scale of booze production and was subject to greater law enforcement. This chapter establishes that women's participation in the illicit alcohol economy increased during Prohibition, but organized crime and its diversified markets largely ignored women's localized illicit establishments that produced and sold alcohol.

Chapter 6 presents the organized crime network of Prohibition, its centralized leadership, and the thirty-eight women involved in organized crime. Prohibition shifted organized crime to a large, sparse network with a powerful central core. In turn, these structural shifts dramatically increased gender inequality, with women composing only 4 percent of the network. Much of what was to become of Chicago organized crime during the Prohibition years was imprinted by a particular trajectory that began in the early 1900s: the districts, the blocks, the illicit entertainment economy, and some of the male persisters. The same was not true for organized crime women, whose relationships to organized crime became increasingly dependent on their marital and familial relationships to organized crime men—more so than women's involvement in and proprietorship of 49 percent of Chicago's Prohibition era brothels.

The conclusion in chapter 7 summarizes the book's main arguments and reviews how the pieces of the *Syndicate Women* puzzle fit together. The theoretical contributions and broader implications in chapter 7 return the reader to the larger question of what this unique case illuminates. I wrote *Syndicate Women* in an accessible style to bring social network analysis to a wide audience. Readers will learn some basics of social network analysis throughout some of the chapters. My hope is that social network scholars will see the value in providing an account of social network analysis that is accessible to readers from a variety of backgrounds using the simplicity I try to bring to this case, and that those scholars might find this book a meaningful introduction to the field for their students and nonspecialists.

# 2. Mapping Chicago's Organized Crime and Illicit Economies

Archives are not neutral spaces. They house the records of powerful families, churches, and states; privilege institutional histories over individual and household histories; silence historically marginalized groups; and wield the power to shape memories and index collective histories.[1] No historical record is 100 percent complete, but women's histories are more incomplete than men's. Archives have obscured women's history when male-dominated archiving efforts have ignored women's contributions to social life, repositories have physically separated women's records from men's, and women have considered their own writings inconsequential and unworthy of storage.[2] Archives' obscuring women's history is even truer for criminal women's history, in which secrecy, privacy, and cover-ups are key features of successful crimes.

Locating syndicate women in the archives required a relational approach that relied on publicly available information on the criminal men in women's lives. Using a relational approach meant that rather than searching for individual organized crime women, I searched for organized crime men's relationships to others. In the folders and boxes dedicated to Chicago's most infamous gangster, Al Capone, his cronies, and other public enemies are occasional mentions of the names of women and brief descriptions of women's criminal and noncriminal activities. Women's criminal and noncriminal records are in the archives, but they are entangled with men's history, much as a relational approach would assume. The historical records on women in organized crime are incomplete and often pose more questions than they answer, but the records contain detailed information on relationships among men and, sometimes, between men and women.

One particularly fascinating example of this archival entanglement is the case of Betty Schwartz, which highlights some of the challenges in archival research on women in organized crime. Schwartz's story was archived twice in the Capone files at the Chicago Crime Commission.[3] Capone's files were the most voluminous I found in the archives because he was Chicago's favorite rags-to-riches mobster; he ascended from brothel doorman to syndicate boss during Prohibition. According to the Capone files at the Chicago Crime Commission, in 1930 police in Florida arrested three men, Fred Eberhardt, Frank Ralls, and Henry Helsema, who were suspects in a plot to assassinate Florida governor Doyle Carlton. Police found one of the suspects, Eberhardt, in a hotel room with eighteen-year-old Chicago native Betty Schwartz. When she was taken in for questioning, Schwartz implicated Capone in the plot to assassinate the Florida governor. Capone and his family had moved to Miami Beach that year and had frequently appeared in local newspaper headlines, so the connection between a high-profile Florida murder and Capone was not extraordinary. While being questioned, Schwartz claimed that she was a Capone gang affiliate in Chicago and Miami.[4] Her wild claim of Capone gang affiliation received little attention from the arresting officers.[5] According to the *Chicago Tribune*'s reporting of the event, when "[r]epeatedly questioned regarding what information she may have in connection with the reported plot, the Schwartz girl finally retorted: 'I have lots of information, but try and get it.' Questioned further she became so enraged that she attacked the jail matron."[6]

When investigators questioned Capone about the assassination plot, he denied any involvement but was not surprised that he had been implicated. He was becoming more and more familiar with his name being besmirched any time a scandal erupted in Illinois or Florida. There was no mention of whether he knew the three suspects, Eberhardt, Ralls, and Helsema, or if he knew Schwartz. A *Chicago Tribune* reporter interviewed Schwartz's mother, who lived in Chicago, about her daughter's involvement in the assassination attempt. Mrs. Schwartz doubted her daughter's claims and credibility: "Pretty Betty Schwartz has run afoul of the law before in the course of her eighteen years, her mother admitted yesterday. . . . But her claim to membership in the Capone gang or knowledge of their activities is braggadocio intended to impress the police, she added. Mrs. Schwartz explained that Betty, at sixteen, was sentenced to the home for wayward girls at Geneva. Afterward she was committed to an asylum in Wisconsin."[7]

If there was more to Schwartz's story, it is no longer available to us. Answers to why a young woman from Chicago, spending time with the publisher of the *Tallahassee State News*, would want to implicate Al Capone and claim to be part of his gang would be pure speculation. Betty Schwartz was, however, the only woman on record who ever claimed membership in

Capone's syndicate during Prohibition, and I found her intriguing story in archival documents preserved for Capone. For whatever reason, an investigator at the Chicago Crime Commission took the newspaper articles on her seriously enough to clip them from the newspaper and file them in the Capone folders.

Betty Schwartz's story also raises questions about veracity in the archives. Al Capone never mentioned her, and her mother disputed the young woman's membership in Capone's gang. Whose account should be taken seriously for historical research purposes? Historical research on organized crime requires sifting through a century of allegations, triangulating accounts, and reading between the lines. In the end, I included Betty Schwartz in the Prohibition era organized crime network, as I did hundreds of men and dozens of women whose details in the historical records were similarly thin or based on a single allegation. This project required building a detailed relational database that included allegations and questionable claims, but I applied the tools of social network analysis and spatial mapping to the database to sort out much of the noise and allegation within the archives.

THE ARCHIVES

To build a relational database on organized crime, I accessed files and boxes at four physical archives located in Chicago, downloaded files from four online archives, and coded pages from a selection of historical and contemporary secondary sources. Table 1 presents an exhaustive list of all the sources and the distribution of the 5,001 pages of documents and notes coded to create the database. Missing from this table are the additional thousands of archival pages that I skimmed through in search of organized crime individuals and their relationships. The types of documents in the physical and online archives ranged from newspaper clippings and obituaries to details of police investigations, bail bond cards, tax documents, and court testimony.

At the Chicago Crime Commission, I accessed the original public enemy reports that designated Al Capone as Chicago's—and America's— first-ever public enemy number 1. At the National Archives and Records Administration–Great Lakes Region, I accessed all of the documents from the federal lawsuits that attempted to bust Capone, which included charges of conspiracy to violate the Prohibition Act, contempt of court, and of course, the more successful charge of conspiracy to violate the Revenue Act (better known today as tax fraud). (In 1931, two years before Prohibition

TABLE 1. Primary and Secondary Sources in the Capone Database

| Physical Archives | Collection | Pages |
|---|---|---|
| Chicago Crime Commission | Various criminal and correspondence files | 2,081 |
| Chicago History Museum | Institute for Juvenile Research Life Histories | 178 |
| National Archives–Great Lakes Region | Criminal Case files | 1,072 |
| Newberry Library | Waller & Beckwith Realty Company Collection | 6 |

| Online Archives | Collection | |
|---|---|---|
| Internal Revenue Service | Historical documents relating to Alphonse Capone | 86 |
| FBI FOIA Electronic Reading Room | Gangster Era: Al Capone | 6 |
| Northwestern's History of Homicide in Chicago, 1870–1930 | | 130 |
| ProQuest Newspapers: *Chicago Tribune* | | 788 |

| Historical Secondary Sources | | |
|---|---|---|
| Asbury, Herbert. 1940. *Gem of the Prairie.* | | 172 |
| Landesco, John. 1929. *Organized Crime in Chicago.* | | 231 |
| Pasley, Fred. 1930. *Al Capone: The Biography of a Self-made Man* | | 23 |
| Reckless, Walter. 1933. *Vice in Chicago.* | | 12 |

| Contemporary Secondary Sources | | |
|---|---|---|
| Abbott, Karen. 2007. *Sin in the Second City.* | | 3 |
| Eig, Jonathan. 2010. *Get Capone.* | | 159 |
| Russo, Gus. 2001. *The Outfit.* | | 45 |
| Stelzer, Patricia. 1997. *An Examination of the Life of John Torrio.* | | 9 |
| | Total | 5,001 |

ended, Capone was found guilty of tax evasion.) Electronic access to the *Chicago Tribune* archives provided search functions for hundreds of historical accounts of organized crime people, their activities, and places. Together these documents provide an outsider perspective on Chicago organized crime—as none of the documents was written by organized crime insiders— but a perspective that was recorded concurrently with the organized crime activities. For the insider perspective, I read dozens of life histories from the Institute for Juvenile Research Life Histories Collection at the Chicago History Museum. These life histories have a nearly one-hundred-year-old confidentiality protection, which meant that I was not able to add the names and activities listed in these documents to the database and the organized crime network. Instead, I typed 178 pages of notes from these life histories for the context and voice they provide to some of the criminal activities in Chicago that I discuss throughout this book.

There was much redundancy across these sources, as they saturated similar details of particular events and particular people in Chicago organized crime. Although the documents were fascinating, I did not discover any hidden secrets of Al Capone. I relied on the same archives and read the same documents that prior writers and historians did. The details, individuals, and events were the same as in previous accounts, but my approach to these archival sources was novel because I used them to construct a relational database on historical organized crime. The archives were not nicely arranged for this analysis, with links and actors clearly defined. Rather, what makes this project unique is that I dug into each court document, investigator's note, and newspaper clipping to reconstruct Capone's web of crime strand by strand.

## THE CAPONE DATABASE

Across the 5,001 pages of sources listed in table 1, I found 3,321 people who were in some way referenced to organized crime activity and its investigations in Chicago in the early 1900s, 15,861 social relationships among these people, and 1,540 locations where they spent their time. I organized, sorted, and classified these people, relationships, and addresses in a relational database called the Capone Database. Al Capone offered the starting point to build Chicago's historical organized crime network.[8] Although his was an impressive organized crime success story, no hustling entrepreneur has the time or the memory to recall three thousand names and describe the fifteen thousand relationships among them. Importantly for a social network perspective, Capone's view of his own personal network would not be the same as a bird's-eye view of his network. Social networks locate individuals in a massive web of connection, and individuals are only privy to their most local section of the network. One of the amazing aspects of social network analysis is that it reveals how embedded we are in the web of social life beyond what we can ever imagine.

The Capone Database is unique in its scope, detail, size, and historical moment, as most social science databases lack any information on relationships among actors. Thick data on relationships (e.g., the different types, time, and sometimes location of social interactions and connections) have the potential to reveal much about criminal groups' actions and outcomes, even when the information on individual criminals is thin (e.g., sometimes nothing more than a name). In other words, we often do not have much detail on the background of criminals from history, but we can learn a lot by examining the patterns of their relationships to co-arrestees and co-offenders.

People in the Capone Database include attorneys, judges, police officers, witnesses, and of course, criminals. Addresses in the Capone Database include saloons, brothels, and gambling dens, as well as hotels and restaurants. Importantly, the Capone Database contains detailed information on more than one hundred different types of relationships, such as business associations, criminal associations, family relationships, romantic partnerships, friendships, financial exchanges, funeral attendance, legal charges and rulings, courtroom witnesses, travel companions, political associations, rivalries, union associations, and violence exchanges. The majority of these relationships occurred during Prohibition, but the database includes relationships dated as early as 1882 and as late as 1952. Some of the relationships were directed, such as one person paying a second person's bail or one person shooting another, while others were undirected, such as two brothers or a group traveling to the Bahamas together. Some relationships were negative in type or action, such as those that involved rivalries and violence, whereas others were positive associations, such as friendships and political campaign contributions.

In its entirety, the Capone Database captures the messiness of social life; a positive, undirected relationship such as a romantic partnership is a very different type of social connection than a negative, directed relationship such as ordering a hit on someone. Rather than analyzing the Capone Database in its entirety, I subset the Capone Database to generate samples of theoretical and empirical interest. I used two subsets from the Capone Database for the research in this book: (1) the criminal relationships comprising Chicago's organized crime network and (2) the address data mapping the geography of Chicago's illicit economies. I discuss these in detail in the following sections.

## THE ORGANIZED CRIME NETWORK

After building the Capone Database, the next step I took to reconstruct Chicago's organized crime network was to create a subset of data that included only the criminal relationships. As I have mentioned, there are more than one hundred types of relationships in the Capone Database, but the networks covered in this book use only the criminal ones. Criminal relationships encompassed general criminal associations, co-owners of illegitimate businesses, coworkers in illegitimate business, making graft (i.e., extortion and bribery) or protection payments, co-arrests, criminal mentorships, and political corruption. I treated all the criminal relationships in this subset as undirected and equally weighted. Undirected relationships do not distinguish between who sent and who received the criminal relationship. Treating the criminal relationships as equally weighted means that for the purposes of this analysis, a $50 graft payment to a collector is equal to the criminal relationship between top crime bosses; both appear in the network as a single criminal link between the two criminal actors. Historians might take issue with such a crude collapsing of historical context, but this is an important step in aggregating the data to reveal the structure of organized crime. In the Capone Database, a criminal relationship between two individuals—such as the owner of a speakeasy buying booze from a bootlegger—does not equal organized crime. This relationship was merely a case of criminalized employment or market connection. Rather, the constellation of how multiple criminal relationships came together and centered on particular individuals within particular markets reveals the larger structure in which this single criminal transaction fits.

The last step was to decide which criminal relationships in the subset were part of organized crime and which were not. Early on in my research, it became clear that some of the information on criminal relationships in the archives was not actually part of Chicago organized crime (e.g., the uncertainty around the Betty Schwartz case). Some investigator or reporter assumed that a particular event was connected to organized crime and stuffed a newspaper clipping into an organized crime folder, but the presence of the clipping did not mean that these people and events were all connected. Moving from the subset of criminal relationships to an organized crime network therefore required a process of identification that could remove petty criminals who existed outside the sphere of influence and protection of powerful Chicago mobsters.

I relied on theory to distinguish the networked organization of organized crime from everyday criminal groups. Scholars have been debating the usefulness of the term "organized crime" for decades.[9] In fact, one of the earliest uses of the term has a unique connection to Chicago in the early 1900s. Criminologist Klaus von Lampe traced the term's origin and found that the Chicago Crime Commission (whose archives I accessed for this research) coined the term "organized crime" in 1919 in reference to

Chicago's estimated (and likely exaggerated) "10,000 professional criminals" who conducted "crime as a business."[10] It is historically interesting that the label came from an outside, private law enforcement organization. However, central to my conceptualization and measurement of the Chicago organized crime network were the following insights from organized crime scholarship: (1) the primary activity of Chicago organized crime was dominating and protecting shifting illicit markets; (2) Chicago organized crime included state actors through exploiting and corrupting law enforcement, politicians, and judges; (3) violence was a means of enforcement and market protection, especially during Prohibition; and (4) the organization was durable over time, withstanding assassinations and the incarceration of various figureheads.[11]

Organizations are bounded networks with density around powerful roles.[12] An organization requires the intentional relational formation of a group of people for some purpose, production, or set of tasks.[13] The goals of Chicago organized crime were to make a lot of money, control the illicit market and its politics, and avoid prosecution within shifting legal fields. These goals required many complicit actors who contributed their resources and talents, took risks, engaged in some level of trust, and privileged secrecy. Conceptualizing Chicago organized crime as a networked organization assumes that the following were its relational resources: (1) access to crooked politicians, police officers, judges, and fixers who provided protection from legal prosecution; (2) proximity to influential and violent gangsters, who controlled who participated in criminal markets and their income-generating opportunities; and (3) flows of trust and information that limited market competition, quashed rivals, and developed durable positions and promotions. Thus, the central difference between low-level Chicago criminals and criminals within organized crime was differentiated access to the relational resources of organized crime.

Following these theoretical insights, I needed a method to distinguish everyday criminals from the members of organized crime. This required social network analysis. Thus, the last step of building the organized crime network was identifying the "components" in my subset of Chicago criminal relationships to operationalize the network's "giant component" as organized crime. Components identify and measure each section of the network in which all of the actors are reachable through paths to or through each other but have no paths to other actors in other sections of the network.[14] Components can be of different sizes, ranging from as small as one actor, which would be an isolate or an actor with zero relationships or connections in the network, to as large as the maximum size of the entire network, with

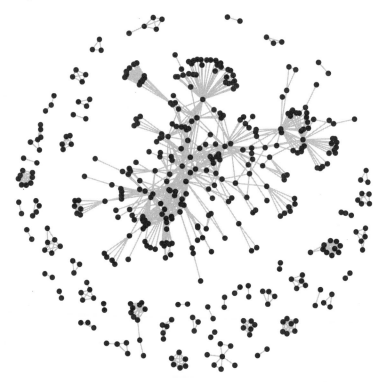

FIGURE 2. Network of all components with criminal relationships, 1900–1919.

every single actor being connected in a single component. In a disconnected network, the component that connects the greatest number of actors is called the "giant component."

Figure 2 plots all of the criminals and their criminal relationships in the Capone Database from 1900 to 1919. Each circle (or node) represents an actor or individual in the network, and each line (or link) represents a criminal relationship or tie between actors in the network. The figure shows a disconnected network containing multiple components with no paths that connect or bridge different sections of the network.[15] It reveals a network of fifty-one components. At its center is the giant component, with a structure distinct from all other sections of the network. Based on the preceding theoretical discussion, the giant component, unlike the smaller components, contains the definitional requirements of Chicago organized crime as established by organized crime scholars and the relational resources required of networked organizations. For the Capone Database, the giant component is the best measurement of the organized crime network.

Organized crime did not include all of Chicago's criminals, as some of them operated independently from organized crime activities and characters. As pictured in figure 2, surrounding the giant component, but never connecting to it, are dozens of smaller components containing just a few individuals. These smaller components represent co-offenses (e.g., bank robberies, illegitimate businesses' activities, brothels' operations, street gang activities) that showed up in the archival searches related to organized crime but never connected to organized crime individuals through criminal relationships. The lack of connection to the giant component suggests that these criminal groups were distinct from organized crime and had no overlapping criminal relationships with members of organized crime. Their apparent independence from organized crime could be an issue of missing historical data. However, the giant component was the most complete part of the Capone Database because of the particular archives I accessed and the saturation I reached in coding the same events across multiple archival documents.

## THE ORGANIZED CRIME NETWORK'S PROPERTIES

Measuring the Chicago organized crime network required two steps of data analysis from the Capone Database: (1) subset only the criminal relationships and (2) identify the giant component. With this technique, I was able to measure Chicago's organized crime at two points in history. I generated the network for two time periods: 1900 to 1919 (Progressive Era) and 1920 to 1933 (Prohibition). This restricted timeline required me to drop all criminal relationships that did not have approximate years, although I attempted to approximate a year or time period whenever possible.[16] The resulting organized crime network contained 789 criminal relationships among 267 people from 1900 to 1919 and 3,250 criminal relationships among 937 people from 1920 to 1933.

Figure 3 presents the Chicago organized crime network at two points in time. Each circle in figure 3 represents an organized crime individual. Black circles designate organized crime men, and white circles designate organized crime women. Each line between the circles represents some type of criminal relationship between pairs. At the dyad level (pairs of actors), each line in the criminal network indicates some form of criminal collusion or co-offense between two people. At the level of the giant component, the larger structure of organized crime and its changes over time finally become visible. In this abstract form, this network provides precise measures of who was involved in organized crime and their positions within organized crime.

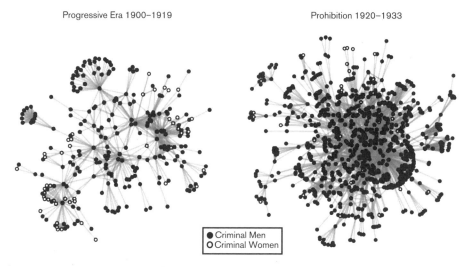

Progressive Era 1900–1919         Prohibition 1920–1933

● Criminal Men
O Criminal Women

FIGURE 3. Chicago organized crime network, 1900–1919 (n = 267) and 1920–1933 (n = 937).

Figure 3 visualizes how the organized crime network changed between the Progressive Era and Prohibition. Only twenty-seven individuals (twenty-six men and one woman) endured the structural changes in organized crime and persisted across both time periods of the network (see chapter 6 for a discussion of the persisters).

The network visualizations in figure 3 map out distances in social space rather than geographic space. This visualization places the people most central in the network toward the middle and those most peripheral to the network toward the outside. This is why we see so many individuals with only one criminal relationship around the edges of the network and why the center of the network is so dense. Even with this general rule, there are some unique sections around the outside of the network where we can see a single individual connecting a large number of people to the denser center. One notable example is at the top of the Progressive Era organized crime network. This one individual is connecting all the individuals above him to organized crime. (I discuss the importance of this network property, called "brokerage," in more detail in the coming chapters.)

To establish the structural changes in organized crime, I calculated indices that measure the whole of the network: size, number of ties, density, degree centralization, betweenness centralization, and diameter. These structural measurements are not independent of each other. They are all

TABLE 2. Properties of Chicago Organized Crime Network, 1900–1919 and 1920–1933

|  | Progressive Era 1900–1919 | Prohibition 1920–1933 |
| --- | --- | --- |
| Number of individuals | 267 | 937 |
| Number of criminal ties | 789 | 3,250 |
| Density | 0.022 | 0.007 |
| Degree centralization | 0.140 | 0.331 |
| Betweenness centralization | 0.398 | 0.707 |
| Diameter | 8 | 12 |

different ways of examining network size and connectivity. Table 2 presents the precise calculations of these structural measures by listing network properties from the Progressive Era organized crime network and the Prohibition era organized crime network. These properties are based on graph theory and have explicit definitions and often technical formulas. I provide some additional detail in the endnotes.[17]

Network *size* is the number of actors (or nodes) in the network. Size measures how large or how small a network is. Related to size is the *number of criminal ties* among actors present in the network. Network *density* is the percent of all ties present in a network given all the possible ties that could exist among a set of actors.[18] Density measures how connected the network is. *Degree* measures how central each actor is in a network by counting the number of ties or links each actor has. Degree tells us which actors are the highest and lowest in concepts such as popularity, social capital, or power. *Degree centralization* measures the distribution of degree across the whole network, ranging from zero, when ties are equally distributed across individuals (e.g., a circle of connections between people), to one, when all ties concentrate on a single individual (e.g., a star of connections, with one person at the center). Degree centralization tells us how concepts such as popularity, social capital, and power are unequally spread across the whole network. *Betweenness* measures intermediaries or "gateways" within components to identify which actors are essential to connecting others to the component.[19] Every actor within a component can reach every other actor in the same component. Examining the shortest path between any two actors in a component (called the *geodesic*) shows that some of those paths require brokers or intermediary actors whose positions in the network help complete the path. Betweenness identifies who the brokers are and who is brokered. *Betweenness centralization* measures the distribution of betweenness in a network on a scale of zero (when each actor in the network has the same betweenness) to one (when a single actor is the intermediary on all of the geodesic paths in the network).[20] Brokerage is a powerful position that maintains networks, and betweenness centralization measures the inequality of brokerage spread across an entire network. Finally, the *diameter* of a network is the largest geodesic distance between two actors in a component, which is counted as the number of links along the shortest path connecting the farthest actors.[21] If a resource needed to travel to everyone in the network, diameter measures the longest distance that resource would have to travel.[22]

Table 2 shows that the Progressive Era organized crime network was relatively small in size, with 267 people, and quite sparse, with only 2 percent of all possible ties present in it. Degree centralization reveals that the network was quite decentralized, with a more equal degree distribution across it. Betweenness centralization reveals that Progressive Era organized crime required intermediaries and gateways connecting people to different parts of the network. The diameter shows that the people farthest from each other in the network could be connected through eight links. All of the properties in table 2 are visible in figure 3. The decentralized structure of the Progressive Era network is visualized as people with high degree scores spread out around the component. We can also see the people who are important intermediaries for keeping different parts of the network connected to the component. We can see the people farthest from each other in the network and follow the shortest paths between them.

Visually and statistically, the Prohibition network was very different. Prohibition brought incredible growth to Chicago organized crime. During Prohibition, the network included three times as many individuals and four times the criminal relationships as organized crime in the Progressive Era. The Prohibition era organized crime network was sparse; only 0.7 percent of all possible ties actually existed during Prohibition. When networks get larger, they become sparser because of how difficult it is to maintain social ties to large numbers of people. In criminal schemes, selective relationships are a strategic choice to maintain secrecy and protection, even if the small criminal scheme is embedded in the larger organized crime network with important relational resources. Degree centralization for Prohibition organized crime was 0.33, which suggests that powerful individuals held a large proportion of criminal ties in the network. Even though the large network was sparse and most people had few criminal connections, those in the core of the network hoarded the bulk of the criminal relationships. One of the most dramatic measurements of the Prohibition network is the betweenness centralization score of 0.7, which indicates that this network was held together by powerful brokers through which the majority of paths had to go. Figure 3 makes clear that these brokers are in the powerful center of the component. Finally, the diameter of the Prohibition organized crime network was 12, meaning that it took twelve steps along the shortest path between the people farthest from each other in the component. These statistical shifts in the network, especially in terms of size and centrality, are also visible in figure 3. To summarize, size determined these networks' structural results. The smaller organized crime network from 1900 to 1919 meant that the network was decentralized and locally clustered. The exogenous shock of Prohibition dramatically grew organized crime from 1920 to 1933, which in turn generated a sparse and centralized structure.

Network size and resulting structure have consequences for people who are already marginalized in organizations. Research on legitimate organizations finds that dense and decentralized networks are more equitable, whereas sparse and centralized networks are inequitable.[23] The reason for this is that any resources contained in dense, decentralized networks are redundant and accessible to more people in the network. On the other hand, large, sparse, and centralized networks generate a hierarchical structure that permits resource hoarding, which creates a bigger division between the people who control the resources in the network and those with limited access to those resources.

Returning to the case at hand, the Chicago organized crime network contained many resources—some more tangible and measurable than others—including access to powerful men in legal positions to fix cases and provide protection from prosecution. When the organized crime network was small, clustered, and decentralized, a woman in organized crime might only be a few network links away from a fixer who could bribe a judge or get her out of jail. If she was arrested or being exploited, she could turn to her network and ask for help. If she was not directly connected to a corrupt alderman or police chief, she could turn to the men to whom she was directly connected, and they would likely know a man to fix the case. In contrast, if a woman in organized crime was arrested in the large, sparse, and centralized network, there were increased chances that the men to whom she was directly connected might still be a few network links away from any of the men who could fix the case. In the large and centralized network, the people with the most influence were most concentrated at the center, where they hoarded the network resources of protection and criminal opportunities. Women, who were already marginalized in organized crime, were farther removed from the powerful centers.

The social network analysis of Chicago organized crime revealed one other important change over time: women made up a substantial 18 percent of the Progressive Era organized crime network, but during Prohibition they were only 4 percent of the network. The remainder of this book digs into layers of explanations to solve the puzzle of why the gender gap in organized crime increased so dramatically during Prohibition. Part of the puzzle's solution hinges on a second set of data from the Capone Database on the addresses of Chicago's illicit businesses over time.

## THE GEOGRAPHY OF CHICAGO'S ILLICIT ECONOMIES

Al Capone's Four Deuces at 2222 South Wabash Avenue is a feature of Chicago organized crime history. In the early 1920s Capone ran one of Chicago's bawdiest brothels there, which doubled as a headquarters for the syndicate.[24] Although today nothing remains of 2222 South Wabash except an empty lot, the property had an organized crime history before Capone even arrived in Chicago.[25] Sol Friedman ran a saloon at 2222 South Wabash Avenue in 1903, one of the many Wabash Avenue saloons that upset Mayor Carter Harrison and the neighborhood vigilance committee.[26] Sol Van Praag was operating a gambling joint at 2222 by 1916 that was syndicated with Mont Tennes's gambling ring.[27] Martin Guilfoyle took over a small space on the 2220 side in July 1919 to run his own gambling joint with a cigar shop front.[28] These men at this address are compelling examples that, as was the case for 2222 South Wabash, location provided more stability for organized crime than did the people. The organized crime network described in this chapter was not bound to a single address even though most activity in the organized crime network took place in the city of Chicago. Mobsters were mobile, and their schemes were not confined to city or state boundaries. We know this because of detailed documentation on addresses and locations in the archives.

In the archives I found addresses of saloons, speakeasies, breweries, brothels, cabarets, dance halls, hotels, and restaurants that violated sex work and alcohol laws; small shops and pharmacies selling alcohol illegally during Prohibition; and domestic spaces of apartments and houses where women and men sold sex or booze. There were addresses for murder scenes and raids on office buildings that served as organized crime headquarters. When investigatory committees and reporters were unable to identify offenders by name, they often relied on the stability of an address for details in their reports. I found archival documents that contained nothing more than lists of twenty to thirty addresses of illicit establishments with no names accompanying them. It was not always clear if these addresses were actually organized crime locations, like 2222 South Wabash Avenue, or unprotected locations that were more susceptible to raids. I transcribed all of the addresses I found across the archives into a spreadsheet in the Capone Database to make sense of what these addresses meant for organized crime and the geography of Chicago's illicit economies.

Overall, the addresses in the Capone Database provide a broad snapshot of locations under the investigatory spotlight in Chicago. Much like the data on relationships, an address in an archival document provided a cross section of history. When a business opened, how long it operated, and when it closed were details often not available in the archival documents. For example, a blind pig (slang for a speakeasy or illicit alcohol establishment) raided in 1924 may have been at that location and in operation before 1924 and may have operated long after 1924, but the archival document only recorded that address in 1924. Although the data on historical addresses are still incomplete, they offer a meaningful lens with which to consider the geography of Chicago's illicit economies.

In total, I found 1,540 addresses during my archival research that included legal and illegal establishments. For the purposes of this book, I limited my analysis to establishments involved in sex work and alcohol operating during the Progressive Era from 1900 to 1919 and Prohibition from 1920 to 1933. This sample included formal and informal brothels controlled by organized crime, but importantly, it also included similar spaces that were not part of organized crime. Mapping the illicit economies of sex work and alcohol allowed me to examine whether the gender exclusionary processes that occurred within the organized crime network were also occurring more broadly in the illicit economies outside of organized crime.

Gambling was an important part of Chicago's illicit economy and organized crime. Although my data collection included addresses on gambling locations, these addresses did not appear as frequently in the archives as did saloons and brothels, except for the saloons that had gambling. There were sixty-three gambling-only (no mention of a saloon or alcohol sales) establishments with named owners and operators during the Progressive Era (none of whom were women). However, I dropped the gambling-only establishments from the spatial analysis because there were only twenty-six such establishments with named owners and operators during Prohibition (two of whom were women). The small number of gambling-only establishments did not lead to convincing gender analysis results, and it became clear in my analysis that much of the illicit gambling economy occurred in saloons and occasionally even in brothels.

I used only sex work and alcohol addresses that included names of proprietors, managers, and co-owners for the comparative analysis. (Establishments with no named proprietors were used only to construct maps.) These names were critical to my comparative analysis for two reasons. First, this step allowed me to establish which addresses were managed or owned by individuals in the organized crime network. I matched names associated with sex work and alcohol addresses to names in the organized crime network to classify establishments as involved in organized crime. Second, named proprietors identified which addresses included women in the management and ownership of the establishment. Some of these women appear in the organized crime network, but many do not. I used gendered pronouns (she, her, hers) and titles (Mrs. and Miss) with the names to identify which addresses included women as managers, operators, or proprietors (women sex workers were seldom mentioned, let alone named in the archives). Removing establishments without any named proprietors from the comparative sample dropped 41 percent of Chicago's sex work addresses and 22 percent of the alcohol addresses. In the following discussion I calculate percentages of addresses that involved women or members of the organized crime network. I use the term "involved" a bit passively because it was not often clear how many people were involved and how many were missing, how long named individuals were involved, or what exactly their role was at the establishment.

In total, I identified 480 unique sex work–related addresses with named owners and operators within the thirty-four-year time period. These locations included formal spaces such as brothels, as well as cabarets, dance halls, restaurants, and saloons that violated sex work laws.[29] The sex work–related addresses also included the domestic spaces of apartments and houses where women and men sold sex. There were nineteen sex work–related addresses that spanned both the Progressive and Prohibition eras. I identified 480 unique alcohol-related addresses with named owners and operators within the thirty-four-year time period, including saloons, speakeasies, and breweries, as well as restaurants, small shops, and pharmacies selling alcohol illegally.[30] These addresses also include domestic spaces such as blind pigs, beer flats, and homes providing domestic sales of moonshine. There were nine alcohol-related addresses that spanned both eras. In the Progressive Era, there were ninety-one addresses that sold both sex and alcohol (seven of which included women as managers, operators, or proprietors). In the Prohibition era, there were thirty-two addresses that sold both sex and alcohol (seven of which included women as managers, operators, or proprietors). These addresses appear in both illicit economies in map 1 and table 3.

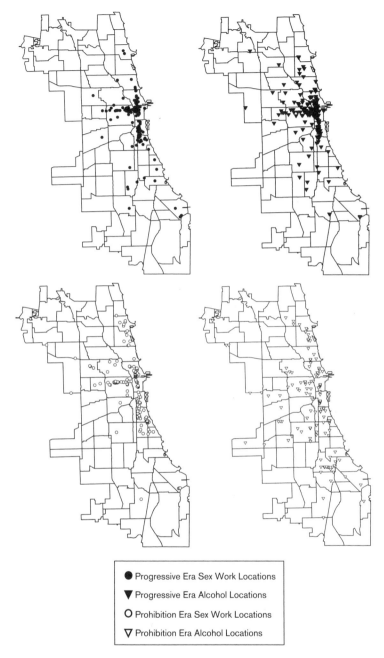

MAP 1. Chicago sex work and alcohol establishments, 1900–1919 and 1920–1933. *Sources:* Chicago Data Portal, "Boundaries—Community Areas (current)," 2018, https://data.cityofchicago.org/Facilities-Geographic-Boundaries/Boundaries -Community-Areas-current-/cauq-8yn6, accessed June 24, 2018; Andrew Ba Tran, "Mapping with R," 2017, https://andrewbtran.github.io/NICAR/2017/maps /mapping-census-data.html, accessed June 24, 2018.

TABLE 3. Sex Work and Alcohol Establishments with Named Proprietors, 1900–1919 and 1920–1933

|  | Sex Work Addresses | | Alcohol Addresses | |
|---|---|---|---|---|
|  | Progressive Era | Prohibition | Progressive Era | Prohibition |
|  | (1900–1919) | (1920–1933) | (1900–1919) | (1920–1933) |
| Total number of addresses | 576 | 288 | 367 | 261 |
| Number of addresses with named proprietors | 322 | 177 | 321 | 168 |
| Percent addresses missing names | 44% | 39% | 13% | 36% |
| Number of women-involved addresses | 125 | 86 | 13 | 45 |
| Percent women-involved | 39% | 49% | 4% | 27% |
| Number of organized crime–involved addresses | 80 | 39 | 48 | 38 |
| Percent organized crime-involved | 25% | 22% | 15% | 23% |

NOTE: Percentages of women-involved (i.e., as proprietors, coproprietors, operators, or managers) addresses and organized crime–involved addresses use the total of addresses with named proprietors for calculations, not the total set of addresses that includes unnamed or missing proprietors. Criteria for organized crime–involved addresses required proprietors who were in the organized crime network during the corresponding time period.

I used contemporary mapping software on the historical address data with named and unnamed proprietors to examine the geographic spread of the illicit economies. Not all of the addresses I identified appear in map 1. Some were too old to approximate a matching contemporary address. Street names have changed, and highways have replaced old roads. Overall, map 1 shows that the geography of Chicago brothels and sex work establishments was quite consistent between the Progressive and Prohibition eras. Map 1 also shows that saloons and alcohol establishments were located in the same districts as the brothels during the Progressive Era but spread out more from the city center during Prohibition. I discuss these changes and their implications in more detail in the coming chapters. Here I introduce these addresses to provide context regarding the illicit geographies within the urban space of Chicago to show what these patterns meant for women.

The address data provide evidence regarding the changing markets around sex work and alcohol and women's and organized crime's involvement in the changing illicit economies. Table 3 includes the counts and percentages by era of illicit establishment addresses in the sex work and alcohol economies that involved women as proprietors, coproprietors, operators, or managers. These were not women-only establishments, because many of the addresses that involved women also involved men as co-owners, comanagers, or property owners with women managers. These percentages do not indicate gender segregation, as women's relationships with men clearly shape the locations of the criminal economy, but these percentages point toward trends in women's involvement, most often alongside men, within Chicago's criminal landscape.

The percentage of women involved in operating the sex work addresses increased between the Progressive Era and Prohibition: women were involved in 39 percent of the sex work–related addresses from 1900 to 1919 and 49 percent from 1920 to 1933. Women's involvement in operating alcohol establishments was much lower than their involvement in sex work establishments. However, women's involvement in alcohol distribution and sales still increased during Prohibition. Women were involved in only 4 percent of alcohol-related addresses from 1900 to 1919, but in 27 percent of addresses from 1920 to 1933. Here the puzzle deepens, as these address data demonstrate that women were a growing presence in two of the major illicit economies in Chicago during Prohibition, even while they had a shrinking presence in the organized crime network. In the following chapters I return to this part of the puzzle and detail the reasons this contradictory pattern occurred.

Table 3 also includes the counts and percentages of organized crime proprietors, coproprietors, operators, or managers involved in the illicit establishment addresses. These calculations summarize the changing proportions of individuals involved in the sex economy and the alcohol economy who were part of the organized crime network (see figure 3). The percentages show how many addresses with named proprietors included a named person who appeared in the organized crime network of the corresponding era. The archives did not always make clear this person's role at the establishment, but for these instances I found documents associating the organized crime person with a specific illicit place. Across most of the columns, I actually found more women involved in these establishments than named organized crime individuals. I also found less dramatic change in the percent of organized crime–involved addresses between the two eras. Organized crime individuals were involved in 25 percent of the sex work–related addresses from 1900 to 1919 and 22 percent from 1920 to 1933. Organized crime individuals were involved in 15 percent of the alcohol-related addresses from 1900 to 1919 and 23 percent from 1920 to 1933.

The growth in the organized crime network during Prohibition is inconsistent with the stability and low percentages in the illicit establishment address data. Perhaps this inconsistency points to the success of the protection market. Organized crime was powerful enough to keep its properties away from investigation and raids and to direct attention toward unprotected properties, especially in the early years of Prohibition. Likely the domestic spaces, where women had increased opportunities for participating in the illicit economies during Prohibition, were more susceptible to raids and investigations. (I return to this point in more detail in chapter 5.)

## THE LIMITATIONS

This research faced the same challenges and limitations that arise in all social network analysis studies dealing with crime data and dark networks. Dark networks refer to hidden networks that cannot be seen by researchers and sometimes even by network members themselves. Networks are not dark because they are necessarily criminal. They are dark when they are clandestine and members prefer to conceal their identities and their activities (e.g., secret organizations, HIV-infected people, hate groups).

The main challenge in the analysis of dark networks is incomplete data. I likely encountered incomplete data on Chicago historical organized crime networks (a) where investigators and reporters did not record and archive events and relationships because the events and relationships were either unremarkable, hidden, or backstage and (b) where investigators and reporters recorded and archived events incorrectly, either intentionally because of lying and cover-ups or unintentionally because they did not know the full story. *Chicago Tribune* reporters, Chicago Crime Commission investigators, and federal Prohibition and Internal Revenue Service (IRS) agents had a special interest in uncovering and prosecuting a particular version of organized crime that went after a few high-profile men and largely ignored the associates at the margins.

Gaps in the historical record resulted in underestimating organized crime networks, especially at the margins where women's and low-level men's criminal relationships were located. For example, the *Chicago Tribune* reporter never named the "henna-haired madam" working at Capone's Four Deuces in 1922.[31] I never found even one mention in the archives of a sex worker's name connected to a Capone brothel during Prohibition. I found no mention in the archives of waitresses or barmaids connected to organized crime saloons, even though urban workingwomen formed the class of waitresses in all the major Chicago restaurants, where they performed the same kind of labor that was required of workers in speakeasies and parlors.[32] Meridel Le Sueur's novel *The Girl* (written in 1939 but not published until 1978) detailed this gendered, behind-the-scenes work of Midwest speakeasies, in which young women found jobs and formed romantic relationships with men boot-leggers.[33] But it was novelists, not reporters or organized crime investigators, who detailed these backstage Prohibition era relationships.

I am similarly convinced that marginal men, such as bartenders, drivers, plumbers, and couriers, are also likely to be underestimated in the networks. Archival coverage of organized crime was greater during Prohibition than in the Progressive Era, in large part because of the coordinated efforts of the Federal Bureau of Investigation, the Chicago Crime Commission, and the IRS to bust Al Capone in the late 1920s and early 1930s. Any investigatory spotlight on Capone and his inner circle would have excluded women because they were not part of the inner circle, but many men participating in organized crime were also not part of the inner circle. As long as the men at the margins performing mundane, behind-the-scenes labor of organized crime's illicit economy were as likely to be missing from the archives as women, then missing data on organized crime associates at the margins should not dramatically impact the overall results of my analysis by gender.

Where missing information on women is most consequential is the limited information I was able to find on wives of organized crime figures. Reporters and investigators documented gangsters' wives as notable individuals and occasionally documented their financial connections to organized crime. However, there were so few cases of wives connected to Progressive Era and Prohibition organized crime that I suspect other influences on missing information about wives in the archives. These influences could include the trope of the silent wife who either knew everything or nothing but would never say, and this trope clouded journalists' and investigators' accounts.[34] Perhaps the gender bias of law enforcement, investigators, and journalists assumed that women were innocent, less capable of crime, or inconsequential as criminals.[35] Perhaps husbands involved in high-risk organized crime activities went to greater lengths to protect their homes and families from investigation. All three of these propositions would be fascinating additions to this historical case and could potentially speak to the empirical puzzle, but the archives are remarkably silent about the wives of organized crime. Data limitations may influence some of my findings, such as the low numbers of women in organized crime. However, I have no reason to believe that the limitations differed so substantially across the two time periods that they would generate dramatic gender differences in organized crime. Data limitations, such as scant information on organized crime wives and women at the margins, were prevalent during both time periods of my analysis.

The Capone Database is just one possible iteration of the social world during a particular historical moment. Data on criminals often feel partial and flawed, and this is especially the case for historical women criminals. Political scientist Peter Andreas, the author of *Smuggler Nation: How Illicit Trade Made America*, advises: "[I]t is better to tell the story with admittedly imperfect and incomplete data than to simply throw up one's hands and pretend that the world of smuggling doesn't exist because it cannot be precisely measured. After all, that would be the equivalent of a drunkard looking for his keys under the lightpost because it is the only place he can see."[36] I agree with Andreas's sentiment. It is better to pursue the analysis and dig into what remains of the historical record while acknowledging the limitations of incomplete data than to leave dominant narratives unchallenged. Adding to Andreas, researchers should use analytic tools that can draw the signal from the noise in historical data and bring fresh perspectives to classic debates.

## THE MOVE FROM EVIDENCE TO ARGUMENT

The historical analysis and organized crime network analysis in this book explain syndicate women's inclusion and exclusion from organized crime relationships that occurred simultaneously with women's increasing locations in illicit economies across the city of Chicago. My argument is that the increasing gender gap found in organized crime during Prohibition was inconsistent with women's increased participation in Prohibition era crime. Central to syndicate women's stories are the broader contexts of population and industrial growth of Chicago as the Second City of the United States; the fluctuating enforcement of laws and municipal regulations responding to the activism of the Progressive Era; the nontraditional pursuit of the American Dream through corruption, exploitation, and crime; and an organizational shift centering on a few infamous men hoarding resources and blocking opportunities.

The mixed-methods approach of historical research plus social network analysis provides the intellectual room to interrogate the meaning of the social relationships in organized crime networks and to examine closely the historical moment in which the networks developed. With social network analysis, I am able to address the generic network processes that occur writ large in our social worlds—such as preferences, similarity, status, power, and influence—and measure and compare these processes to provide insight into my case. I adhere to a back-and-forth approach between the networks and the historical narrative and context to evolve meaning and develop theory. Inherent to this is that I have treated social network analysis as a logic of discovery for a particular set of events, group of people, and historical moment more than as a logic of proof.

# 3. Chicago, Crime, and the Progressive Era

From 1880 to 1890 Chicago's population more than doubled, making it the second largest city in the United States, with a population of just over one million. By 1910 Chicago claimed more than two million residents. Rural laborers, waves of migrants from southern and eastern Europe, and the great migration of African Americans from the South, all moving to Chicago in pursuit of food, work, and money, fueled urban growth in the early 1900s. As the city's population grew, urban entertainment thrived on the wages of industrial capitalism. Workers' demands for leisure redefined city blocks, outpaced regulations, and brought together men and women from all walks of life.

Unaccompanied young men and women arrived in Chicago in unprecedented numbers. In 1909 Jane Addams, a charter member of the American Sociological Society, sociology instructor at the University of Chicago, and founder of Chicago's settlement house Hull House, lamented the changes she observed in urban youth and young adults: "Never before in civilization have such numbers of young girls been suddenly released from the protection of the home and permitted to walk unattended upon city streets and to work under alien roofs; for the first time they are being prized more for their labor power than for their innocence, their tender beauty, their ephemeral gaiety.... Never before have such numbers of young boys earned money independently of the family life, and felt themselves free to spend it as they choose in the midst of vice deliberately disguised as pleasure."[1] While Addams's sentiments exemplified the social movement politics of the Progressive Era and progressive activists' concern for white women's exploitation in the urban labor force, her alarm at "vice deliberately disguised as pleasure" referred to the lucrative and growing urban entertainment economy of sex work, gambling, saloons, cabarets, and dance halls.[2] White women found rather decent returns "more for their labor power than for their innocence" in Chicago's licit and illicit entertainment centers. As Addams noted, the growing city redefined traditions of labor, family, gender, and crime.

Chicago organized crime staked its own claim to these urban entertainment profits by coordinating the protection and exploitation of illicit gambling and sex work businesses with the complicity of political and law enforcement offices. Progressive Era organized crime developed and maintained a territorial protection market that exploited Chicago's red-light districts, where brothels, gambling dens, dance halls, and saloons were concentrated. Today this type of protection market is more commonly referred to as a "protection racket," but the term "racket" to describe illicit businesses or the extortion of money came into use about a decade later, originating in Chicago to describe Prohibition's illicit and violent markets.[3] As the political organizing of Progressive Era activists increased and local regulations and enforcements cracked down on gambling, sex work, and saloons, the illicit entertainment economy had increasing need for a protection market. This formed the foundation for Chicago organized crime. As I show in chapter 4, women were a substantial part of organized crime during the twenty years of the Progressive Era, in which they paid collectors and fixers, owned or managed protected brothels, and trafficked other women.

In this chapter I detail the legal and geographic conditions that permitted organized crime to develop and thrive in Chicago at the turn of the twentieth century. I begin with a discussion of Progressive Era activism and its influence on shifting sex work regulations. State laws and municipal codes expanded what was considered a sex work violation, but these regulations were irregularly enforced at the local level. Thriving red-light districts in Chicago openly flaunted their violations of the law, often with few negative consequences. Second, I explain the work conditions for men and women in the sex economy as gendered labor and how gendered labor generated leadership opportunities for women in brothel management and ownership in 39 percent of Chicago's brothels during the Progressive Era. I then show how the illicit entertainment economy was spatially concentrated in three red-light districts in Chicago. Organized crime developed a territorial protection market in the red-light districts where politicians, law enforcement, and men and women owners of illicit entertainment businesses coordinated a loose and profitable syndication of graft payments, collections, protections, and extortion. This chapter establishes the historical conditions of the Progressive Era—ambiguous and shifting regulations targeting illicit entertainment, local law enforcement's discretion and corruption, the importance of gendered labor in illicit entertainment, and the spatial concentration of illicit entertainment—under which women had increased opportunities for participation in Chicago's illicit entertainment economy and consequentially in organized crime.

## THE LAWS AND THEIR ENFORCEMENT

Chicago's most lucrative urban entertainments were risky businesses. When police and local politicians tolerated gambling dens, brothels, and saloons, the business owners of the illicit entertainment economy operated successfully with only mild risk. Though not illegal, saloons and dance halls were highly regulated by city statutes and frequently raided by Chicago police and morals inspectors. Saloons and dance halls faced violations when women entered those establishments without male escorts, when interracial couples danced or socialized, and when the establishments failed to follow municipal closing hours. These regulations were municipal attempts to enforce boundaries around gender, race, and ethnicity. The Progressive Era's politics and its broad and varied concerns about social improvements assumed that unaccompanied women in saloons were prostitutes, that interracial mixing would destabilize the racialized boundaries intended to separate whites from Chicago's growing population of African Americans, and that neighborhood saloons in ethnic enclaves generated a riotous class of drunken and disorderly immigrants.[4]

The Progressive Era was a period of diverse social and political activism that lasted from the late 1800s to the early 1900s, a period when activists believed that the social problems of the United States—such as corruption, delinquency, poverty, working conditions, housing, and sanitation, but also interracial mixing, immigration, women's presence in public, and sex work—could be solved by a stronger state.[5] The Progressive Era did not have a unified agenda, as there was little agreement among activists about which social problems of the day were the most pressing and what were the best methods for promoting social improvements.[6] However, one of the broader ideological stances characteristic of the Progressive Era was that the problems were social in origin rather than resulting from individuals' moral deficits.[7] This ideological orientation shifted the understanding of sex workers, for example, from naturally depraved women to women as victims in need of laws to protect them.[8] Saving women from sex work became an easy and public issue for some Progressive Era activists, who referred to themselves as "vice crusaders" or "purity crusaders."[9] Activists even leveraged popular Progressive Era language of antimonopolization and anticorruption to describe the need to abolish formal red-light districts.[10] Through protests, debates, legislative pressure, and legal changes, Progressive Era activists reshaped laws and regulations regarding urban entertainments in Chicago and across the United States.

The state of Illinois technically criminalized sex work and gambling, but the laws were ambiguous, and their enforcement at the local level was discretionary. Although all laws are actually ambiguous because of the multiple ways they can be interpreted, the laws and their enforcement impacting the illicit entertainment economy of Chicago were dramatically changing in the early 1900s.[11] The 1874 Illinois Criminal Code prohibited the keeping or leasing of a "house of ill fame" or "disorderly house" that encouraged "idleness, gaming, drinking, fornication, or other misbehavior."[12] This law focused on property and property owners rather than on individuals engaged in illicit entertainments. Sex work faced the brunt of shifting Progressive Era regulations. Acts passed in 1887 updated Illinois laws to "prevent the prostitution of females" by prohibiting running a brothel, enticing women to work as prostitutes, or keeping women against their will or under false pretenses while they worked as prostitutes.[13] This change in Illinois law moved beyond property to prosecute operators, traffickers, and pimps in order to reduce prostitution, but there was no clear statement criminalizing the sex workers themselves or their selling of sex. During this period in US history, sex workers were considered more of a public nuisance, like beggars and vagrants, than criminal offenders.[14] "Prostitute" was even a US Census vocation category as late as 1900.[15]

Chicago's municipal codes were no less ambiguous than state codes regarding the criminalization of sex work. The first set of Chicago municipal codes from 1837 (the year of the city's incorporation) was only twenty-one pages long and focused mostly on sanitation and fire prevention. Its few sections on nuisances and preserving order targeted gambling and alcohol sales to minors and American Indians, but there was no mention of prostitution in the document.[16] Almost fifty years later, the 1881 Chicago municipal code incorporated Illinois state law and, in its eight-hundred-plus pages, clarified the city's authority to restrain and punish vagrants, beggars, and prostitutes. In a separate section, the document declared that anyone found in a "house of ill fame" would be fined under the regulation of nuisance properties.[17] Even city regulations, like state regulations, focused on property and maintaining order—not on the criminalization of individuals selling sex.[18] Things changed in 1905, when Chicago's revised municipal code targeted individual sex workers under a new subheading, "Night Walkers." All prostitutes, solicitors to prostitution, and all persons of evil fame or report, plying their vocations upon the streets, alleys or public places in the city, are hereby declared to be common nuisances and shall be fined not to exceed one hundred dollars for each offense."[19] The 1905 code, in contrast to Chicago's previous regulations, called for the regulation of sex workers themselves rather than of brothels and disorderly houses. However, the nuisance ordinance fell under the municipal code on misdemeanors, which included other benign violations such as wearing a hat in the theater and installing barbed wire fencing.[20] At the state level, it was not until 1915 that an amendment to the disorderly conduct laws criminalized the solicitation of sex, which was the first Illinois criminal statute to impact sex workers directly.[21]

Disorderly house criminal codes and nuisance ordinances provided law enforcement with tools to prosecute, but police and judges irregularly enforced these criminal and municipal codes. Sociologists of law Ryken Grattet and Valerie Jenness argue that disparities between laws and their local enforcement occur because of extralegal interests (such as the strength and influence of activists or political organizers), discretion, and legal ambiguity.[22] All three of these factors were apparent in Progressive Era Chicago. Chicago police officers were not students of Illinois state law; rather, their power to arrest focused on local ordinances, Chicago's shifting regulations, and demands from the mayor.[23] From the earliest days of the Chicago police department in the 1850s, most arrests of Chicago men were for drunk and disorderly conduct, and most arrests of Chicago women were for their being "keepers and inmates of houses of ill fame."[24] Nevertheless, in the 1900s Progressive Era, activists drew attention to the police and courts' inaction and their failure to enforce the laws about social improvement.

Multiple commentators pointed out the discretionary enforcement of prostitution law in the city of Chicago. For example, *Chicago Tribune* journalist John Callan O'Laughlin noted Chicago's failure to enforce state law in 1909: "I am told an Illinois state law prohibits prostitution. This law is not enforced in the city of Chicago. I am told there is a city ordinance so constructed that it permits by wide interpretation the regulation of this moral crime. In Chicago vice is neither prohibited nor is it well regulated."[25] University of Chicago sociology student Walter Reckless provided a better explanation of the legal ambiguity in his 1933 survey *Vice in Chicago*: "Prostitution was never quite legalized or even tolerated in Chicago or in other American cities. It merely had been permitted to exist (in spite of statutory law) during a period when public discussion of it was tabu [taboo]."[26] Legal leverage and cultural taboos gave Chicago law enforcement officials a useful upper hand, as they had discretion to go after any "disorderly" brothel or saloon or to turn a blind eye to the popular activities occurring within some of Chicago's most profitable establishments. Within this gray area of law in the early twentieth century, the rules and regulations targeting brothels and sex work certainly landed women selling sex, men buying sex, or men and women managing the selling of sex in jail and in court.

Meanwhile, the cacophony of sex work regulations grew louder during the Progressive Era. Regulations changed and came to include women calling down to men and soliciting them from brothel windows, the leasing of property to operate brothels or "houses of ill repute," liquor sales at brothels, and boarding women against their will. Chicago police altered their enforcement of the sex economy's rules and regulations when proclaiming themselves reformers or bowing to the pressures of loud Progressive activists. In 1909 Chief of Police Leroy Steward issued a new directive against Chicago's red-light districts.[27] He single-handedly banned swinging doors, colored lights, and delivery boys under the age of eighteen in brothels. He banned brothels outside of the segregated red-light districts; within two blocks of a school, church, hospital, or other public institution; and located on Chicago's elevated train line. Steward also promised rigid enforcement of a ban on women entering saloons without a male escort.

Chief Steward's actions had real consequences for legal enforcement. Immediately following the three-day grace period to comply with the new orders, police made over fifty arrests (of about thirty men and twenty women).[28] Later in the week twenty more women were arrested at North Side saloons because they were without male escorts.[29] Enterprising unescorted women banned from the saloons turned their attention to cheap theaters, where they could "sit and solicit drinks from the men in the audience," or hired men to sit with them in saloons and cafés.[30] When police arrested women assumed to be sex workers in raids, they took the women to the police stations but held off booking them until 1:00 a.m. Inspectors argued that this departmental policy kept women off the streets and out of the brothels, as their bail would not be posted until after mandatory city-wide closing hours.[31] The irony of this supposedly protective action was that women had to complete more sex work in order to pay back their bail. Thus, the regulations meant to protect women during the Progressive Era effectively increased the criminalization of women—sex workers or not.

Steward's regulations were a startling display of power, considering that there were already laws on the books targeting brothels and sex work. The regulations caused immediate confusion among the red-light district workers, and they swarmed precinct stations with questions.[32] The most public opposition came from William A. Brubaker, chairman of the Prohibition Central Committee of Cook County, in an open letter published in the *Chicago Tribune*. Brubaker admonished Chief Steward for abusing his power: "Permit me to ask: Who clothed you with legislative powers and authorized you to nullify the ordinances of the city of Chicago and the laws of the state of Illinois? When and by whom was the chief of police of Chicago made superior to the governor, the legislature, and the Supreme Court of Illinois?"[33] Even though Brubaker chaired a committee calling for the criminalization of sex work and the closing of Chicago's red-light districts, the contents of his letter focused on law enforcement's failure to follow and administer state law. Perhaps Brubaker recognized that a rogue chief of police could not bring lasting change to the city of Chicago. Chief Steward refused to read Brubaker's letter or acknowledge its contents, and he had no qualms about discrediting Brubaker's position on the criminalization of sex work as being unrealistic.[34] Two years later, the *Chicago Tribune* noted that Police Chief Steward's order had been "hailed generally as one of the best regulative orders that Chicago ever had known and it worked a wonderful change in the [red-light districts]."[35]

This fluctuation of law enforcement occurring in the streets was paralleled by changes in the courts. New, specialized courts in Chicago's judicial system added to law enforcement's discretion directed at the sex economy. The Morals Court was a specialized branch of the Municipal Court that processed sex work–related arrests.[36] Chicago officials established the Morals Court in 1913 in response to the Chicago Vice Commission's 1911 report. The Morals Court operated as a public clearinghouse, record keeper, and enforcer of sex work regulation.[37] The morals upheld in the Morals Court preserved an ideal of white women's femininity (mainly preserving virginity until marriage) during a time when mentions of sex work and women's sexuality were taboo.[38] In effect, the criminalization of moral transgressions was largely a criminalization of women. Men booked at the Morals Court could leave quickly if they could arrange bail.[39] Women were held overnight to undergo medical examinations and appear in court the following morning. If women tested positive for venereal diseases, they were sent to Lawndale Hospital for treatment.[40] Judges frequently viewed the hospitalization as punishment and would dismiss the pending cases when women were no longer infected. The moral double standards of this court changed slightly in 1919, when judges could hospitalize infected men as well as women.[41]

Forced to respond to the changing regulations of sex work and the red-light districts, some judges' rulings were inconsistent with Progressive Era activists' attempts to save women victims. In 1911 Municipal Court judge Walker discharged eleven women from his court, striking at the police order that banned unescorted women from saloons. He justified his actions by saying, "A woman has as much right in a saloon as a man," and criticized the police for not also targeting unescorted high society women at the "fine hotel cafes."[42] Judge Walker's call for gender and class impartiality in the application of saloon regulations came as a surprise to moralizing *Chicago Tribune* reporters who were chronicling law enforcements' failures to enforce municipal regulations. However, in other instances, judges' rulings in favor of greater gender parity were punitive. For example, Morals Court judge Hopkins was the first judge in the state of Illinois to charge women, alleged sex workers from South Side brothels, with vagrancy. Police often used vagrancy charges to book men buying sex in brothels, which is why Judge Hopkins's ruling against the women came as a surprise. Reporters commented that he had "annihilated the double code of morals when he announced his intention of punishing in equal measure men and women alike found in resorts."[43] These inconsistencies in judges' rulings were part of the larger discretionary law enforcement around sex work and illicit entertainments in Chicago; it was not always clear what folks could get away with and which folks could get away with it.

Law enforcement discretion and ambiguous, fluctuating regulations made illicit entertainments—especially sex work—risky business.[44] Increased police raids cost brothel owners money when posting bail, and judges' vagrancy and disorderly house rulings cost brothel owners money when paying legal fees and fines. New Morals Court judges and inspectors, with their heightened convictions, were more difficult to bribe and pay off.[45] These payments cut into profits, and thus there was money to be made if a protection market could undercut the price of bail, legal fees, and fines. An elaborate syndication of protection, graft, and corruption could also force businesses into the protection market with threats of frequent police raids. Consequently, organized crime developed in this criminally opportune space.

## THE SEX ECONOMY

The role of brothels and the sex economy in the protection market meant that women and their gendered labor were critical to Chicago organized crime. However, the gendered labor occurring in the red-light districts was more than women performing sex work. Chicago's red-light districts produced an elite class of brothel madams coordinating their own relationships and participation in organized crime's protection markets. As I show in the coming chapters, women brothel owners were a substantial part of the Progressive Era organized crime network but not of the Prohibition era organized crime network, even when the economic necessity of the sex economy persisted for men, women, and organized crime.

Working women—women who had left Midwest family farms, immigrant women, and African American women—were a growing part of Chicago's workforce.[46] But Chicago's gender-stratified labor market paid women paltry wages that did not go far in the city. Women earned about $8 per week in manufacturing or sales and about $5 to $6 per week plus tips in waitressing.[47] Adjusted for inflation, these wages would be approximately $130 to $200 per week in 2018 dollars.[48] Women could earn more lucrative wages in the growing urban entertainment economy of sex work, saloons, cabarets, and dance halls. White women working at modest or midrange brothels could earn just as much salary per week as white shop girls and waitresses while working fewer hours and receiving free room and board.[49] Carrie Watson, with her successful brownstone brothel on Clark Street, told British muckraker William Stead that if women had youth, health, and good looks, their assets were valued more in the brothels on Clark Street than in offices and retail shops.[50] Sex work, she explained, was "an easy lazy way of making a living" for women, and all of her employees were each supporting three to four dependents with their wages.[51] Based on the estimated counts of sex workers in Chicago, it is clear that a substantial number of women agreed with Carrie Watson. In 1911 the Chicago Vice Commission estimated that there were five thousand sex workers in Chicago and $15 million spent each year in Chicago's brothels (about $380 million in 2018 dollars).[52] Although it would have been in the Vice Commission's interest to inflate its figures, its claim of an influential underground economy in which many women found work went undisputed.

Chicago's elite brothels permitted a select few women to accrue wealth during a time when conventional business investments were largely not available to women. The elite brothels of Chicago wined and dined distinguished clients with live music, luxury furnishings, premium champagne, and talented women. The elite and notorious Everleigh Club banished all visitors who spent less than $50 per visit, and the women working at the Everleigh Club pocketed $100 per week (about $2,500 per week in 2018 dollars).[53] Upon the closing of the Everleigh Club, the never-married Everleigh sisters retired to New York with their collection of luxury items and died comfortably of old age surrounded by their Chicago-accrued wealth.[54] Another brothel madam, Bessie Hertzel, who had "more diamonds than any landlady on the West Side" and a serious heroin addiction, sold her brothel in 1910 when she woke up married to Eddie Jackson after a "binger."[55] Hertzel made somewhere between $15,000 and $20,000 on the sale of her brothel—approximately $375,000 to $500,000 in today's dollars, accounting for inflation.[56] If the Everleigh sisters and Bessie Hertzel had unconventional businesses, their motivations for profits were as conventionally American as they could possibly be.

Chicago brothel owners recognized the moral implications attached to their wealth, but they understood their engagement in the local sex economy through the lens of early 1900s capitalism. On October 19, 1909, preacher Gipsy Smith led a revivalist parade of hundreds of evangelical men, women, boys, and girls through the segregated red-light district.[57] His anti-red-light-district and anti-sex-work parade to save women was an eccentric, albeit effective, advertisement for brothel owners. One unnamed woman who managed one of the largest brothels in the district joked and moralized to reporters about the boom in business that the preacher had brought to her part of the red-light district:

> I have been in this neighborhood more than five years, and I can truthfully say that I never saw anything like the crowds that are coming to the houses tonight. Several times since the parade this place has been so full that we have had to refuse any more admittance. From a business standpoint I suppose we should be highly pleased. However, notwithstanding all the easy money that has drifted our way this evening, I am sorry that it happened. I am sorry for the young boys that were attracted to the district—many of them for the first time in their lives. And the young girls that walked along the street and gazed into the houses cannot escape a tinge of corruption. But far be it from me to moralize. I'm here to make the money, and it certainly is coming in fast tonight. If Gipsy Smith would lead a few more parades down here I would soon make money enough to retire and live on the interest of my wealth.[58]

In addition to the irony of this successful brothel madam's "moralizing" about the evangelical preacher's protest methods as corrupting young minds, the madam's discussion of "wealth" and "retirement" in this quotation showcases the reality that brothels were a reasonable means for women to navigate a gender-stratified labor market. This madam's frank explanation of her presence in the district—"I'm here to make money"—did not fit the traditional victimization narrative of the Progressive Era, but rather evoked a conventional narrative of an ambitious business owner looking forward to retirement. The size of the wealth accrued by this unnamed madam, the Everleigh sisters, or Bessie Hertzel was, however, not the norm for the majority of Chicago brothel owners.

Most men and women of Chicago never came near acquiring the start-up capital necessary to open an elite brothel in Chicago's red-light districts. Vic Shaw (discussed in chapter 1) went from being a burlesque dancer to owning two elite brothels because of the large cash bribe she received from a Chicago millionaire family to keep quiet about crossing state lines for a tryst with their son.[59] The majority of Chicago's brothels were nothing more than shanties or small apartments where men and women coordinated the buying and selling of sex. Most brothels provided homes by day and workplaces by night for many men and women of the red-light district, but brothels varied greatly in terms of comfort and profits. Annie Plummer's brothel at 13½ Peoria Street was a "miserable shack" that she struggled to keep open because of increasing rents and her abusive ex-husband.[60] Sex workers on the West Side rented horse stalls and rooms in dilapidated buildings by the night for a place to conduct their trade.[61] These were not rooms sporting the gold-plated piano and fountains filled with perfume of the Everleigh Club.

The wages for women in the lower tiers of the sex economy varied dramatically. Prices for sex work in Chicago ranged from 25 cents to $20 (approximately $6 to $500 in 2018 dollars), with African American women sex workers receiving the lowest wages.[62] According to historian Cynthia Blair's analysis of Chicago's 1900 Census, African American women made up 17 percent of registered brothel sex workers but were only 2 percent of Chicago's population.[63] African American brothel owners and sex workers earned less than their white counterparts, but occasionally they accessed niche markets catering to the racialized curiosities of the white male clientele.[64] Historians have identified that much of the moral panic of the Progressive Era was in reaction to racial mixing, especially when white women socialized and coupled with black men.[65] The moral panic did not apply to black women selling sex to white men, as this transaction reinforced the system of racialization linking black women to depraved sexuality.[66]

In their efforts to save young, poor white women, Progressive Era activists targeted and vilified men who profited from women's sex work. Activists and reverends produced books and films that exaggerated and perpetuated enslavement and trafficking narratives, including books such as *Chicago's Black Traffic in White Girls* (1911), *The Vice Bondage of a Great City* (1912), and *Can Such Things Be? A Story of a White Slave* (1912), and the silent film *Traffic in Souls* (1913), to name a few examples.[67] These narratives painted men in the sex economy as abductors and enslavers and black men as rapists of enslaved white girls.[68] The Progressive Era activists were not wrong about men generating income from the sex economy. The activists did, however, fail to acknowledge that many of the men, including black men, working in the sex economy were low-earning brothel staff such as piano players, waiters, and porters.[69]

In 1909, when Chief of Police Steward single-handedly changed red-light district regulations, one of his reform measures targeted the men profiting from the sex economy.[70] He prohibited men from owning or operating brothels and promised to arrest all men subsisting off the income of sex workers on charges of vagrancy.[71] Certain Progressive Era activists were enthusiastic about this new policy because it reinforced the notion of protecting women from the "white slavers" and the male "undesirables" living off the profits of women.[72] However, the powerful men of the red-light districts were immune to Steward's regulations.[73] Brothel owners paying into organized crime's protection market avoided Chief Steward's raids and arrests. Men working as porters, doormen, and piano players were at heightened risk as targets of vagrancy charges because of their race; their service jobs, which were visible to the police and public; and their wages, which were inadequate to offer bribes. Other men owning brothels who should have been the targets of Steward's regulations bypassed the technicality by registering their wives as the brothel owners or promoting a woman to brothel manager.[74] There were plenty of women to promote in the red-light districts who profited from selling sex work performed by other women.

Women's work in the sex economy was not just as sex workers; entrepreneurial women ran brothels, employed and managed sex workers, and recruited other women. Estimates of the gender gap in brothel ownership and the percentages of men and women in Chicago's sex economy are crude and variable, but some are available. The captain of the 22nd Street police station estimated in 1909 that women owned 50 percent of the 140 brothels in his district.[75] In the same year, Chief Steward estimated that women owned 75 percent of Chicago's four hundred brothels.[76] Sociologist Walter Reckless estimated 1,020 brothels in 1910—more than double Chief Steward's estimate—but Reckless did not provide information on how many of those were owned or operated by women.[77] Historian Cynthia Blair analyzed British muckraker William Stead's 1894 "Black List" of some of the most notorious brothels in Chicago's red-light district, finding that women owned 24 percent of the brothels on that list.[78]

My estimate of women's participation in the ownership and management of the sex economy during the Progressive Era falls between these estimates, at 39 percent. This calculation comes from the sample of sex work–related addresses in the Capone Database (described in more detail in chapter 2 and table 3). I identified 322 sex work–related addresses that contained names of owners, operators, and managers during the Progressive Era, and 125 of these addresses had women named among the proprietors. My emphasis on brothel managers, owners, and operators is analytically important because my research on women in Chicago organized crime uncovered very few references to sex workers themselves. Although the sex workers and their gendered labor were central to the commodification of sex, they were mostly not the named women participants and associates in Chicago organized crime. Rather, it was women's participation in the management and selling of sex that permitted their increased participation in organized crime.

There are some data limitations to consider in my estimate. These 125 establishments involved women but were not necessarily solely owned by women. The historical documents listing these addresses only named proprietors for 56 percent of the sex work establishments, and the documents mostly named women among a list of proprietors that also included men. The history of Chicago's discretionary law enforcement (as detailed in this chapter) is an important context for interpreting estimates of women's participation in the management and ownership of the sex economy. During the first decade of the 1900s, men experienced greater police and media scrutiny in sex work businesses and faced gender-specific ordinances that criminalized men's work while tolerating women's work in brothels, which could explain women's ownership or management involvement in only 39 percent of the establishments.

In general, women's participation in crime and illicit economies increases when crime is enhanced or dependent on women's gendered labor. "Gendered labor" refers to the assumptions around masculinity and femininity that shape differences and generate inequality in work, positions, power, and compensation.[79] The sex economy of the early 1900s was almost entirely based on women selling sex to men, but women's gendered labor is foundational to other illicit economies as well.[80] For example, human smuggling requires women's gendered labor when families view women participants in smuggling chains as safer in negotiating the smuggling of women and children.[81] Drug robbers use women accomplices to lure male targets into vulnerable situations in which the robbers can more successfully victimize them.[82] Businessmen rely on women's knowledge and expertise in their low-level staff and secretarial positions to complete white-collar corporate crimes.[83] Across these examples, the gendered labor of illicit economies and crime increases success and opportunity while reinforcing gendered hierarchies of women as objects of men's sexual desire or the assumption that women are less dangerous and less capable of crime than men. Women's gendered labor in crime also receives lower financial compensation than men's gendered labor, affirming that gendered labor is more about exploitation and opportunity than about any form of equality in participation.[84]

A relational perspective on gendered labor in illicit economies points to the recruitment, exploitation, and manipulation of women's gendered labor in illicit economies as another avenue for women's increased participation in crime: men and women criminals need access to women who will perform gendered labor. Contemporary research on sex work in the United States and in Mexico shows that pimps' and managers' access to women sex workers predominantly comes through their individual social networks.[85] Research on sex work networks in Canada shows that women sex workers will take on management tasks for other sex workers when pimps refuse to do the work.[86] Women's relationships to other women thus provide increased opportunities for women to broker women's participation in illicit economies.[87] An increase in criminal opportunities will not generate important or powerful positions for women in illicit economies, but women's access to women who perform gendered labor in crime makes money. Profits can cross barriers of trust and experience that usually keep women out of illicit economies.

The legal and labor market conditions that made sex viable work, the percentage of women brothel owners and managers, and the theoretical discussion of access to gendered labor in sex work presented in this section are important contexts for the comparisons I make later in this book. Sex work grew in Chicago during Prohibition. I find that there was a higher percentage of women involved in the ownership and management of sex work establishments and that organized crime maintained its interests in brothels. As I show in the coming chapters, the sex economy in Chicago did change in just the twenty years between the Progressive Era and Prohibition, but that change was growth, not decline. How then did organized crime leave women behind during Prohibition?

## THE THREE LEVEES

Spatially, Chicago was, and continues to be, a large city in terms of square miles (234 square miles), especially compared to older eastern cities such as Boston (90 square miles) and Philadelphia (143 square miles). During the Progressive Era, brothels existed across Chicago, but the segregated red-light districts provided a profitable concentration of illicit entertainment establishments. Chicagoans and visitors referred to these districts as "the

Levees." "Levee" referred to districts along the river ward.[88] The Levees provided segregated space for social order. Chicago historian Sam Mitrani explains how the Chicago police were a tool for maintaining order, and this task required considerable leverage in deciding how and when to deploy local power. Permitting brothels to operate in the Levee districts gave Chicago police a place to contain sex work when elite residents complained about it.[89] The spatial concentration of the Levees helped the police maintain order, but it also helped organized crime develop a localized territorial market of protection and payments. Because women could own or operate brothels in the Levees, women's risky establishments were also profitable establishments, paying into the localized protection market.

Using contemporary mapping software, I plotted the addresses of the 576 Progressive Era sex work and 367 alcohol establishments with named and unnamed proprietors within a map of Chicago's community areas. (Many of the addresses were too old or too incomplete to map.) The dots on the left panel of map 2 plot the brothel and sex work addresses. The triangles on the right panel of map 2 plot the saloons and alcohol-associated addresses. Approximately 25 percent of the locations sold booze and sex, and these establishments appear in both panels. Map 2 shows the concentration of the brothels in Chicago's three Levee districts, which are labeled with dotted lines in the left panel. Map 2 also shows how the saloons and alcohol establishments followed a similar spatial pattern as most of the brothels in the Levee districts, although the alcohol establishments have greater geographic spread outside of the Levees than do the brothels.

The original Levee was located just south of the central business district, bounded by Clark Street and State Street from west to east and by Van Buren Street and 12th Street from north to south.[90] It was in this Levee that organized crime in Chicago began. In the shadows of the Loop high-rises, Chicago's tolerated vices of gambling, brothels, dance halls, and saloons were all condensed into several blocks. Locals, laborers, and visitors had no trouble finding their way to the entertainments of the Levee. The Levee district was a prominent feature of central Chicago, and naysayers were quick to ask: "Do the people of Chicago know that their business district, known as the 'loop,' can hardly be reached except by passage through or in close proximity to infected districts?"[91] The sounds, smells, and sights of the "infected district" included music, train arrivals and departures, cigarettes, alcohol, interracial mixing, modern dancing, and a steady traffic of clients and sightseers. Cabarets of the Levee district brought together an unfamiliar combination of "saxophone music, fox-trotting, risqué entertainment, open promiscuity, wholesale intoxication and cigarette smoking, prostitutes, shop girls, and

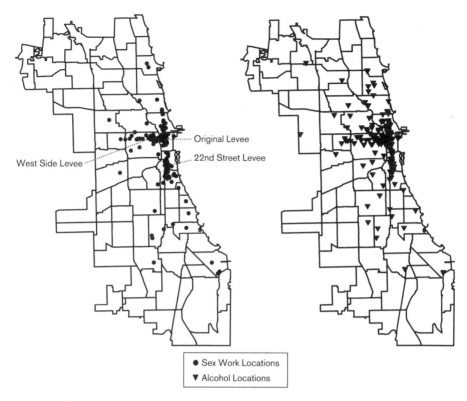

West Side Levee

Original Levee

22nd Street Levee

● Sex Work Locations
▼ Alcohol Locations

MAP 2. Chicago sex work and alcohol establishments, 1900–1919. *Sources:* Chicago Data Portal, "Boundaries—Community Areas (current)," 2018, https://data.cityofchicago.org/Facilities-Geographic-Boundaries/Boundaries-Community-Areas-current-/cauq-8yn6, accessed June 24, 2018; Andrew Ba Tran, "Mapping with R," 2017, https://andrewbtran.github.io/NICAR/2017/maps/mapping-census-data.html, accessed June 24, 2018.

slumming society folk."[92] Dance halls called "black and tans" catered specifically and illegally to both white and black patrons.[93] A room at the Hotel Queen would be rented eight times in a single day, though under oath the owner explained that the eight visitors a night were due to room changes from the insects or uncomfortable temperatures rather than short visits by sex workers and their clients.[94] A visitor to Chicago in 1909 described the Levee district and Levee lore with horror:

> I have been through the red light districts of Chicago, and I am filled with a great loathing. I have seen your dance halls, where temptation to sin is offered in the form of lights, and music, and drink. I have seen saloons which are but the ante-rooms to iniquity. I have visited your

vice quarters, and have been astonished at the open traffic that exists therein. I have learned of how "white slavery" is conducted in Chicago. I have been told of women imprisoned behind bars and forced to do the will of their keepers. I have learned of police service to prevent the escape of unfortunates. The condition that exists is at once heartrending and disgusting. It is a blot upon the fair name of Chicago.[95]

The Levee and its lore of "temptation to sin" and "women imprisoned behind bars" acted as a lightning rod for Progressive Era activists. Objectively, the Levee was a rough place with a tough reputation. It was the kind of place where travelers to Chicago would find themselves robbed by thieving gangs of women, exemplified by August Bloemfon's allegations that four women thieves at 377 State Street stole $55 from him while he was lost in Chicago looking for his cousin.[96] But Bloemfon's allegations and the visitor's reference to the Levee as a "blot upon the fair name of Chicago" were also thinly veiled critiques of the poor and working-class residents of the Levee.

The Levee provided sex workers, hoboes, and drug addicts a segregated place to live, hustle, and work.[97] Other residents of the Levee included working-class, immigrant, and African American families renting filthy and cold rooms in dilapidated hotels and boarding houses.[98] Their children played in the streets next to soliciting women, much to the dismay of some police officers.[99] In 1911 the Chicago Vice Commission calculated that 3,931 children lived in Chicago's First Ward, which contained the Levee district.[100] However, saloons functioned as the primary social service agencies, providing warmth, toilets, stew, and bread to residents and visitors.[101] Much of the hand-wringing over the Levee's entertainment establishments was due to the geographic proximity of Chicago's poverty to its wealth. The other two Levee districts developed later than the original Levee, and they were farther from the Loop and its wealth.

The second Levee was in West Side Chicago, where brothers Mike and Joseph Heitler owned and controlled entire blocks of shanties and flophouses, especially along Green Street, Sangamon Street, and North Peoria Street, as pictured in figure 4. Rents in the West Side Levee typically ran about $15 (about $350 in 2018 dollars) per month for working-class residences, but within the prosperous Levee economy the Heitlers could charge up to $300 (about $7,500 in 2018 dollars) per month for their shacks used as brothels or gambling dens.[102] Around 1910 the Heitlers expanded into Curtis and Carpenter Streets, buying all the available houses near their existing monopoly on properties in the West Side Levee.[103] The West Side Levee did not receive as much attention from the press, tourists, and Progressive activists as the original Levee because it was farther from the central business district,

FIGURE 4.   Exterior of the Heitler Resort, a house of prostitution at 310 North Peoria St. (formerly 169 Peoria St.), in the Near West Side community area of Chicago, Illinois, 1910. *Source:* DN-0008171, *Chicago Daily News* negatives collection, Chicago History Museum.

but it was no less important as an organized crime territory. Mike and Joseph both became figures in organized crime, and Mike came to be one of the most connected people in the Progressive Era organized crime network. The West Side Levee paled in comparison, however, to the organized crime legacy of Chicago's third Levee on 22nd Street.

In 1903 the Citizens' Vigilance Committee, an activist organization with the goal of banishing brothels from the First and Second Wards of Chicago, complained to Mayor Carter Harrison about a third "encroaching" red-light district spreading Chicago's vices farther south, to 22nd Street.[104] This was not a desirable, high-class neighborhood, even though the Citizens' Vigilance Committee claimed to represent residents and property own-ers.[105] Historian Cynthia Blair's research found that brothels started open-ing around the area that was to become the 22nd Street Levee as early as the 1880s, when brothel entrepreneurs were attracted to the low rents for shabby houses unsuitable for working-class families.[106] Nearly ten years after the opening of the 22nd Street Levee district in 1914, a Chicago police officer using the pen name Officer 666 wrote in the *Chicago Tribune*: "There had been a lot of talk about the disgrace to the city of a levee district in the shadow of the big loop office buildings. All of a sudden it was announced there was a new segregated district out around 22nd Street."[107] This announcement came from Mayor Harrison and his political wing in their efforts to push the Levee district out of the South Loop to the area around 22nd Street.[108]

The new Levee segregated the hoboes, sex workers, drug addicts, and poor families to second-rate properties away from the valuable streets and real estate near the Loop frequented by Chicago's business elite. Located on the northern side of what was becoming Chicago's Black Belt, the 22nd Street Levee included the twelve blocks between 18th and 22nd Streets from north to south and between Clark Street and Wabash Avenue from west to east.[109] These neighborhood borders were porous, however, with brothels, saloons, and gambling dens stretching farther south and deeper into Chicago's Black Belt.[110] By 1911 the district police captain estimated that there were 152 brothels in the 22nd Street Levee.[111]

The 22nd Street Levee brothels were as fascinating and grand as the brothels of the original Levee. The district was illuminated late into the night by electric lights; women wore real diamonds at the "gilded" brothels; and when twenty state's attorneys toured the district in 1907, they declared the "chatter of the geisha girls to be the most attractive thing of the evening."[112] If any of the walls in the 22nd Street Levee could talk, we would want to listen to the buildings of the 2000 blocks of South Wabash Avenue. This was where bondsmen accompanied police officers during raids; love triangles ended in murder; illegal gambling occurred in nearly every apartment, barber shop, and cigar store; and Al Capone would eventually run his Four Deuces (at 2222 South Wabash Avenue).[113]

The thrill and legend of the 22nd Street Levee coalesced at Colosimo's Café, 2126–2128 South Wabash Avenue. Jim Colosimo and his wife Victoria Moresco had been successful brothel owners in the original Levee. Folks referred to Colosimo as "Diamond Jim" for the jewels he wore on each finger and carried around in his pocket to shuffle while sitting.[114] Around 1910 Colosimo and Moresco opened an Italian restaurant and cabaret in the 22nd Street Levee. They fully intended to run a classy establishment, but their close association with Chicago's criminals made their high-society aspirations difficult to achieve. The small dining room was modestly decorated in rose and gold, hanging lamps ran down the center of the ceiling, and tables and chairs crowded the edges of the dance floor and orchestra in the middle of the room.[115] Accustomed to being immune from legal trouble, Colosimo and Moresco violated liquor laws, paid bribes to maintain licenses, illegally served alcohol to uniformed soldiers and sailors during wartime, and had "immoral" appearing women flirting and selling cigarettes table to table.[116] Some of these legal violations caught up with them. In 1914 Jim transferred all of the properties to Victoria's name, but the locals only ever knew Colosimo's Café as Jim's place.[117] According to an unnamed *Chicago Tribune* reporter, the reputation of Colosimo's Café was as large as the man himself:

> "Colosimo's" as "Big Jim made it" wasn't just a cabaret. It was a place of interest, a rendezvous, an enticing lure and one of the best known in the world, a gathering spot for men and women of all classes. . . . Yes, there was lure in Colosimo's, and thrills. Its reputation was naughty, but its character was not unnice. There seldom was any "rough stuff" there. When there was, it was promptly stopped. You saw painted women and maudlin women, and drunken men. You saw thieves and gamblers and crooked coppers and lords and dukes of the badlands. But you could see, too, millionaires and merchants and bankers and novelists and teachers of kindergarten.[118]

Colosimo's popular café and its tables filled with "gamblers and crooked coppers" illuminated his importance in organized crime. As I show in the next chapter, he became the most connected person in the Progressive Era organized crime network through his intimate and trusting relationships with underworld gamblers, brothel owners, traffickers, and local ward politicians. The politicians and their corruption within the Levees solidified the legacy of Chicago organized crime.

## THE CORRUPTION

In 1929 John Landesco, the only scholar of the Chicago School of Sociology to study Chicago organized crime at that time, argued that the history of organized crime in Chicago went back twenty-five years, to the early 1900s.[119] Landesco's scrupulous detailing of who was who in organized crime revealed a legacy of immune people and untouchable places going back to the syndicated sex work and gambling rings at the turn of the twentieth century. In response to Landesco's research, his adviser, Ernest W. Burgess, argued that "the position of power and affluence achieved by gangsters and their immunity from punishment was due to an unholy alliance between organized crime and politics."[120] The syndication of protection in the Levee districts laid the foundation for Chicago organized crime well before some of Chicago's most influential mobsters even arrived in the city.

In the Levees, the underpaid city officials came to expect generous donations from brothel, saloon, gambling den, and dance hall owners.[121] Progressive

Era activists were especially keen on exposing organized crime and corrupt officials because doing so provided even greater evidence for their crusade against the red-light districts.[122] Activist Kate Adams ran the Coulter House, a reform house for sex workers, and she regularly testified about the system of graft payments from brothels, in which money was split among police officers, bondsmen, doctors, and the "higher up."[123] Adams was vague about who the "higher up" were. She failed to name names or identify how high up these people were. Chicago officials and residents assumed, however, that the "higher ups" of Levee organized crime were two aldermen of the First Ward, nicknamed the "Lords of the Levee."[124]

Aldermen Michael "Hinky Dink" Kenna and "Bathhouse" John Coughlin of the First Ward, the ward containing the South Loop Levee and the 22nd Street Levee, drove much of the political wing of organized crime during the Progressive Era. They were the well-known political arm of the Levee "vice trust": the syndication of graft payments and protection among the thieves, saloons, gambling dens, and brothels in coordination with the police and politicians.[125] Alderman Kenna owned a saloon on Clark and Van Buren Streets that catered to a rough crowd. When Carrie Nation, the hatchet-wielding Kansas saloon smasher, visited the Chicago Levee in 1901, she labeled Kenna's saloon a "hell hole," crying, "You are sending scores of persons to hell every day."[126] Had Carrie Nation focused her hatchet on the broader corruption and organization of crime, she might have aimed even stronger insults and accusations at the alderman.

The most public moments of Aldermen Kenna and Coughlin's influence and criminal connections were their annual First Ward Democratic Balls. The balls were grand affairs, attended by twenty-five thousand guests who were entertained by masquerade dancing, thirty-five thousand quarts of beer, and ten thousand quarts of champagne.[127] Aldermen Kenna and Coughlin's constituents were not Chicago's tycoons and elite; rather, the First Ward voters included thieves, saloon owners, gambling den operators, and men brothel keepers. Madams and sex workers of the Levee were unable to vote, but many women relied on the aldermen's protection and influence to keep the Levees open. *Chicago Tribune* reporters writing about the annual First Ward balls focused much of their criticism at the lower class and social standing of the majority of the guests intermixing with the political and legal arms of Chicago: "They packed the Coliseum so full of gentlewomen of no virtue and gentlemen attached to the aforesaid gentlewomen that if a great disaster, thorough in its work, had befallen the festive gathering there would not have been a second story worker, 'dip,' thug, plug ugly, porch climber, dope fiend, or scarlet woman remaining in

Chicago."[128] The reporters padded their criticisms of Chicago's criminal class with fodder on the fashion, drinking, smoking, dancing, flirting, and swearing of women attending the ball. The balls gained a reputation for debauchery and were eventually referred to only as "orgies" in the *Chicago Tribune* headlines.[129] When the press threatened to report the names of public figures attending the balls, politicians and business elites developed elaborate alibis as evidence that they were no longer attending.[130]

The First Ward Democratic Club raised thousands of dollars from these balls, and though Alderman Kenna described the educational and social services the funds would provide to First Ward residents, donors understood that the profits paid for the aldermen's reelection campaigns.[131] Saloon and brothel keepers purchased up to $200 (around $5,000 in 2018 dollars) worth of ball tickets, which they liberally distributed to their employees and customers to increase the presence of constituents.[132] Levee business owners were expected to purchase bottles of wine at the ball based on the size of their businesses.[133] Even though many of the guests and constituents did not or could not vote, the increasing attendance and profits each year were successes for the political party.[134] In 1902 Alderman Coughlin commented on the addition of five thousand guests from the previous year: "The increase means just one thing—victory for the democratic ticket at the spring election."[135] His prediction was correct.

Aldermen Kenna and Coughlin had strong ties to the mayor's office because they could deliver votes. Their demand in return was that the two First Ward Levees were theirs to regulate. Local beat police officers "winked" at the aldermen's protected establishments operating in direct violation of laws and ordinances when Kenna and Coughlin were "Lords of the Levee."[136] In one instance, when a New York gambling ring operator made plans to take over a floor in a downtown Loop hotel to expand his operations in the open city of Chicago, the aldermen interfered and shut him down to protect local gambling establishments as well as secure more local donations in their pockets.[137]

In another instance, the aldermen banned the "grizzly bear" dance from Chicago. The ragtime grizzly bear dance originated in black dance halls, and its movements included leaning into partners' chests and wrapping arms around each other.[138] Critics of the dance considered it overtly sexual because of how closely dance partners embraced and because of its origins in black culture. The aldermen were among its critics. Their ban began at Frieberg's dance hall, where they had deep financial interests. In the interest of Frieberg's more respectable and higher-class dances, such as two-steps and waltzes, the aldermen organized a citywide ban on the grizzly bear dance, cursing it as immoral. Business at Frieberg's plunged as a result of the ban, because Chicago patrons loved the ragtime steps of the grizzly bear dance. Their dance hall competitors, who ignored the citywide ban and permitted the grizzly bear dance, faced so many raids that eventually one of them tore the entire dance floor out of his establishment in surrender.[139]

Aldermen Kenna and Coughlin orchestrated much of the political corruption of the Levee districts, though their interests seemed to be in their own personal, financial, and electoral gain rather than in broader organized crime. The ban on the grizzly bear dance, for example, had ramifications for other dance hall owners and operators who were paying into and receiving protection from Levee organized crime. Nevertheless, Aldermen Kenna and Coughlin staked their claim as persistent members of Chicago organized crime from the Progressive Era to Prohibition.

## SUMMARY

This chapter details the legal and geographic conditions of Chicago's illicit entertainment economy, from which organized crime developed. It also discusses the importance of brothels and sex work to the origins of organized crime and how they created unique opportunities for women's participation. At the turn of the twentieth century, ambiguous, shifting laws targeting sex work and other illicit entertainments were irregularly enforced, making sex work a risky, but profitable, business in Chicago. The gendered labor of the sex economy required thousands of women sex workers, but the requirements for gendered labor also created increased opportunities for other women to manage and broker sex workers. Women were managers and proprietors of 39 percent of Chicago's brothels in the Progressive Era.

Chicago's vices of sex work, gambling, and alcohol were concentrated within the Levee districts, and in turn organized crime developed in the Levees as a loose protection market connecting illicit entertainment business owners with corrupted ward politicians and police officers. The protection market and the geography of Chicago required organized crime to be territorial and spatially concentrated. Together ambiguous and fluctuating laws, law enforcement discretion and corruption, gendered labor in illicit entertainment, and spatial concentration of the Levees were the conditions under which women had increasing opportunities for participation in the illicit entertainment economy. As I show in the next chapter, this economy, and the decentralized structure of Chicago's organized crime network, increased women's participation in organized crime during the Progressive Era.

# 4. Syndicate Women, 1900–1919

The Progressive Era organized crime protection market provided immunity from raids by police and moral investigators, a payment plan with judges to release sex workers quickly, and ward politicians who fought to keep the Levees open. Organized crime's protection market did not include all of the illicit businesses of the Levees, nor was the protection market always good for business. Paying off organized crime still cut into profits, but there was no alternative.[1] The *Chicago Tribune* reported in 1906: "No man in the First ward Levee opened a saloon, started a handbook or poolroom, and no woman opened a disorderly house without first gaining the consent of at least one of the members of the syndicate."[2] Organized crime had the power to absorb businesses that wanted protection and connections as well as the power to exploit businesses that it wanted to protect or close.

Former mayors, Chicago School sociologists of the 1920s, and urban historians have made the connection between early twentieth-century Chicago organized crime and the sex economy by focusing on a few key men.[3] This chapter extends previous conceptualizations of organized crime by demonstrating that women of the sex economy were relevant actors in Chicago's Progressive Era organized crime network and establishes the decentralized, brokerage structure of the network, which was an essential condition for women's increased participation in organized crime. As detailed in the previous chapter, women were involved in the proprietorship of 39 percent of Chicago's brothels. Women's brothels were among the many illicit entertainment establishments requiring protection in the Levees, and women connected to organized crime through their payments into and their benefits from the protection market just as the male business owners of saloons, handbooks, poolrooms, and brothels did.

This chapter explains the implications of the decentralized, brokerage structure of Progressive Era organized crime, in which men connected with entrepreneurs of illicit business, including brothel madams such as the Everleigh sisters and Victoria Moresco. This structure stands in contrast to the structure of organized crime bosses at the center of the network hoarding resources and criminal opportunities found in Prohibition era Chicago. Women fared better in the small, flat, decentralized structure, when organized crime was predominantly a territorial protection market. Brokers, rather than bosses, were foundational to the structure of Progressive Era organized crime, and brokers scooped up illicit businesses regardless of the gender of the owners and managers. Women connected to organized crime through the locations of their illicit businesses in an era when organized crime continued to thrive, despite the Progressive Era activists' successes in formally closing the Levees.

### THE VICE SYNDICATE

Organized crime in Progressive Era Chicago did not have an official name or lasting moniker like some of the criminal organizations that grew out of Chicago, such as the Outfit of the 1930s and the Gangster Disciples of the 1960s, names still used by Chicago street gangs today. Recorded references to Chicago's criminal organization and its protection included the language "vice combination," "vice trust," "organized vice," "vice syndicate," and "vice ring."[4] Historian Mara Keire argues that this selective language and labeling was intentional and instrumental during the Progressive Era. Activists fighting against sex work and red-light districts purposely deployed the rhetoric and labels "syndicate" and "trust" in their efforts to exploit the antimonopolization sentiments of the Progressive Era.[5] The people involved in the vice syndicate were not using these labels, and membership in the vice syndicate was fickle rather than formal. Nevertheless, social network analysis is best suited to provide a bird's-eye view of the organizational and structural patterns of Progressive Era organized crime.

Organized crime in Progressive Era Chicago included 267 people and 789 criminal relationships among them. Figure 5 illustrates that the structure of the organized crime network from 1900 to 1919 was small, sparse, and decentralized, and it comprised several localized clusters. As introduced in chapter 2, each circle in figure 5 designates a person in organized crime; the white circles represent organized crime women and the black circles, organized crime men. Each line in the network represents a criminal relationship between two people that occurred at some point between 1900 and

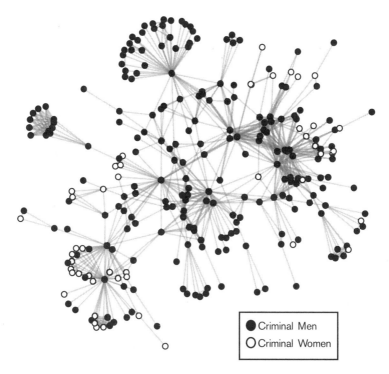

FIGURE 5.   Chicago organized crime network, 1900–1919 (n = 267).

1919. Based on the archival research, the majority of the criminal relationships in the organized crime network occurred within Chicago's Levee
districts. The Progressive Era organized crime network was relatively small
considering the size of the Levees and their levels of illicit activity.
The network was also quite sparse, as only 2.2 percent of all the potential
criminal relationships among this set of organized crime people actually
existed.

The most unique feature of the organized crime network during this
period was its decentralization. Figure 5 shows no clear, identifiable center to
the organized crime network. Instead, the network was relatively flat (i.e.,
nonhierarchical) and consisted of multiple large, distinct clusters connected
by certain individuals brokering the different clusters of the network to other
clusters. There were areas of the network with a lot of activity and many
people, but these areas were not in the center. Some criminals looked powerful in terms of the number of relationships connecting them to other criminals. In fact, the number of criminal relationships a person had in the network
provides a meaningful measure of power and influence in organized crime. In

a resource-rich organized crime network, the number of relationships reflects involvement in multiple criminal schemes, the size of a particular scheme, and/or the number of trustworthy conspirators. However, in this network the powerful individuals were spread out and not concentrated in the center. The unique network structure of the Progressive Era becomes more meaningful in the sections below, in which I detail the individuals and their historical relationships that contributed to this structure.

## THE BOSSES

Progressive Era activists and observers convinced themselves that corrupt Aldermen Kenna and Coughlin were the leaders of organized crime. The aldermen stoked these suspicions with their balls, voting base, and business interests, but especially by appointing and keeping the "notoriously corrupt or notoriously incompetent" Captain Michael Ryan of the 22nd Street police station as chief of police of the First Ward—a position Captain Ryan held until 1914, when he was transferred after being accused of maintaining the "vice" conditions in the Levee.[6] Even with fingers pointing at Kenna and Coughlin and their police captain, the "bosses" of organized crime were largely undefined. Investigators and journalists had little knowledge of the names or the number of organized crime bosses and at times referred to the "Big Three," "Big Four," "Big Five," and "Big Seven" of the vice syndicate, sometimes in the same breath.[7] In one particular two-page spread, "Inside Story on Vice's Grip on Chicago," the unnamed *Chicago Tribune* reporter actually referred to both "the Big Four" and "the Big Five" in a single sentence:

> While every "vice ring" is described as a wheel in a political machine, the situation in Chicago is said to permit the carrying out of the details of the figure of speech to an unusual length. In other cities, the "ring" has been found to be a clique of gambling kings who ruled the situation. In Chicago, the ring is extended to the formation of a complete wheel. [Captain Michael] Ryan [of the 22nd Street police station] is the hub. His plainclothes policemen, his "confidential men," are the spokes, and the sections of the rim are the "Big Four" or the "Big Five" as conditions happen to be at the time, the dive owners and keepers controlling the strings of saloons and resorts that travel along without interruption. But—more important than any or all of these parts—the one thing without which the wheel could not revolve—is the axle, and this axle is "the little fellow" [Alderman Kenna] to every denizen of the district.[8]

Perhaps the reporter's "inside story" was less of an inside scoop than the *Chicago Tribune* editors and headline writers wanted readers to believe. The reporter also incorrectly described the "vice ring" as structured by a "hub" and "spokes," with Alderman Kenna at the center. From the bird's-eye perspective gained through social network analysis—in this case perhaps more useful than an inside scoop—the organized crime network from 1900 to 1919 did not have a "hub and spokes" structure. There was one area of the network that somewhat resembled such a structure as part of the larger decentralized, clustered pattern (in the upper middle part of the network in figure 5, connecting all men), but this was not the part of the network where Aldermen Kenna and Coughlin and Captain Ryan were situated. Kenna and Coughlin resided in a dense part of the network (on the right side of figure 5) with many overlapping ties between individuals and no hierarchical structure pointing to a clear boss.

Reporters and investigators occasionally attempted to identify the ambiguous leadership, with conflicting results, but their reports did have one thing in common: the names provided for the Big Three through Seven were all men and often owners of large, successful, and not always legitimate businesses in the Levees. Katie Adams, a vocal Progressive Era activist, alleged that this group of syndicate men owned and managed two hundred of the Levee districts' better-known brothels and disorderly establishments.[9] Over time the list attempting to name the Big Three through Seven came to include twenty more names in addition to Alderman Kenna, Alderman Coughlin, and Captain Ryan: Roy Jones, George Little, Frank Wing, Ed Weiss, Jim Colosimo, Ferdinand Buxbaum, Ike Bloom, Samuel Hart, Samuel Harris, Ben Hyman, Tom Costello, Mike Heitler, Mont Tennes, Solly Friedman, Jakey Adler, Harry Hopkins, Andy Craig, Louis Weiss, Bob Gray, and John Jordan.[10] It would have been difficult to find a dining table large enough to fit this entire group, not to mention the organizational challenges and interpersonal conflicts that would have occurred had there actually been this many crime bosses in Chicago.

If there were crime bosses in Progressive Era Chicago organized crime, social network analysis can clarify who they were and what their structural importance was based on the number of criminal connections each actor had in the network (technically their degree score). For the most part, reporters' and investigators' lists that included these twenty-three "bosses" were congruous with the most-connected criminals in the Progressive Era organized crime network, but there were some inconsistencies. Three of the names identified by reporters were Chicago criminals, but I never uncovered evidence of their connection to the Progressive Era organized crime network. Of the remaining twenty "bosses" on the lists, all but three had a large number of criminal connections in the network. One of these three was Captain Ryan, who only had five criminal relationships in the network, when the average for the network was six. Ryan's few criminal connections would hardly establish him as the "hub" of the vice "wheel," whereas Kenna's twenty-seven criminal relationships and Coughlin's twenty-three criminal relationships established their position among the criminal elite— although not necessarily as "bosses."[11]

Moreover, there were a few notable oversights in the reporters' lists of "bosses." Four men who were never named in those lists were more criminally connected in the network than 65 percent of those on the lists. These oversights included Maurice Van Bever and Johnny Torrio, two men who worked for Jim Colosimo and had strong influence and connections in the organized crime network. Torrio would become the actual syndicate boss during Prohibition, as measured by both the organized crime network and the historical record. The other two oversights were Inspector Edward McCann and Louis Frank, who were co-conspirators in a large protection ring on the West Side Levee around 1909 (discussed in more detail later in this chapter).[12]

According to the social network measure of criminal degree, Big Jim Colosimo was the closest thing Progressive Era organized crime had to a boss—but barely. Colosimo had the most criminal relationships (forty-three), but gambling king Mont Tennes had forty-two, and graft collector Louis Frank had thirty-nine. In other words, there was a near tie for who was the most criminally connected in this organized crime network. Importantly, Colosimo, Tennes, and Frank were also located in different regions of the network, suggesting that the most criminally connected people were not in cahoots with each other but were indirectly connected to each other through brokers. Even within the spatial concentration of organized crime in the Levees, mastermind criminal coordination was not occurring within the Progressive Era organized crime network.

The lack of bosses and the decentralized structure of organized crime go hand in hand; each is a necessary condition for the other. A centralized network requires certain actors with a high degree score, and a decentralized network requires degree scores to be more evenly spread out. In this network, high degree scores identify the most criminally active and criminally connected. Criminal degree might not be a perfect measure of organized crime bosses, but it does show us what the reporters and activists missed. The qualifications for making reporters' lists of bosses might have been based more on organizational roles, the infamy of their local establishments, or details not otherwise preserved in the archives. The organized crime network in figure 5 requires an aggregation and a cross section of history that were unavailable to the reporters. This bird's-eye view of the decentralized and clustered structure of organized crime shows another thing that reporters missed: the women at the margins of organized crime.

## THE SYNDICATE WOMEN

Shifting from the ambiguous center of organized crime to the margins reveals individuals with fewer criminal relationships who were more weakly connected to organized crime but still appear in the network. The margins of the network contain configurations of gambling den and brothel owners, thieves, sex workers, housekeepers, and traffickers, who all contributed to the size and structure of the syndicate. These people were not the political bosses or the Big Five, but they were individuals coordinating and benefiting from the organization of crime and protection in the Levees. What is often ignored in this historical case is that the margins of organized crime included dozens of women. Of the 267 criminals in the Progressive Era organized crime network, 47 (18 percent) were women. These women operated brothels, paid extortion fees, got arrested, posted bail, trafficked other women, and attended political galas while embedded in Chicago's organized crime network from 1900 to 1919. The gender gap in Progressive Era organized crime occurred both in terms of the gap between the ratio of men to women and in terms of the gap between the relationships women had compared to men, as presented in table 4. When organized crime was small, decentralized, and clustered, women were a part of 19 percent of the criminal relationships in the network: 3 percent of all ties in this network were between two women, and 16 percent of all ties in this network were between one man and one woman.

The extent to which women's criminal relationships within organized crime connected them to men is noteworthy and is entirely consistent with research on contemporary co-offending. Research regularly shows that men co-offend with men, women co-offend with men, but women seldom co-offend with women.[13] When the majority of offenders are men, mathematically the majority of co-offenders will also be men. This is considered the pool of eligible people who could be selected as co-offenders. Selection of co-offenders requires identifying cooperative, trustworthy individuals who have criminal experience or particular knowledge. This selection process privileges masculinity and men's criminal competence and requires available conspirators who are more likely to be men.[14]

When men and women co-offend, one possible orientation is that male offenders might be neutral to women as co-offenders under the right

TABLE 4. Men, Women, and Their Relationships in Chicago's
Organized Crime Network, 1900–1919

|  | *Men* |  | *Women* |
|---|---|---|---|
| Nodes | 220 |  | 47 |
|  | (82.4%) |  | (17.6%) |
| Men-only criminal relationships | 641 |  |  |
|  | (81.2%) |  |  |
| Women-only criminal relationships |  |  | 26 |
|  |  |  | (3.3%) |
| Man-and-woman criminal relationships |  | 122 |  |
|  |  | (15.5%) |  |

conditions of trust, cooperation, knowledge, and opportunity. If women
have what it takes for the crime at hand, the co-offenders may focus more
on the desired outcome and less on the gender of who is cooperating.
However, even if men are gender-neutral in their selection of co-offenders,
male offenders have fewer opportunities to select women co-offenders
because the pool of eligible women who are experienced offenders is smaller.
A second orientation to men and women's co-offending is the advantages
that men might gain when working with women. The obvious example is
the importance of women in sex economies, but other feminine stereotypi-
cal roles may be advantageous to certain crimes, such as setting up a male
target, an unassuming woman holding contraband, or requiring a female
secretary's knowledge of corporate bookkeeping. In this orientation, the
gender gap in co-offending comes from fewer crimes having a feminine
advantage. Last, and related to the second orientation, it is also of course
possible that men might be exploitative of the gendered labor that women
are able to perform in crime and will select women as co-offenders for their
own criminal success.[15] Since women's gendered labor is not necessary in
many criminal opportunities, women might only be exploited for particular
criminal and co-offending needs. These three orientations to men and
women's co-offending are not mutually exclusive. As sociologist Randol
Contreras shows in research on violent drug robbers in New York, women
co-offenders are needed and exploited for their gendered labor, but the
men's personal relationships to the women include trust and opportunities
for the women co-offenders.[16]

These orientations of gender-neutral cooperation, gender advantage, and/ or gender exploitation are also at play when women select co-offenders. When women select men as co-offenders, they are selecting from a larger pool of eligible men with criminal experience or particular knowledge, but they are also likely privileging masculinity and assuming men's greater criminal competence. When women select other women as co-offenders, it could be a gender-neutral decision based on the availability of women with trust, knowledge, and opportunity; a decision based on cooperation and shared goals; or a need to access other women's gendered labor. Certainly preferences and the pool of eligible co-offenders shape patterns of co-offending, but these are well-entangled factors that are difficult to separate and measure independently in most examinations of co-offending, including this analysis of historical organized crime networks.

I closely examined the criminal relationships of all forty-seven syndicate women to identify the type of criminal activity that generated women's presence in organized crime. Nearly all of them (89 percent) were involved in the sex economy, whether as brothel owners, managers, operators, sex workers, clerks, or traffickers. Of the remaining 11 percent, only one woman in the organized crime network clearly had no connection to the sex economy; she connected to organized crime through a co-arrest with her husband. The remaining four women in the organized crime network were arrested by the police with four men while at a saloon. These men and women were all regulars at the saloon, and they called upon Louis Frank to fix the judge in their case.[17] It is possible that these four women were sex workers, but police and morals inspectors often arrested unmarried women at entertainment establishments, incorrectly assuming that they were sex workers. With these five possible exceptions, women of the organized crime network in the first two decades of the twentieth century were almost entirely operating within the sex economy. As a point of comparison, only 33 percent of the men in the organized crime network were involved in the sex economy; 30 percent of men in the organized crime network were involved in the gambling economy, with some men overlapping in both the sex and gambling economies. Organized crime individuals included those involved in the gambling and sex economies plus collectors, fixers, and corrupt police officers and local politicians. There were no women collectors or corrupt officials; it was the location of women's brothels and establishments within organized crime territories that facilitated their entrée into organized crime.

It is likely that some of the women brothel owners were exploited by organized crime and forced to pay into the protection market or face closing.

Historical research on New York City's brothel districts shows that underworld protection markets involving police officers and local politicians were just as exploitative of illicit entertainment businesses as they were protective.[18] In Chicago, this challenging arrangement exchanged profits for protection against raids and prosecution, but protection was still expensive. May Ward operated a brothel at 25 North Carpenter Street. She testified to the Civil Service Commission in 1911 that Mike Heitler and Mike Fewer had threatened to close her brothel on multiple occasions unless she paid them $150.[19] When May told collector Mike Fewer that she would testify, he threatened that if she did testify, Chicago would not be a pleasant place for her. She ran away to Michigan shortly after testifying, whether by choice or by force is unclear.[20] May's payments to Fewer and Heitler were the criminal transactions that connected her to the organized crime network, but the details of her case suggest gender exploitation by male members of organized crime rather than May herself seeking access to the resources of organized crime.

Women's access to organized crime through the sex economy is not surprising. As I discussed in the previous chapter, in general, women have greater access to crime when the illicit economy requires access to other women.[21] In this case, syndicate women had essential access to women sex workers. I also looked at women's marital status and romantic relationships to see if syndicate women's presence in the network was through their male romantic partners. The most surprising finding in this context was the importance of brothel locations in the Levees in generating women's criminal relationships to organized crime rather than their prior marital and romantic relationships to organized crime men. This finding is surprising because contemporary research on women's networks and initiation into crime and delinquency tends to find that women's criminal activity is associated with their romantic partners' criminal involvement.[22]

Only ten of the forty-seven women in organized crime had documented romantic, marital, or familial relationships to men in organized crime. These romantic or family ties co-occurred with criminal ties within the organized crime network—for example, husbands and wives co-owning a brothel or operating a trafficking ring together.[23] It is remarkable that only 21 percent of women from the early 1900s connected to organized crime through their husbands or male relatives. In predominantly male organizations, men are the gatekeepers to the organization, and having a trusting relationship with a husband, boyfriend, or male relative might be the only way for a woman to access an organization that is largely closed to women. It appears, however, that unmarried, illicit business-owning women could do fine for themselves, and even married women did not necessarily need their husbands to connect to organized crime in early twentieth-century Chicago—a pattern that did not persist during Prohibition. Among the ten married women, not all entered organized crime through their husbands. At least two women, Vic Shaw and Victoria Moresco, were brothel owners in the Levees before their marriages to organized crime men. It was Shaw's and Moresco's previous wealth and Levee success before their marriages that arguably catapulted the organized crime careers of their husbands, Roy Jones and Jim Colosimo. These husbands and wives may even have met through other organized crime connections. In the end, these two women's marriages to organized crime men pushed both of them out of organized crime after their divorces.

Organized crime husbands were sometimes a liability for the wives of organized crime. Husbands' business failures entangled their wives in ways that the husbands' successes did not. Listings of brothels owned by men could have failed to acknowledge wives' contributions to the business, but when men failed to escape prosecution, their wives were often implicated with them in the legal cases. For example, Julia Van Bever worked directly with her husband, Maurice, in trafficking and selling women to Colosimo and Moresco for their brothels. Julia Van Bever's success in the trafficking business was dependent on her husband's organized crime connections, but his convictions also implicated her. When police and prosecutors uncovered the Van Bever–Colosimo trafficking operations, Colosimo and Moresco were insulated from prosecution because of their legal connections and organized crime protection, whereas the Van Bevers both received sentences at Leavenworth prison because they were clearly not connected closely enough to the protective resources in organized crime. It is not clear why Colosimo was able to leverage his protective resources for him and his wife to evade prosecution whereas the Van Bevers could not. Certainly there are limits to social network resources and how they are deployed.

No brothel in the Levee districts received as much attention—positive or negative—as the Everleigh Club at 2131 South Dearborn Street. The mysterious, glamorous, and unmarried Everleigh sisters, Minna and Ada, owned and operated the brothel from 1900 to 1911. The club had a reputation as the most elite and luxurious brothel of Chicago, with its gold piano, gold spittoons, gold-plated room, and perfume fountain. On one occasion a German prince and his entourage all drank champagne from the shoes of the women working at the club.[24] The Everleigh sisters were regular features of Aldermen Kenna and Coughlin's First Ward Democratic balls, and they escorted the aldermen during the grand march.[25] During the 1908 ball,

Minna and Ada were spending $50 an hour on wine for their box, and organized crime collector Ike Bloom called out to Minna, "Keep it up, Minnie. You are the only live one around here."[26] The Everleigh sisters funneled money to the aldermen outside of the balls as well. Minna testified that they contributed $3,000 (approximately $75,000 in 2018 dollars) to Kenna and Coughlin when the aldermen needed funds to defeat a legislative bill forbidding the sale of liquor in brothels.[27] Although they were competitors with many of the men business owners of the Levee, the Everleigh sisters secured their position in the syndicate through a single tie to Alderman Coughlin. Their criminal ties to organized crime were the privileged protection their establishment received from Coughlin as thanks for their legitimate political donations.

The Everleighs' establishment was immune to raids and forced closings for almost twelve prosperous years, until 1911, when Mayor Carter Harrison started to crack down on the Levees and specifically ordered the closing of the Everleigh Club.[28] The Levee was shocked by the news, but the Everleigh sisters kept their poise:

> "I don't worry about anything," [Minna] continued. . . . "You get everything in a lifetime. Of course, if the mayor says we must close, that settles it. What the mayor says goes, so far as I am concerned. I'm not going to be sore about it, either. I never was a knocker, and nothing the police of this town can do to me will change my disposition. I'll close up the shop and walk out of the place with a smile on my face. Nobody else around here is worrying either," she went on with a smile, waving a hand literally coruscated with diamonds toward the parlor, from which came sounds of music and bursts of laughter. "If the ship sinks we're going down with a cheer and a good drink under our belts, anyway."[29]

There was a bit of a kerfuffle during the actual closing of the Everleigh Club. The official orders were lost on someone's desk for about forty-eight hours, but allegations were made that the Everleigh sisters had paid a large sum of money for one final night of operation.[30] By 1925 the former Everleigh Club building on Dearborn Street had been converted into a rooming house for African American residents, which was demolished in 1933 by a wrecking ball.[31]

The one African American woman in the Progressive Era organized crime network was May Douglas, a brothel madam who provided light-skinned black women sex workers to an exclusively white male clientele.[32] Douglas was one of several "eminent" madams arrested with Levee district "vice lords" in October 1912.[33] Organized crime protected this group of eminent Levee characters by securing their "immediate release on bail."[34]

In this case, Douglas connected to the organized crime network through co-arrest relationships with Jim Colosimo and his associates. The racialized hierarchy of Chicago in the early years of the Great Migration (around 1916) of southern African Americans to northern urban centers was apparent in Douglas's niche of the sex economy. It was also evident in the near exclusion of African Americans from the Progressive Era organized crime network even while organized crime activities were concentrating in and around Chicago's growing Black Belt.

The Everleigh sisters, and women like them, were important and fascinating figures in Chicago organized crime, but to say that women were part of organized crime does not imply any sort of equal standing to men within the organization. Women were at the margins of organized crime, mostly making regular graft payments and arrangements with fixers. In some cases, such as May Ward's, organized crime men exploited women brothel owners, forcing women into their protection market. Given the choice, brothel owners like Ward probably would have preferred to operate without the interference of organized crime and law enforcement, but that was not an option in Chicago's Levees. The Everleigh sisters were not prominent or well-connected actors in the organized crime network, but that did not seem to matter because their single connection to an alderman provided more than a decade of immunity. Even in the decentralized structure of Progressive Era organized crime, women were not the collectors, fixers, or bosses, but rather were paying members of the protection syndicate. Across these relationships was a combination of availability, cooperation, and perhaps exploitation of women's gendered labor in criminal economies forming the basis of women's connection to organized crime. Organized crime had profits to gain by incorporating women business owners into its protection market, and profits are much more gender-neutral than personal preferences and selections.

## THE BROKERS

Brokerage was important to organized crime when the network needed to disseminate information, provide access to legal and political protection, or select potential co-offenders for developing schemes, but the term "brokerage" has an important double meaning in criminal network contexts.[35] First, it refers to intermediaries or middlemen in illicit economies who link buyers to sellers, collect payments, offer protection, or threaten violence.[36] Brokers in the sex economy, often pimps, reduce women sex workers' control over their work and lower women's wages.[37] In the second meaning, brokerage is a crucial network position that measures gateways within a component of a network. Brokers in a network are the actors who reside on paths connecting other actors within the network. Without brokers, fewer actors would connect to the component. Brokers do not always have the most connections in the network, but they are often the most powerful actors in a network and essential for a network to maintain its particular structure.[38]

Under Progressive Era organized crime, many of the brokers (in both senses of the term) were middlemen who collected graft money from illicit business owners and delivered cash to their bosses or paid off judges and police officers. These individuals were also in brokerage positions controlling the flows of and access to networked resources. Brokers connected different sections of the organized crime network and were the gatekeepers to organized crime, often deciding which illicit entertainment businesses were in and which were out. The diversity of brokers and their localized territorial interests increased women's chances for connecting to the vice syndicate, even though all of these brokers were men.

Louis Frank's connections reflect the broker position in a network. His high number of criminal relationships (thirty-nine) had more to do with his long list of graft collections than any sort of kingpin position in organized crime. Frank's organized crime activity was incredibly localized, included many women, and was one of several peripheral sections of the decentralized network, located in the bottom left of figure 5. Frank was in his fifties when he became a notorious public figure in 1909, which was the year he was facing serious legal trouble. To get out from under his own indictments, Frank became a state's witness against police inspector Edward McCann (a well-connected criminal located just above Frank in figure 5), who was charged with police graft and malfeasance in a Cook County grand jury case.[39] Frank's testimony under oath was that he was a saloon owner who became Inspector McCann's collector in the Levee district:

> I asked [Inspector McCann] what I could offer the sporting people in return for the contributions he demanded. He said they would get protection from arrest, unexpected raids and hounding by patrolmen and detectives.... I called for all the fellows I knew who were running houses and said they would have to pay $20 a month and that the inspector ordered it.... I got about $300 on the first collection. I gave it to Detective Griffin, the one who was indicted just before the inspector. He came to the saloon for it.[40]

Inspector McCann, of course, denied all of Frank's claims, and the colonel acting as McCann's defense attorney tried to establish that Frank was feeble-minded, simple, illiterate, and uncultured. When the colonel questioned Frank's knowledge of what pajamas were, Frank responded, "I know pajamas, the gentlemen's kind."[41] Frank's testimony named many names, detailing his own and Inspector McCann's criminal relationships in the Levee. It is reasonable to be suspicious of the veracity of Frank's testimony, given that the police inspectors accused him of singing to the district attorney in exchange for leniency in his own stack of indictments, but the Cook County grand jury must have believed some of Frank's testimony, because they found Inspector McCann guilty.[42]

Louis Frank was an unusual, equal opportunity broker when it came to women in his section of organized crime activity. Of his thirty-nine criminal relationships, nineteen were to women and twenty were to men. Frank directly connected 40 percent of the total organized crime women to the network and demanded the same $20 in protection payments from the women that he did from the men. Prices rose when bigger favors were needed. For example, when Annie Plummer's landlord demanded higher rent for her "miserable shack" on Peoria Street, from which she ran her brothel operations, she went to Frank, who in turn went to Inspector McCann. Plummer's rent was fixed for a $50 contribution.[43]

Without brokers or gatekeepers like Louis Frank, women's position in Chicago's Progressive Era organized crime network would have looked very different. The protection market of organized crime was limited enough in scope that the gendered labor of sex work and the localized sex work establishments of the Levees meant that women and men brothel owners faced comparable protection and graft demands. Frank was in the more strategic structural position to exploit these conditions for women, and his position connected many women to organized crime. Perhaps scholars should be suspicious of his impact on women in the organized crime network since he was a snitch, but in this decentralized, clustered network structure, it was exactly people like Frank, with their smaller and localized schemes, who generated organized crime opportunities for men and women. The main difference between Frank's section of the network and the similarly large cluster of all men at the top of the network in figure 5 was that he connected women to organized crime. Frank's graft collector brokerage position was less common when the organized crime network shifted in response to the exogenous legal shock of Prohibition.

## THE SHIFTING LEVEES

The Levee districts were lightning rods for the Progressive Era cultural debate about sex work. On one side, the "segregationists" declared that the

Levee districts were a necessary evil in order to contain disease, enforce regulations, and keep sex work out of residential neighborhoods.[44] Segregationists even pressed the discipline of sociology into service as the "practical proof" for their argument, though they failed to offer any sociological specifics.[45] On the other side their opponents, the "abolitionists," wanted an end to sex work, which they equated to slavery, bondage, and the trafficking of women.[46] Abolitionists wanted the Levee districts shut down and the courts to go after brothels, madams, pimps, and anyone who profited from women's bondage.[47] In 1912 Chicago aldermen organized a special aldermanic committee chaired by Alderman John Emerson to settle the "vice question" regarding which position—segregation or abolition—was better for the city. The sides debated for five and a half hours. The segregationists argued on the grounds of practicality and history: "You can't club morality into a person with a policeman's club. . . . There always has been vice and there always will be. The thing to do is to place all those women in a single district and force these illegal flats out of the residence sections. You can't drive out vice; you can only shift it."[48] The abolitionists rebutted with their own counts of the number of women trafficked to the segregated red-light districts and argued that segregation inflated the supply of sex workers beyond the demand. They also incited fears of racial mixing between African Americans and whites through comments on white slavery and allegations that the majority of male brothel workers and pimps were black: "Segregation creates a neglect on the part of the public. It fosters a 'don't care' spirit toward the question, while scattering incites the public to attention, puts the public on guard. . . . This 'don't care' spirit on the part of the public allows the vice interests to overestimate the demand and establish ways of recruiting the supply by most obnoxious methods. This recruiting has given rise to the awful white slavery of today."[49] The aldermanic special committee and debate did not resolve the "vice question" for Chicago, largely because city officials attempted to remain agnostic in the broader cultural debate. Members of the Chicago Police Department argued that abolition would scatter sex work around the city, requiring ten times as many police officers to maintain similar levels of control.[50] Mayor Harrison said that the matter should be left up to the voters.[51] Officials were more comfortable riding out the impassioned debates with a neutral position than risking upsetting the voters and disrupting the cash flow from the Levee districts.

Chicago abolitionists believed they had won, however, when Illinois state's attorney John Wayman formally closed the Levees in 1912.[52] The closure occurred shortly after Congress passed the Mann Act, officially the

White Slave Traffic Act of 1910, which prohibited crossing state lines with women for immoral purposes.[53] It was also the case that segregationists and city officials had a harder time defending the Levees against abolitionists as investigations continued to uncover the presence of organized crime there. Segregationists' arguments faltered in the face of a new conception of the problem: pimps and "male parasites" were no longer just profiting off women, they had organized a vice syndicate that was infiltrating and corrupting public offices.[54]

The state of Illinois forced the closing of the Chicago Levees, and the Levees transformed in response to the edict. In 1914 a bartender in the 22nd Street Levee waxed philosophical: "The levee is on th' bum for true. They's no telling' when things'll be opened up right again."[55] In 1916 *Chicago Tribune* writer Henry Hyde walked the Levee for his series on the aftermath of its closing:

> It is 1 o'clock in the morning. The trolley car stops at State and Twenty-second streets. . . . This is the heart of the old red light district, the bad lands, the lava beds, of international notoriety. At this hour, little more than three years ago, the "line" was just waking up for its night's work. . . . Tonight the district is dark and silent. There are no lights of any color. It is like landing in some remote and ruined city devastated by the plague. . . . Not only are the House of All Nations, the Everleigh club, the California, Tokio, the Mecca, and all the other notorious resorts tightly closed, but the buildings which they occupied are utterly deserted. Not only are they deserted, but many of them stand only as empty shells. They have been looted and gutted until nothing but the outer walls and an occasional stairway is left in place. In many of the buildings, which formerly rented for $200 or $300 a month, the front door swings open to the touch. One steps in and his feet crunch an inch deep layer of plaster and glass. The very doors are gone. All the lead pipe, plumbing fixtures, gaspipe, and hardware long ago disappeared. The plastering has been ripped off the walls. An internal cyclone could have wrought no more complete havoc.[56]

This abolitionist win was a different kind of win for organized crime. Organized crime networks that are the most flexible are also the most profitable when they can adapt to exogenous shocks to the legal field. The closing of the Levee districts forced brothels underground and scattered them throughout working-class residential neighborhoods.[57] With the brothels underground, the large dance clubs, all-night saloons, and cafés that coordinated meetings between sex workers and clients had even less competition. This was not a new type of sex work in the Levees, but it was more covert than the sex work of the former, large, infamous brothels that Hyde described.

In spite of reports like Hyde's about the destruction and abandonment of the Levees, contradictory accounts of raids and massive arrests suggested that the former 22nd Street Levee remained under the rule of "vice kings."[58] These unnamed men were mentioned again when a private detective and ex-police officer, Harry Cullett, attempted to bribe the head of the Morals Inspection Bureau, William Dannenberg, to permit the reopening of the 22nd Street Levee district.[59] Cullett claimed to represent ten times more resort owners than had been around in the old Levee district and promised the inspectors up to $2,200 a month in bribes (about $55,000 a month in 2018 dollars).[60] Cullett's claim of "ten times more resort owners" in the former 22nd Street Levee suggests that the unofficial protection market had grown dramatically following the official closure of the Levees.

Even with organized crime's increasing protection market, the network's powers still remained scattered and largely undefined. Officer 666's anonymous account in the *Chicago Tribune* alleged that in 1914 there were three protection rings competing with each other: one led by Jim Colosimo with Maurice Van Bever and Johnny Torrio; one led by Julius and Charles Maibaum, who took Ed Weiss's places under their wing; and the third by brothers Joe and Bill Marshall.[61] Officer 666 was among the first to acknowledge Torrio's and Van Bever's importance to organized crime. These two were among the criminal elite of the organized crime network, but reporters and investigators underestimated their roles when naming vice syndicate "bosses." Julius and Charles Maibaum were in the organized crime network, each with five criminal ties, and the Marshall brothers never connected to the organized crime network. From the perspective of the organized crime network, the Marshall and Maibaum brothers were far from competitors with Torrio and Van Bever, who were among the most criminally connected.

In 1917 a big case for State's Attorney Maclay Hoyne that painted a centralized organized crime triumvirate appeared to be largely for prosecution purposes rather than showing evidence of having cracked the decentralized, clustered organized crime network. Hoyne's men raided a luxury office at 109 North Dearborn Street and discovered Tom Costello, Mike Heitler, William Skidmore, and Lieutenant Martin White sorting through packages of money secured by rubber bands.[62] The raid also uncovered White carrying a small Moroccan leather notebook that included lists of protected hotels, brothels, and saloons. A page in the notebook contained the heading "Can be raided," and underneath the heading was a list of names and partial addresses.[63] Hoyne submitted this notebook as evidence of the police departments' control and efficacy in the newly forbidden red-light districts.[64] He argued that the "rulers of the vice world" were Costello, Heitler, and Skidmore—names familiar from the days before the Levees closed and all well-connected members in the organized crime network.

In figure 5, these four organized crime associates are located up and to the right of Louis Frank's section of the network, and their region of the network includes the two actors with very high degree scores. Heitler and Costello were among the most connected criminals in Progressive Era organized crime; Heitler had thirty-five criminal connections and Costello had thirty-two. Heitler was also the top broker in the Progressive Era network; 14,367 paths, or 41 percent of all the paths in the network, went through him. Heitler's brokerage position was consistent with his organized crime biography. He was a kingpin and property owner in the West Side Levee district. (Figure 4 in chapter 3 is a photograph of one of his brothels.) He received tribute payments and had political connections. Illicit business owners wanting or requiring legal and political protection had to go through Heitler, and Heitler brokered several women to organized crime. Skidmore and White were not as powerfully connected as Heitler and Costello. Skidmore had ten connections in the network, and White had thirteen. Although they had fewer relationships than other key people in the network, these relationships still secured them a relatively powerful location far from the margins of organized crime. These alleged "rulers of the vice world" were protected by Chief of Police Charles Healey, who personally netted about $25,000 annually as beneficiary to the vice ring (about $530,000 in 2018 dollars).[65] Hoyne built his case only against the West Side vice ring, but he noted the existence of a second vice ring operating in Chicago about which he had nothing to say.

Tom Costello of the West Side vice ring turned state's witness in the case against Healey. In his testimony, Costello detailed how the Chicago Police Department had become "a veritable bribe assessing and collection machine with Healey the master grafter."[66] One of the details that got buried in Costello's hours of testimony against Chief Healey was an interaction that Costello had had with Jim Colosimo's right-hand man, Johnny Torrio.[67] Torrio knew that Costello had connections to Chief Healey and to members of the anti-sex-work investigatory Committee of Fifteen, so Torrio went to Costello to buy into the protection syndicate for his brothel and five of his associates' brothels. Costello agreed. The next day, Torrio took Costello and Harrison Streeter of the Committee of Fifteen for a drive in his Studebaker to show them the six brothels requiring protection. Torrio drove the men to the former 22nd Street Levee, where the six brothels were located. Near the Vestibule and the De Luxe were two women-owned brothels, Emily Marshall's and Georgie Spencer's places. Marshall and Spencer passed their envelopes of cash to their broker, Torrio, who passed them to his broker, Costello, who passed them to Chief Healey. This chain of money passing through the organized crime network secured these two women brothel owners' positions. Marshall's and Spencer's brothels were forced underground when the Levees closed, making the protection market even more lucrative and necessary. Women's brothels, even when underground and covert, were still able to enter the organized crime network, but the wheeling and dealing negotiations and corruption among the criminal elite, law enforcement, and politicians never directly included women.

The official closing of the Levees in 1912 was essentially the closing of the large, prosperous, and most infamous Chicago brothels—brothels owned by men and women. Several organized crime women, such as the Everleigh sisters, closed shop and left their Chicago playground to retire in New York. Others, like Vic Shaw, moved to smaller and more discreet locations within the former Levees or farther out into residential districts.[68] Mayor Harrison closed Jim Colosimo's café and cabaret, but he transferred the title over to his wife, Victoria Moresco.[69] She was able to keep it open in the 22nd Street Levee until she and Colosimo divorced in 1920. Marshall and Spencer accessed the protection of organized crime and the bawdy reputation of the former Levees with their brothels years after the closing. Organized crime women continued to traffic women for the sex work rings run out of brothels, hotels, and saloons.[70] Sex workers even returned to their old Levee haunts. According to a 1914 Committee of Fifteen complaint to Mayor Harrison, the old "vice kings" had purchased the brothel buildings, converted them into hotels and saloons, and rehired sex workers to solicit from the back rooms.[71] Though the Levee districts shifted in response to legal shocks, geographical locations still mattered for women's entrée to the organized crime network toward the end of the Progressive Era.

SUMMARY

In chapter 3 I argued that several social and political influences—such as the shifting legal changes regarding sex work, discretionary law enforcement, the gendered labor of managing and selling sex, and the spatial concentration of the Levees—provided conditions under which women had increasing opportunities for participation in Chicago's illicit entertainment economy and, consequently, in organized crime. In this chapter I have examined the network conditions that increased opportunities for women's participation in the margins of the organized crime network even after the official closing of the Levees.

The organized crime network from 1900 to 1919 was small, sparse, and decentralized. Although men had the most criminal connections in the network and were its brokers, my analysis shows that Progressive Era organized crime did not have one single boss or even a clear set of bosses. Rather than being a hierarchy, the network was shaped by local actors brokering their schemes and associates to others across the network. Brokers, rather than bosses, generated the structure of Progressive Era organized crime. Brokers selected women as co-offenders either through gender-neutral decisions based on cooperation and trust or through advantageous (and possibly exploitative) access to women's gendered labor in the sex economy. These brokers were not always husbands, relatives, or boyfriends, but rather middlemen coordinating protection and payments. This chapter extends previous conceptualizations of organized crime by situating women of the sex economy as relevant, though marginal, actors in the Chicago organized crime network from 1900 to 1919. Establishing the conditions that increased women's presence in organized crime during the Progressive Era is necessary to understand what happened during Prohibition, when organized crime left women behind.

# 5. Chicago, Crime, and Prohibition

From 1920 until 1933, the United States conducted the "noble experiment" of Prohibition; the mocking epithet "noble experiment" stuck based on comments made by President Herbert Hoover in 1928.[1] The state of Illinois had largely ignored the Wartime Prohibition Act that went into effect in July 1919, so January 17, 1920, was the first day of major consequence regarding the antialcohol legislation and its enforcement.[2] The eve of Prohibition was an especially busy day for liquor sales as citizens of Chicago stocked up on their home supplies.[3] The law permitted personal consumption and storage of alcohol—a Prohibition perk available to the wealthy. At midnight the Chicago "drys" (i.e., supporters of Prohibition) sang songs to a symbolic John Barleycorn, Chicago's head of Prohibition enforcement discussed a ten-day grace period for saloon owners to register their alcohol stock with federal agents, and police responded to twenty incidents of alcohol theft.[4] Prohibition-related crimes had begun.

In this chapter I detail the political momentum that resulted in the Eighteenth Amendment to the US Constitution. The prohibition in 1920 of the production, transportation, and sale of intoxicating beverages was an exogenous legal shock to illicit markets that was especially opportune for Chicago's preexisting organized crime network. Although the Eighteenth Amendment contained less legal ambiguity than local and state regulations regarding sex work, the enforcement of the law was uneven and discretionary. Prohibition ushered in income-generating opportunities for many Chicago residents from all walks of life. This included women, such as Moonshine Mary, and families outside of organized crime, whose domestic bootlegging at home contrasted with the industrial scale of alcohol production and distribution coordinated by organized crime. This chapter establishes an important piece of this book's puzzle: women's participation in the illicit "booze" economy increased to 27 percent of alcohol establishments during Prohibition. Even though organized crime and its restructured protection market largely ignored women's and families' localized illicit establishments that produced and sold alcohol, the illicit economy did not push women out.

## THE CONSTITUTIONAL AMENDMENT

Progressive Era activism achieved two constitutional amendments in 1919: the national prohibition of alcohol and women's right to vote. The antialcohol temperance and women's suffrage movements coincided temporally and overlapped in membership.[5] Both were strong movements that had multiple successes at state levels. The temperance movement engaged in some of the largest and most aggressive lobbying efforts the United States had ever seen.[6] The Woman's Christian Temperance Union had more members than entire suffragists' movements, but there was considerable overlap between the two.[7] Elite and educated women organized around saving poor women from violent, drunk husbands who were squandering the household income at the local saloon.[8] The momentum of women's increasing political involvement and influence in the temperance movement motivated national brewers and distillers to lobby against women's suffrage.[9] States that passed suffrage laws tended to be in the West, where there were more opportunities for women in education, work, political organizing, and property ownership.[10] In 1913 Illinois became the first state east of the Mississippi to grant women the right to vote in municipal elections and presidential primaries, but women's ballots were counted separately from men's.[11]

The temperance movement gained momentum during World War I (1914–1918) with increasing anti-German sentiment, "bread, not beer" campaigns to support the soldiers abroad, and anti-immigrant alarm targeting the growing populations of urban poor.[12] As a result, World War I effectively silenced working-class and immigrant opponents to Prohibition. In 1919 both the temperance and suffrage movements achieved constitutional reform with the passing of the Eighteenth and Nineteenth Amendments to the US Constitution. The Eighteenth Amendment, referred to as Prohibition, banned the production, transportation, and sale of intoxicating beverages. Prohibition went into effect on January 17, 1920. Congress also approved the Nineteenth Amendment, giving women the right to vote, in 1919, but it was not ratified by the states until August 1920. Although Prohibition and women's suffrage were in many ways politically linked, Prohibition came first.

The Eighteenth Amendment was the first amendment to the Constitution that limited, rather than protected, individual freedom.[13] Prohibition's controversial invasion of home and leisure generated massive disregard for the law and, as a result, incredible profitability for those who organized the production and sale of booze. Prohibition triggered new forms of corruption: Chicago's elite received alcohol home delivery, politicians voted for dry laws while wetting their palates with bootleg booze, judges had access to the best Canadian imports, law enforcement salaries multiplied through bribes, and federal Prohibition agents engaged in graft.[14] Short supply and high demand kept Chicago's local bootleggers busy. Four years into Prohibition, reporter Arthur Evans wrote a three-part series for the *Chicago Tribune* on the conditions in Chicago. Evans and the unnamed politician he interviewed for the article accused "alien" immigrants of supplying Chicago's "Americans" with poisonous booze:

> Homemade wine has no patrons for it is considered too tame, while beer is larded as nothing more than a chaser. The call is for something with quick and fiery action, something volcanic. . . . There are spots on the west side where at night when the clouds are low, the streets reek with smells like a distillery in prewar days. . . . Bootleggers with bottles in their pockets in black grips prowl the streets. The hooch addict has no trouble in locating a source of supply. As fast as the police hammer it down in one spot it rises in another. . . . The stuff goes at 25 or 50 cents a flask in the general run. . . . "And for the most part the moon is being made and bootlegged by alien foreigners who are not citizens, but who are getting rich poisoning Americans. There are some foreign districts in Chicago where half the alien population seems to be moonshining and those who don't make moon are bootlegging the stuff."[15]

Evans and the anonymous politician's accusations against Chicago immigrants and their "fiery" booze focused on domestic production in tenements and Chicago slums, perpetuating the anti-immigrant sentiment that had propelled the passage of the Eighteenth Amendment. Their reporting was correct in identifying the domestic production of alcohol in Chicago. However, Evans's article failed to mention the small-scale entrepreneurs, experienced brewers, and organized criminals seizing Chicago's alcohol production and distribution opportunities. Across the United States, folks from all walks of life were taking risks to cash in on Prohibition's transformed illicit market.

## THE EXOGENOUS SHOCK

Prohibition was an exogenous shock to US illicit economies. The overnight criminalization of the production, sale, and distribution of alcohol shifted the licit and local market to an illicit and international one. Exogenous shocks are external forces that transform markets; they include social movements, natural disasters, and social disasters (e.g., war, terrorist attacks), as well as governmental regulations or deregulations and other state actions.[16] These examples are all shocks that are external to markets, but they can have immediate and consequential effects on them. The September 11, 2001, terrorist attacks on the United States, for example, immediately caused a short recession in the airline and tourism industries, but this exogenous shock eventually developed a large and durable market of airline travel security that included equipment, training, and personnel.[17] In effect, exogenous shocks create conditions for skilled people to reorganize markets.[18]

Market-based organizations and market-oriented individuals respond differently to exogenous shocks; whereas some might see opportunity, others see an end. Prohibition reshaped the local illicit economy with a lucrative and high-demand product, and participants willing to violate the new law embraced this exogenous legal shift and its incredible financial opportunity. Brewers complying with Prohibition law shifted production or closed shop, and compliant saloon owners boarded their doors and windows or shifted to less profitable food sales. Some German brewing families, such as the Leinenkugel family of Chippewa Falls, Wisconsin, who had been brewing since 1867, responded to the exogenous shock of Prohibition by converting brewing operations to producing nonalcoholic sodas and low-alcohol beers that were permitted during Prohibition—a business decision that barely kept Leinenkugel afloat in the thirsty Wisconsin logging town.[19] Other organizations, families, and individuals accepted the risk associated with the immense profits of Prohibition. Soda shops, pharmacies, and cigar stores became fronts for peddling booze. Doctors' prescriptions; diluted industrial-grade alcohol; and homemade batches of wine, beer, and "moonshine" could not keep up with the dry city's thirst. In 1920 a judge found hundreds of gallons of Canadian whiskey being smuggled across the border and delivered to Chicago.[20]

Chicago's established Progressive Era organized crime network was in the most powerful position to reorganize the illicit markets following the exogenous shock of Prohibition. Economic sociologist Neil Fligstein explains that "new markets are born in close social proximity to existing markets," and this insight is useful in thinking about the impact of Prohibition on the Progressive Era illicit economies.[21] As I detailed in chapters 3 and 4, Chicago's illicit entertainment economies were robust and durable even in the face of the shifting regulations of the Progressive Era. Alcohol was an integral product of illicit entertainment that complemented less inhibited spending in card games and brothels. Prohibition did not create a new product, but by criminalizing the production, transportation, and sale of a very popular product, it generated even greater cash flows to the illicit markets already dependent on alcohol. Organized crime's foothold in the illicit economies of gambling and sex work was not just a "social proximity" to the new market; rather, organized crime was the market-oriented organization positioned to reorganize and dominate the transformed market.[22]

## THE ENFORCEMENT

National Prohibition laws were irrefutable and clear in ways that Illinois's and Chicago's sex work regulations had not been. The legal ambiguity of regulating sex contrasted sharply with the legal clarity of Prohibition. The date of January 17, 1920, was clearly defined; sales and production of intoxicating beverages could take place in many locations across the United States the day before, but not that day or on the days to follow. The Eighteenth Amendment to the US Constitution overrode legal variation in state and municipal codes. Certainly there were some legal loopholes that were exploited, such as the distribution and prescription of medicinal liquors, but the real variation in Prohibition market successes and failures occurred because of discretion in enforcement.

Unlike in the illicit economies of the Progressive Era, Prohibition law enforcement fell under the purview of federal agencies (the Bureau of Prohibition and the Bureau of Justice), with support from local and state law enforcement. The situation was much like that of immigration law today, in which some local and state law enforcement agencies' concerns for local crime control and social order supersede their enforcement of federal immigration law, while other agencies actively deploy local law enforcement resources to enforce federal immigration laws even without guidance from local elected officials.[23] Moreover, it was clear in the early days of Prohibition that the federal government was unable to provide the level of enforcement that the federal law required. Prohibition commissioner John Kramer started off the federal agency in 1920 with fifteen hundred men (the Chicago Police Department had approximately forty-five hundred patrolmen in 1923) and a budget of $2 million (nearly $26 million in 2018 dollars), but his agency required national urban and rural coverage and enforcement.[24] It was not long before the underfunded and inexperienced federal enforcement agents reeked of corruption.[25]

The local/federal dynamic of enforcement of a despised law created conditions for unique relationships among bootleggers, organized crime, and local law enforcement.[26] Chicago was one of the "wettest" cities in the United States.[27] Mayor "Big" Bill Thompson (1915–1923, 1927–1931) mostly permitted Chicago police to ignore Prohibition law except when it was politically convenient for him to enforce it.[28] Mayor William Dever's (1923–1927) short term represented a brief attempt to crack down on Prohibition violators and violence in Chicago, but putting the city's power into Prohibition enforcement actually escalated gangland violence and pushed organized crime into the suburbs of Chicago, outside of the mayor's jurisdiction.[29] The goal of local politicians and local police officers was not erasure of the illicit market of alcohol—although they were certainly in a position to make arrests or to report Prohibition-related crimes to the federal agents.[30] Rather, local actors used Prohibition violations as a mechanism of social control.[31] Local politicians and law enforcement could make an arrest whenever they wanted or needed, but often the threat of reporting was enough to gain the social order, benefits, or graft payments they demanded.[32]

Chicagoans ridiculed federal Prohibition agents as incompetent, under-resourced, and corrupt Washington, DC, socialite outsiders with no understanding of Chicago and its hierarchies. Chicago's most public case of chasing out a DC agent was its riddance of Count William Yaselli. "Dapper" Count Yaselli was a federal Prohibition agent whose sleuthing and entrapment tactics included disguises ("his forty pairs of shoes, his twenty hats, his adjustable Van Dyke beard") and pleasure seeking ("a thirsty bon vivant") so over the top that they landed him in the pages of the *Chicago Tribune*.[33] Yaselli ran around Chicago, charged huge tabs, drank with his women escorts, and extorted payments from local establishments, then turned and was to serve as the expert witness in sixty-five Chicago Prohibition cases.[34] Chicago detested Yaselli. When Yaselli appeared in court as a witness in a Prohibition case against Henry Horn of the Green Mill Gardens, attorney David Stansbury punched Yaselli in the nose, sending him falling over the railing of the jury box.[35] Yaselli himself faced entrapment when a young woman detective was hired to plant a flask of whisky under the table while dining with him. His arrest and his eventual dismissal were subjected to public mockery: "At the station the prisoner gave his name as 'Count' William D. Yaselli. 'You're an American citizen, ain't you?' asked Desk Sergeant Myers. Yaselli twisted the waxed ends of his mustache, flecked a speck of dust from his sleeve, stooped to shake some snow from one of his fawn colored spats, and nodded in the affirmative. 'Well, we have no counts over here,' returned the sergeant. 'You go down on the blotter as Bill Yaselli.'"[36] The *Chicago Tribune* publicized its version of the Chicago Police Department's derision of Yaselli's "waxed" moustache and grooming habits as characteristic of a socialite DC outsider while also emphasizing nativist sentiments by refusing to refer to Yaselli as "Count" and prying into his immigrant status. The Bureau of Justice was so embarrassed by Yaselli that it dismissed him and agreed to drop the sixty-five pending Prohibition violation cases in which he was to have served as a witness. When Yaselli asked for carfare to arrange his transportation back to his home in Philadelphia after being discharged, the Bureau of Justice office in Chicago told him to sell off some of his fancy suits.[37]

The Yaselli case shows how, in the early years of Prohibition, Chicago's local machine politics had little to no tolerance for interference in their relationship with the illicit economy of Prohibition. As historian Lisa McGirr has documented, the later years of Prohibition established the broader state-building project that successfully centralized federal authority.[38] But throughout the fourteen years of Prohibition, Chicago organized crime's power and influence to negotiate with corrupt Prohibition agents and local Chicago authorities developed the uneven enforcement of Prohibition law. Those most at risk of being charged with Prohibition violations in Chicago were poor immigrant families outside of organized crime's protection.

THE WOMEN OF PROHIBITION

The profits from pouring beer and liquor in Chicago were unprecedented and, for many, worth the legal risks. Harry Harris of organized crime in Chicago elaborated on the Prohibition cash flow: "Good whiskey was just like gold and it was nothing to get $120 for a case of whiskey them days. . . . It was nothing to see a fellow with a couple of grand in his pocket when before prohibition a five dollar bill would have been lots of money to him."[39] Harris's comments indicate that there was a scale to the production and profits of Prohibition. Actually, there were two separate scales: the domestic household scale and organized crime's industrial scale. On one scale, anyone with access to an appliance store, a screwdriver, and a set of pliers could build a profitable home still; any man with an overcoat full of interior pockets could turn himself into a walking saloon; and any woman could sell single shots from the moonshine jar hidden under her kitchen sink.[40] These were substantial profits for these individuals and their families, but they were domestic profits generated within neighborhoods and from acquaintances. Although bootlegging income could help a struggling family, especially during the Great Depression that began in 1929, average families were not walking around with a "couple of grand" in their pockets like Harris.

On the other scale, Harris and other members of organized crime took over local breweries, divided the city into distribution territories, robbed federal facilities where confiscated alcohol was stored, and coordinated the international smuggling of imported alcohol.[41] A family's production of alcohol was no competition for organized crime's. Organized crime's mass production, coordination, and distribution ignored small batches of domestic product. However, domestic production and small-scale distribution created opportunities for women to take a small cut of the massive profits generated under the Eighteenth Amendment.

Historians have consistently documented women's domestic roles in brewing and distilling throughout history, dispelling popular notions that brewing was only men's work. In medieval England, women brewed and sold the majority of all the beer consumed. Beer production was domestic work, as denoted by the gendered term "brewster."[42] In the 1600s and 1700s, when Europe and New England were developing markets for spirits and beer, women of colonial Chesapeake households continued to produce alcoholic ciders for drinking, cleaning, medicine, and beauty as part of their regular domestic labor.[43] During Reconstruction in the United States after the Civil War, the distillers of "mountain dew" in the southern Appalachian Mountains were predominantly men, but in the rural mountain communities where distilling was family labor, some wives gave the tax collectors unreliable information regarding the location of distilleries, warned the neighbors when government raiders were approaching, or even fired shots at the raiders.[44] Occasionally, widows and daughters inherited the equipment, skills, and knowledge to continue producing moonshine after the men in their families had died.[45]

Women were an important part of bootlegging and moonshining during Prohibition across the United States, and especially in Chicago. Historical research on Prohibition in the rural United States found that women turned their kitchens into moneymaking machines with home brewing and distilling.[46] Chicago cases suggest a similar economy for urban women when residents complained in letters to Mayor Dever that Italian women were selling barrels of wine and booze from their apartments.[47] Observers of Chicago moonshine cases noted that even though fewer women than men were sent to Bridewell prison, women's cases were increasing.[48] The Illinois Humane Society handled 221 moonshine cases in 1922, and nearly 12 percent of them involved women defendants, an increase from the previous year's figure.[49]

On the domestic scale, bootlegging and moonshining were family affairs. According to the *Chicago Tribune*, "Little girls, daughters of moonshiners whose dingy kitchens had been transformed into distilleries, delivered half pints to customers for 35 cents."[50] Children lied to police officers about their fathers' employment. For example, when plainclothes officers asked a seven-year-old Italian boy what his father did for a living, he demonstrated some quick thinking: "[I] told them that he worked on the railroad and I told [them] that he didn't make moonshine when they asked me."[51] One of the officers offered the boy some candy, saying they were friends and customers of his father's and that they were there to buy a few cans of alcohol. The boy explained, "I stuck to my story . . . and when my dad came back and I told him about the incident, he was so tickled with me and so pleased that he took me down, and he gave me a dollar."[52] The attention to children's participation in the illicit economy reinforces the domestic production around Chicago's poor immigrant communities and their "dingy kitchens." The case of the seven-year-old Italian boy highlights the entrapment tactics used by Prohibition enforcement authorities against immigrant families.

Converting the domestic sphere into a profit-generating enterprise meant having and maintaining roofs over families' heads. German families converted their homes into beer flats where neighbors could spend the evening drinking beer and spending time with the family for a small fee. The Mullers were one such family, whose beer flat was an important contributor to the family economy:

> Their home was an old wooden shack. There were at least half dozen children playing on the floor which was greasy and dirty. The family consisted of Mr. and Mrs. [Muller] and about nine children some married who lived there with their wives or husbands. On top of all this there were about seven fellows and girls who lived with them and no one worked. Mrs. [Muller] was a tall slim woman who loved to drink. The old man was a huge giant, he could hardly talk any English. They were the typical German type. I looked over the place, the furniture was scant. For a kitchen table they had an old wine barrel with a board over it. There were not enough chairs and many had to sit on the floor. . . . The old man loved his beer. He bathed in it. The home as a whole looked more like a stable. Nevertheless we went here quite often as a pretty nice bunch of fellows hung here. . . . The old lady [Muller] was rocking one of the kids to sleep on her lap and in one hand she had a drinking glass filled to the brim with whiskey of which she occasionally took a drink now and then. This family could live on whiskey. Even the children drank it.[53]

During Prohibition, family homes such as the Mullers' became important social institutions in Chicago neighborhoods. They reliably had whisky and beer for purchase, the family could broker trusting connections with residents through mutual participation in the illicit economy, and the space provided camaraderie with the family and the "nice bunch of fellows" who hung out at the Mullers' home.

Men and women found the social connections in these informal social spaces important for reasons beyond the alcohol and companionship. Cigarette Mamie, for instance, was Irish, a "short chubby woman with coal black hair," and she and her husband turned their home into an alehouse.[54] They made good money selling beer and whiskey, but Cigarette Mamie also served as a matriarch of the neighborhood: "Mamie could fight like a man and God help the one she hit. All the women in the neighborhood went to her in time of need or whenever any difficulty arose, she would always help them. The people looked upon her as a sort of advisor."[55] The domestic production and distribution of alcohol generated its own social control for poor immigrant neighborhoods. While the Mullers' beer flat and Cigarette Mamie's alehouse fostered community relationships and trust, this position in the illicit economy also established Cigarette Mamie's authoritative position in the community, through which she would intervene on behalf of the women in the community. It is likely that Cigarette Mamie's helping "in time of need" referred to confronting men who were beating their wives or squandering the family wages on booze. Informal social control that relies on community members to resolve conflicts without the assistance of official authorities is a common feature of underground economies.[56]

In many cases, these informal beer flats and alehouses were the same locations as the informal brothels and disorderly flats around the city; homes could function as both. Illicit domestic work meant a home by day and a workplace by night without the additional expense of renting commercial space. Upon his release from prison, a young man returned to his mother's brothel, where he knew he could also get a drink:

> One of the girls my mother had staying with her came over and said, "Hello, Baby. How are you?" I told her I was fine and asked her if I could buy a drink. She said she did not know if Rose had any or not that she would go see. I knew that mother always had it but she told the girls never to say she had whiskey until she saw who wanted it. When my mother came in the front room to see if she knew who wanted the drink she looked at me and started to say something. But when she saw it was me tears stopped whatever she had in mind.[57]

Rose's having her home function as a brothel provided housing and employment for herself and the women who worked for her, as well as a

FIGURE 6. Mrs. Mary Wazeniak (Moonshine Mary), arrested for selling moonshine to a man who later died, in a courtroom in Chicago, Illinois, 1924. *Source:* DN-0076723, *Chicago Daily News* negatives collection, Chicago History Museum.

place to land for family and friends. Brothels generated trust required between clients and sex workers and thus were often safe places to ask for a drink. Alcohol sales increased her profits, but Rose tightly controlled the pouring of whiskey at her establishment to avoid flagrant liquor violations. Women clearly exploited the criminal opportunities during Prohibition, but their businesses and distribution usually did not extend past the walls of their homes.

The informality and small scale of domestic production and distribution made for quick cover in case of a raid. However, when the raids did come, these families lacked the legal resources and connections to escape prosecution, and they were easy targets for federal agents needing to inflate their arrest numbers. Women's domestic moonshining and bootlegging operated outside organized crime's protection market, and the legal consequences and sentences were severe. Moonshine Mary Wazeniak, thirty-four years old, was an immigrant from Poland and a mother of three young children. Her husband was chronically ill, so in 1923 she turned their small cottage into a "blind pig" (slang for an illegal saloon). She sold drinks at 15 cents apiece poured from her bottle of home-brewed moonshine. The Chicago newspapers reported on Moonshine Mary because she was charged with manslaughter for selling moonshine that poisoned a man (see figure 6). The report from the coroner's chemist stated that the man died from wood alcohol poisoning. Moonshine Mary received a sentence of one year to life in Joliet State Prison and was the first woman (though certainly not the last) in the state of Illinois to be convicted of manslaughter for selling poisonous moonshine.[58] Moonshine Mary's indeterminate jail sentence speaks to her complete lack of legal resources—resources that were plentiful within the Prohibition organized crime network.[59]

## THE GEOGRAPHY OF BOOZE

The archival address data on alcohol establishments in Chicago show how the geography of booze changed between the Progressive and Prohibition eras. Alcohol-related spaces included commercial saloons, speakeasies, restaurants serving alcohol illegally, and breweries, as well as domestic spaces such as blind pigs and beer flats. Map 3 plots all of the available alcohol establishment addresses (including those with named and unnamed proprietors) on a map of Chicago's community areas using contemporary mapping software. The left panel shows the geographic distribution of alcohol establishments during the Progressive Era, and the right panel shows the geographic distribution during Prohibition. As I established in chapter 3 with map 2, the alcohol establishments from the Progressive Era were mostly concentrated in the three Levee districts alongside brothels. The Prohibition map shows that when alcohol was forced underground, the establishments that were raided and appeared in the papers were more evenly spread across the city. There was little concentration of these establishments in the center of the city. Even

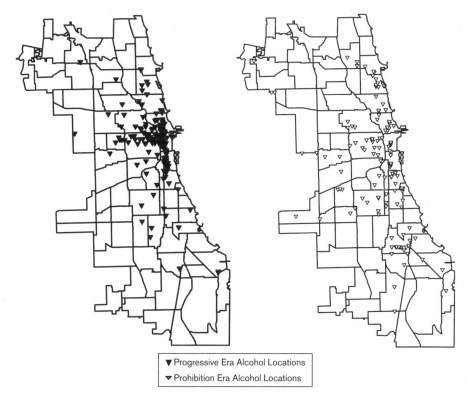

MAP 3. Chicago alcohol establishments, 1900–1919 and 1920–1933. *Sources:* Chicago Data Portal, "Boundaries—Community Areas (current)," 2018, https:// data.cityofchicago.org/Facilities-Geographic-Boundaries/Boundaries-Community -Areas-current-/cauq-8yn6, accessed June 24, 2018; Andrew Ba Tran, "Mapping with R," 2017, https://andrewbtran.github.io/NICAR/2017/maps /mapping-census-data.html, accessed June 24, 2018.

though there were fewer addresses uncovered and mapped, there were clusters of booze locations on the north and south sides of Chicago.

As discussed in more detail in chapter 2, the comparative analysis of women's and organized crime's involvement over time requires establishments with named proprietors. Due to the underground nature of these spaces, I uncovered fewer addresses for alcohol establishments with named proprietors during Prohibition (168) than during the Progressive Era (321), even though alcohol establishments were highly regulated and raided during the Progressive Era. The line graph in figure 7 shows the change in the proportion of addresses that involved women and organized crime members

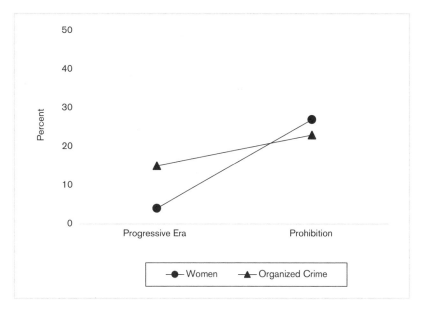

FIGURE 7. Women-involved and organized crime–involved percent of alcohol establishments in Chicago, 1900–1919 and 1920–1933.

as proprietors, co-proprietors, operators, or managers from the Progressive Era to Prohibition. The counts of establishments were low during both eras for women and organized crime. Women's names were listed as being involved at thirteen alcohol establishments during the Progressive Era and forty-five establishments during Prohibition. Names confirmed in the organized crime network were listed as being involved at forty-eight alcohol establishments during the Progressive Era and thirty-eight establishments during Prohibition. However, due to the smaller number of total uncovered establishments during Prohibition, the percentage of addresses involving women increased from 4 to 27 percent, whereas the percentage involving organized crime only increased from 15 to 23 percent.

Women's involvement in the illicit economy of alcohol increased dramatically during Prohibition, from almost no women being involved to women involved in over a quarter of locations. Women found increasing opportunity in alcohol-related crimes and establishments during Prohibition that were not available to them in the male-dominated saloons during the Progressive Era. These address data provide a critical piece of the puzzle on women's exclusion from Prohibition era organized crime. The illicit economy of Prohibition did not exclude women from illegal activities. Instead,

women were a substantial part of Chicago's small-scale, domestic bootlegging and moonshining. Families like the Mullers and individuals like
Cigarette Mamie and Moonshine Mary are examples of criminal relationships that were localized interactions between sellers and buyers. In many of
these cases, women produced their own alcohol; in others, it is not clear
where women bought their product. Regardless, these were never criminal
relationships connected to the larger and more powerful organized crime
network of Chicago. Women were operating in isolation and separate from
organized crime.

Figure 7 indicates that organized crime also had a growing interest and
control in Chicago's alcohol establishments, even though its protection
market likely kept the majority of organized crime locations out of the
newspapers and away from the investigative spotlight. Historian Lisa
McGirr explains the "selective enforcement" of Prohibition laws that targeted poor immigrant communities but protected organized crime rings.[60]
Although I uncovered more women-involved establishments than organized crime–involved establishments from Prohibition, the organized crime
addresses were very different in function and scope. These were not small,
kitchen domestic enterprises requiring many addresses in a single community, but rather sprawling warehouses and breweries at single locations
with greater volume and production. Prohibition demanded urban and sub-
urban space to manufacture and store intoxicating beverages. These had to
be large spaces to accommodate all of the equipment required for brewing
and distilling, and they had to be discreet spaces because brewing and distilling vented strong odors. These spaces required start-up capital, machin-
ery, and property ownership—requirements that were out of reach for the
majority of Chicagoans. The Sicilian Genna brothers of the organized crime
network rented an entire row of empty houses along Miller Street, where
they installed nice curtains and blinds to face the street and used the backs
of the houses to store "barrels of mash and yeast and stuff."[61]

As brewers across the country boarded up their businesses or converted
equipment to nonalcoholic soda production, organized crime embraced
Prohibition and took over the breweries. Johnny Torrio, of Progressive Era
organized crime brothel fame, and his associates took control of multiple
breweries in Chicago, including the Sieben Brewery at 1470 Larrabee Street,
Hoffman Products Company at 2606 West Monroe Street, the Malt Maid
Brewery at 3901 Emerald Avenue, and the West Hammond Brewery—and
this list includes only Torrio's breweries that were raided and made the
papers.[62] In 1929, Prohibition agents discovered a fully operational brewery
at 2340 South Wabash Avenue in a three-story brick building, which they

presumed to be Chicago mobster Al Capone's. There, agents found about $10,000 worth of brewing equipment, including twenty-three sixty-gallon fermenting tanks full of beer. Agents noted that they were not dealing with some "fly-by-night bootleggers."[63] Shortly after Prohibition agents took control of this brewery, bootleggers returned and attempted to recover confiscated brewing equipment.[64] In another instance, a raid in 1930 uncovered the fact that the Wabash Automotive Corporation, an automobile accessory shop at 2108 South Wabash Avenue, was actually a front for a large syndicate brewery also assumed to be Capone's. Agents seized 50,000 gallons of beer and 150,000 gallons of mash—the largest seizure at that time in Chicago.[65] These examples of the scale of organized crime's production and profits reveal how dramatic the exogenous shock of Prohibition was to the illicit economy.

## SUMMARY

Prohibition was an exogenous legal shock to the illicit economy of Chicago, and Progressive Era organized crime was the market-oriented actor best positioned to reorganize and dominate the transformed illicit market. This chapter lays out two histories of the illicit alcohol economy in Chicago, revealing dramatic differences in scale. Organized crime did not control "virtually every pint of illicit liquor sold" in Chicago, as the *Chicago Tribune* proclaimed.[66] The domestically produced pints were outside of the purview of organized crime. Women's earnings, such as Cigarette Mamie's several dollars a night or Moonshine Mary's 15 cents a glass, were not competition for the larger beer barons of Chicago, who held thousands of dollars in equipment alone and were operating large-scale breweries. Women's profits from the domestic sphere were so small that either they went unnoticed by organized crime or organized crime tolerated this minuscule cut into its market. Unlike the shifting regulations and legal ambiguity of Chicago's sex economy, Prohibition law regulating the illicit booze economy was federalized, encompassing, and clear. However, the uneven enforcement of Prohibition law created conditions for the powerful bootleggers of organized crime to negotiate with local law enforcement, while immigrant women and families were more regularly targeted by enforcement agents. Women and families violating Prohibition law did not have access to organized crimes' powerful protection market.

The domestic sphere provided conditions under which women had increasing opportunities for participation in the illicit economy of Prohibition. Alcohol sales complemented spending in brothels, and women's discreet beer flats and alehouses replaced the corner saloon as an important social institution in many immigrant communities. Via the historical record and the analysis of address data on alcohol locations, this chapter establishes the point that Prohibition itself was not an economy that excluded women. This is an important context because, as I show in the next chapter, the shifting structure of the Prohibition organized crime network left women behind.

# 6. Syndicate Women, 1920–1933

Prohibition moved previously legitimate alcohol production and selling establishments into the illicit economy. The legal, exogenous shock introduced by Prohibition not only created the crime of violating liquor laws, but also mobilized and refashioned preexisting criminal organizations. Whereas the organized crime network before Prohibition revolved around the protection and exploitation of illicit entertainment economies in Chicago's Levee districts, organized crime during Prohibition added intoxicating beverages and their entire market. Organized crime's large-scale alcohol interests required start-up capital, equipment, spaces for production and storage, vehicles for distribution, and protection. The Progressive Era organized crime spaces became even more profitable under Prohibition, when illegal booze complemented illicit entertainments. Speakeasies, gambling dens, and brothels formed an important part of the distribution network that connected booze to thirsty customers. Women's participation in domestic bootlegging and alcohol production (as detailed in chapter 5), plus the increasing importance of brothels during Prohibition (presented in more detail in this chapter), should have increased organized crime opportunities for women, but this was not the case.

My central argument in this chapter is that the shifting structures of the Prohibition organized crime network left women behind. I present the organized crime network of the Prohibition era, its centralized leadership, and thirty-eight women of organized crime. Leveraging both the criminal network and the historical research, I detail women's decreasing participation in organized crime. First, I show how Prohibition shifted organized crime from a small, decentralized, clustered network to a large, sparse network with a powerful central core of bosses. I argue that in turn, this structural shift dramatically decreased women's opportunities and participation, thus increasing gender inequality in the criminal organization. The criminal organization shifted from women composing 18 percent of the network prior to Prohibition to only 4 percent of the network during Prohibition.

Much of what was to become of Chicago organized crime during the Prohibition years was imprinted by a particular trajectory that began in the early 1900s: the districts, the blocks, the illicit entertainment economies, and some of the male persisters. I show that the same was not true for organized crime women, with the exception of one female persister, Emily "the Immune" Marshall. I establish that another major shift impacting syndicate women was that their relationships to organized crime became increasingly dependent on their marital and familial relationships to organized crime men, more so than their involvement in and proprietorship of businesses in the illicit entertainment economy. This finding has important theoretical implications regarding gender, trust, and violence in organized crime. The final section of this chapter details women's increasing proprietorship of Chicago's brothel locations in spite of organized crime men's increasing control of the large brothels of Chicago and surrounding areas. Together these critical pieces reveal the conditions that left syndicate women out of the organized crime network. The dramatic restructuring and centralization of organized crime and its spreading geographic influence beyond local protection markets shifted women's relationships to organized crime men from the public sphere and moved women's illicit businesses to a dependence on the private sphere and personal relationships.

## THE SYNDICATE

Chicago's organized crime network shifted dramatically over the fourteen years of Prohibition. Organized crime diversified beyond gambling and brothels and their required protection market to include large-scale bootlegging and labor racketeering. Organized crime laundered its dirty money through legitimate Chicago businesses, such as dog racetracks and dry-cleaning shops, and invested its money in Chicago elections and campaign contributions. That growth, and increasing financial and political power, moved organized crime outside of the Levee districts, across Chicago, into the villages outside the city, and, occasionally, into neighboring states.

Figure 8 plots the criminal sphere of these diverse organized crime activities to reveal the underlying structure of the Prohibition organized crime network. The network contained 3,250 criminal relationships among 937 people. Each circle in figure 8 represents a person in organized crime; the white circles designate criminal women and the black circles designate

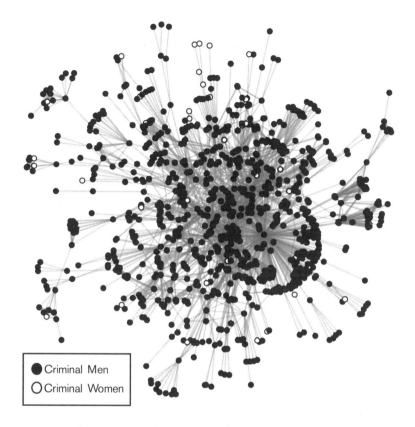

FIGURE 8. Chicago organized crime network, 1920–1933 (n = 937).

criminal men. Each line in the network represents a criminal relationship between two people that occurred at any point between 1920 and 1933.

Social network analysis tools make visible the dramatic change in Chicago organized crime during Prohibition. First, figure 8 shows the explosive growth that characterized the restructuring of the organized crime network during Prohibition. The Prohibition network grew to include three times more individuals and four times more criminal relationships than the Progressive Era network. Second, the organized crime network became increasingly centralized. During Prohibition, powerful men in the center became more powerful.[1] The third notable pattern is that only 0.7 percent of all the potential criminal relationships among this set of organized crime people actually existed during Prohibition. In general, large social networks tend to be sparse because of the social impossibility of coordinating relationships with hundreds of people, so this structural change in network density during Prohibition was a function of the network's growth.

These social network measures matter for thinking about inequality in criminal organizations because dense and decentralized networks are more equitable when networked resources (such as protection, access to state actors or fixers, trust, and information) are redundant and readily accessible to more actors. In contrast, sparse and centralized networks are inequitable because the structure permits the powerful center to hoard networked resources and restrict access to them.[2] The Prohibition era network reveals the structure of power, resource hoarding, and inequality following the exogenous shock of Prohibition to the legal environment.

## THE PERSISTERS

Gone were the decentralized network and ambiguous leadership of organized crime's protection market in Chicago's Levee districts. However, the Levees, the illicit entertainment economies, and some of the men from the Progressive Era organized crime network imprinted on the organizational restructuring during Prohibition. Only twenty-seven individuals (twenty-six men and one woman) endured the structural changes in organized crime and persisted across both networks. As organizations change, individuals get shuffled around, pushed out, or left behind, but the original structure influences the reorganization. The twenty-seven persisters in organized crime reveal some of the continuity in organized crime; this 10 percent of the Progressive Era organized crime network formed only 3 percent of the Prohibition era network. Persisters successfully navigated the exogenous shock of Prohibition by mobilizing or relying on their earlier criminal capital while maintaining and developing it to varying levels of success.[3]

Emily Marshall was the one woman who persisted during organized crime's restructuring in the Prohibition era. She was difficult to trace due to her common surname and her low profile in the archives. What appears to be her story is that she ran an extravagant luxury brothel on Curtis Street, which around 1917 was protected by Johnny Torrio (another persister).[4] However, by 1930 Marshall's brothel had come to be protected by Jack Zuta.[5] Zuta was an immigrant from Russia, a big shot in the Chicago sex economy, a rival of Torrio, and a man with no organized crime record in Chicago before Prohibition (i.e., not a persister).

There are several remarkable aspects to Marshall's career in organized crime. First, she was never a notorious brothel madam, unlike some of the other women brothel owners, such as the Everleigh sisters or "vice queen" Vic Shaw, although Marshall's longevity in Chicago's sex economy certainly indicates some level of success. Second, her career spanned at least thirteen years despite the formal closing of the Levee district, the various legal changes that attempted to impede the sex economy, and the legal shock of Prohibition, which shows that she persisted through multiple sociolegal changes to Chicago's illicit economies. Third, her nickname "the Immune" should imply some level of organized crime protection, but it was likely speaking to the longevity of her establishment rather than legal immunity or even immunity from other criminals; federal agents raided Marshall's brothel in 1918, when they found her knitting near a trapdoor hiding three women; Lieutenant William Schoemaker arrested Marshall and two women for running a disorderly house in 1920; and robbers attacked Marshall, tied her up with a telephone cord, and stole $2,100 cash and $4,100 worth jewelry from her in 1926.[6] For the purposes of analyzing how the organized crime network changed, "the Immune" is a great moniker for the only woman who persisted in organized crime across the Progressive Era into Prohibition. Marshall somehow managed to establish a single relationship to an organized crime man during each era (Torrio then Zuta) that established her fragile connection to the organized crime network.

Much more famous in Chicago lore than Marshall was Chicago's briefest persister, "Big" Jim Colosimo, the most well-connected criminal of the Levees and the Progressive Era organized crime network. Coincidence or not, 1920 was a big year for Colosimo, even though he was largely oblivious to the roar of Prohibition, much to the chagrin of his associate, Johnny Torrio. On May 11, 1920, only one week after returning from his honeymoon with Dale Winter and several months after Prohibition had gone into effect, Colosimo was murdered at his own Colosimo Café at 2126–2128 South Wabash Avenue. He was shot in the head by a single bullet. Theories about the Colosimo murder varied widely, including a political fight, a labor union conflict, his jealous ex-wife Victoria Moresco, a jealous admirer of his new wife, and Torrio—Colosimo and Moresco's right-hand man—wanting greater control of organized crime's direction under Prohibition. Colosimo's murder was never solved.[7]

Colosimo's position as a persister in Prohibition era organized crime was likely a consequence of his strong position in the later years of Progressive Era organized crime. Even though the Progressive Era network was decentralized, Colosimo's position was the most central of the network in terms of his having the greatest number of criminal relationships. Gambling king

Mont Tennes, who was a very close second for most criminally connected in Progressive Era organized crime, also persisted into the Prohibition era network. However, Louis Frank, the equal opportunity broker, snitch of 1909, and third most connected, did not persist. This could partly be a function of age. Frank was about twenty years older than Colosimo and Tennes. It is also possible that Frank did not persist because his criminal relationships to women were not as valuable as the criminal capital Colosimo and Tennes had accumulated before Prohibition. Nevertheless, Colosimo's Progressive Era connections and properties imprinted his transition to Prohibition in ways that women like Emily Marshall could never achieve. Colosimo's appearance in the Prohibition era organized crime network was brief given his early, murderous departure, but some of his previous Progressive Era associates went on to coordinate organized crime unlike anything Colosimo had ever seen.

## THE BOSSES

The most dramatic restructuring of the Prohibition organized crime network was in its size and its accompanying centralization and sparsity. These network conditions reveal a powerful core of organized crime leaders successfully building and protecting their powerful position. The two most infamous persisters at the center of the Prohibition organized crime network were Johnny Torrio and Al Capone. Torrio's rise in organized crime began before Prohibition. Torrio took over management of Colosimo's brothels and expanded his own sex work operations to the Chicago suburb of Burnham around 1916, four years before Colosimo's murder.[8] By 1920, Torrio was well established around Chicago as one of the "vice kings," and he continued to run his brothels during Prohibition, raking in even greater profits. Many historical accounts argue that the dramatic shift for Torrio during Prohibition was Colosimo's death, but perhaps more important to Torrio's rise was his relentless pursuit of flowing beer and liquor into the city of Chicago and its neighboring villages of Cicero, Stickney, and Burnham.[9]

Under Prohibition, what *Chicago Tribune* reporters and Progressive Era activists had occasionally called the "vice trust" or the "vice syndicate" came to be known as Torrio's Syndicate.[10] Torrio organized distribution territories and ensured that buyers remained loyal. As "overlord of the underworld," Torrio charged $50 for a barrel of beer (about $700 in 2018 dollars), but his price included protection.[11] Although there are no estimates of how many people worked for him, Torrio's weekly payroll was estimated at $25,000 (approximately $350,000 in 2018 dollars).[12] Torrio organized crime and collected profits at levels that had been impossible in the Levee district protection market before Prohibition.

Torrio's aide and protégé Al Capone arrived in Chicago from New York around 1919. He came by Torrio's invitation, arriving just in time to make a brief connection to the Progressive Era organized crime network as a bodyguard for Jim Colosimo and a bouncer for Colosimo's brothels and cabaret.[13] When Torrio left Chicago permanently for New York in 1925 after recovering from a shooting attack that had targeted his wife and him, his departure facilitated Capone's ascent into syndicate leadership.[14] Capone's fame and notoriety quickly outpaced Torrio's sensible temperament. Much of Capone's reputation could be attributed to his facial scar, his spending habits, and his big—sometimes violent—personality. In 1936, three years after Prohibition ended, *Chicago Tribune* journalist Guy Murchie wrote a three-part series on Capone's "Decade of Death" in which he alleged that Capone had instigated thirty-three murders during the Chicago Beer Wars.[15] Police Chief Michael Hughes accused Capone of being a Mussolini sympathizer.[16] If these accusations were not enough, Capone was also the target of several failed murder attempts. Legal threats involved prosecutors and judges from Chicago, Philadelphia, and Miami hitting Capone with charges of gun toting, perjury, vagrancy, murder, public nuisance, Prohibition violations, and jury fixing. However, it was the Internal Revenue Service (IRS) that eventually brought Capone down in 1931, for failing to pay income taxes on his illegally generated organized crime income. When federal law enforcement officials finally found a charge that they could make stick, they gave Capone the longest federal sentence ever given up to that time for tax evasion.

Though barely an associate of Progressive Era organized crime, Capone was the center of Prohibition's organized crime network, shown in figure 8. He had 316 relationships to his criminal associates in the network. Due to his early departure from Chicago in 1925 and not being in Chicago as long during Prohibition, Johnny Torrio accumulated only 68 criminal relationships in the organized crime network. Torrio was tied for second as the most criminally connected in the network even though his criminal connections were only 20 percent of Capone's. Many close male associates of Capone and Torrio also had powerful positions in the organized crime network, with influence, protection, and profits that trickled out to those at the periphery of the network.[17]

## THE GENDER GAP

Outside the core of the organized crime network were criminal associates contributing their various activities and relationships to the organizational

TABLE 5. Men, Women, and Their Relationships in Chicago's
Organized Crime Network, 1920–1933

|  | Men | Women |
| --- | --- | --- |
| Nodes | 899 | 38 |
|  | (95.9%) | (4.1%) |
| Men-only criminal relationships | 3,134 |  |
|  | (96.4%) |  |
| Women-only criminal relationships |  | 7 |
|  |  | (0.2%) |
| Man-and-woman criminal relationships | 109 |  |
|  | (3.4%) |  |

structure. The periphery included associates involved in the day-to-day grind of organized crime, such as the drivers, brewers, bouncers, saloon waitstaff, madams, and couriers who were foundational to organized crime activities.[18] These positions resided at the boundaries of the organized crime network and included a small number of women. The last notable pattern in figure 8 is the small proportion of women in the network, and table 5 presents the calculations of the gender gap in the network.

Women were mostly excluded from organized crime's Prohibition growth even when organized crime multiplied in size. There were thirty-eight women in the Prohibition organized crime network, making up only 4 percent of the network and party to only 4 percent of the criminal relationships. There were seven relationships between two women in the entire Prohibition organized crime network (0.2 percent of 3,250 criminal connections). Three of these relationships involved the 1920 arrest of Emily Marshall and two women sex workers at her brothel, three included the women of the Caldwell family who ran a Prohibition era brothel, and the last was between two women labeled public enemies (described in more detail later in this chapter). Table 5 reveals that the growth in criminal relationships during Prohibition was explained almost entirely by men's criminal relationships to other men.

This dramatic shift in the gender composition of organized crime is a puzzle because, as demonstrated in chapters 3 and 5, women's criminal activity and criminal participation in Chicago's illicit economies did not decrease over a twenty-year period. Women's participation in the proprietorship of the sex economy increased between the Progressive Era and

Prohibition (more on this later in the chapter), and women's participation in the illicit alcohol economy increased during Prohibition as women participated in the domestic production and distribution of alcohol (as established in chapter 5). The men of organized crime did not suddenly become increasingly sexist or gender exclusionary on January 17, 1920. Rather, the biggest change in organized crime was the organization itself.

The organizational restructuring and its barriers to access and prosperity developed in ways that were compounded by status, preferences, privilege, and consequently, gender. The core of organized crime was more centralized and powerful and had greater relational resources, but this core only included men. The restructured organization did not incorporate localized brokerage opportunities with equal-opportunity brokers, such as Louis Frank, who collected graft payments from men as well as women. The illicit alcohol economy increased criminal opportunities for men and women, but men's preferences for other male co-offenders were still in play. Women's reliance on male co-offenders is also evident, based on the low number of criminal relationships they had with other women. Access to financial capital for brewing equipment, delivery trucks, and storage facilities was more available to men and less available to women. As the organization became more powerful and profitable, it wasted less time on the local establishments selling moonshine or sex and instead focused on owning and syndicating its own establishments. This organizational reorientation meant fewer opportunities for entrepreneurs of the illicit economy to buy protection, which was the process that explained the majority of women's participation in the earlier era. Each of these restructurings and reorientations of organized crime was based in relational processes, and gender was a category in constant interaction with the inclusionary or exclusionary formation of relationships. This is how networked organizations produce inequality.

This particular case of the production of inequality through the interaction of gender and relational processes can benefit from the theoretical insights from research on legitimate organizations. Research shows that the structure of organizations constrains women's opportunities, and the shape and size of organizational networks influence the level of gender inequality. Although informal relationships within organizations are often based on preferences and positions, the structure of the organization can facilitate or restrict who forms relationships with whom.[19] Less hierarchical, team-based organizations provide greater career opportunities for women than large, durable, and hierarchical institutions.[20] This happens because more open positions and roles within organizations allow participants to form relationships with other people at different levels of the organization.

When an organization is nonhierarchical (such as the Progressive Era organized crime network), people in subordinate positions are increasingly able to form instrumental relationships with people controlling resources (e.g., making connections to the aldermen, working for Colosimo, or being under Torrio's protection). This is a relational process that is less possible with strict hierarchies and divisions of labor.

Research on criminal markets shows that women have greater criminal opportunities when markets are open, flat, and decentralized rather than closed and hierarchal.[21] Women face incredible obstacles to entering criminal organizations in the first place, but the structure of the criminal organization also matters in shaping how relationships form and, in turn, how gender inequality is maintained or mitigated. In its abstract form, the structure of the organized crime network provides foundational evidence for increasing gender inequality. Zooming in on some of the details on the thirty-eight syndicate women further reveals how this structure developed relationally and unequally.

## THE SYNDICATE WIVES AND GIRLFRIENDS

The trope of the silent mobster wife assumes that the wives know either nothing or everything and in any case would never tell.[22] In truth, most wives never connected to Chicago organized crime, or if they did, their activities went undetected or unrecorded by investigators. This was the case with Mae Capone during Prohibition. Irish Catholic Mae Coughlin married Al Capone around 1919, and shortly thereafter the newlyweds moved from New York to Chicago. Mae's involvement in organized crime was uncertain but likely very well hidden. She was arrested once with Capone in 1919 when he was a suspect in a murder. Afterward her connections to organized crime were financial, not criminal.[23] The IRS uncovered a trail of Western Union transactions documenting that Mae received money from Chicago while in Miami, and it also discovered a bank account in Mae's name at West Side Trust and Savings Bank.[24] The investigators believed that the transactions and account were dirty organized crime money, but their allegations were never substantiated. Similarly, in 1928 the Capones purchased their twenty-five-room Miami Beach estate in Mae's name, which the IRS also tried, and failed, to link to organized crime profits.[25] Mae fought the IRS for several years after Al's incarceration and made payments on his unpaid taxes.[26] Mae Capone's role as the silent mobster wife meant that she never connected to the Prohibition organized crime network through criminal relationships—at least never in a way that was detected.

Women made up only 4 percent of the Prohibition organized crime network, but the women of Prohibition organized crime were much more diverse in their roles and organized crime activities than the women of Progressive Era organized crime, who were almost all entirely connected through the sex economy. The thirty-eight women of the Prohibition organized crime network included cabaret performers; a cigarette girl; a waitress; a beer runner from Waterloo, Iowa; brothel owners and managers; a trafficker; and a few sex workers. Detailed accounts exist for some of the Prohibition era organized crime women, which reveal how women's personal connections to men were essential for women's criminal connections to Prohibition organized crime.

The majority of syndicate women (twenty out of thirty-eight, or 53 percent) connected to the network through criminal activities with their criminally involved husbands and boyfriends in ways that were better detected than Mae Capone's. Some of the women (five out of thirty-eight, or 13 percent) connected to organized crime through other male relatives, such as an uncle or a brother-in-law. This pattern was a major shift in women's entrée into or maintenance in organized crime; criminal relationships with organized crime men co-occurred with personal relationships to those men as romantic partners or male family members for 66 percent of the Prohibition era syndicate women, whereas this was the case for only 21 percent of the Progressive Era syndicate women. Most of the women in Prohibition organized crime were involved because of prior noncriminal relationships with the men of organized crime and not because of their illegitimate businesses or work in the illicit economies. This indicates a significant shift from formal inclusion through graft payments and the protection market to informal inclusion through the private sphere.[27] The role of brokers remained fundamental to women's connection to organized crime, but who brokered women changed dramatically. In the decentralized structure of Progressive Era organized crime, collectors who were buying and selling protection brokered many women brothel owners to the network. The men brokering women during Prohibition were mostly family and romantic partners, which increased women's dependence on the private sphere rather than on their illicit businesses in the public sphere.

Often women's criminal connections with organized crime men were through rather ill-timed events, such as being in the company of husbands and boyfriends during raids and arrests and getting caught up in the action, but some organized crime women's connections were more purposeful than guilt by association. Louise Rolfe (see figure 9) was a beautiful model and cabaret singer. She was also the girlfriend of Jack McGurn, a Chicago

FIGURE 9.   Louise Rolfe, reputed sweetheart of Jack McGurn, in Chicago, Illinois, 1929. *Source:* DN-0087855, *Chicago Daily News* negatives collection, Chicago History Museum.

gunman and suspect in the St. Valentine's Day Massacre of 1929. During the investigation of the massacre, police found McGurn at the Stevens Hotel with Rolfe. Rolfe provided his alibi, telling police officers and reporters that he had spent all of Valentine's Day with her and that they had never left their hotel room.

After she was questioned at the police department, Rolfe talked with reporters outside of the police station. Reporters fawned over her fashion and looks. The *Chicago Tribune* article that presented Rolfe's interview showed a reporter convinced of Jack McGurn's alibi because McGurn never would have left such a beautiful woman's side on Valentine's Day:

> She drew the folds of her swanky gray squirrel coat suavely about her hips, tossed back astounding yellow curls from a face Egyptianlike in lines and synthetic coloring, and gazed steadily at the group before her. . . . "Of course, Jack had nothing to do with the massacre. . . . He was in bed—all night and until noon." . . . She admitted that after St. Valentine's Day neither she nor Jack left the room, but, inferring that they had much to occupy them, "we read all the papers," and "when you're with Jack you're never bored." . . . As she talked she smoked constantly, lighting one cigaret [*sic*] from the tip of another. Her face was elaborately made up. Her black dress of crepe over which hung long ropes of imitation pearls, hung modishly beneath the draped fur coat. Dark eyes were heavily mascaraed and her eyebrows were thinned down to the most extreme lines. On one curved ankle a tiny gold bracelet made a line, "with my name on it, so they can't lose me," she offered.[28]

Rolfe's testimony earned her the nickname "the Blonde Alibi," and the alibi apparently worked. The state was forced to release McGurn and other suspects when prosecutors were "not ready to proceed with the trials."[29] However, investigators and prosecutors were hell-bent on hitting McGurn with something. Shortly after his release as a murder suspect, assistant US district attorney Daniel Anderson served the couple with a warrant that alleged McGurn had violated the Mann Act of 1910 when he crossed state borders with Rolfe for immoral purposes and that Rolfe had conspired to violate the Mann Act.[30] The "white slave" charge was based on consensual lovers' romantic vacations that had crossed state lines. Even though McGurn and Rolfe got married in May 1931, just before their case went to trial and after he finalized his divorce from his previous wife, they lost the Mann Act case in Illinois Federal Court—a ruling later overturned by the US Supreme Court.[31] Much like federal tax laws, the Mann Act gave federal prosecutors loopholes to target gangsters when Prohibition cases failed to stick.[32]

A potential insight from this shift in women's romantic relationships to organized crime men may speak to broader issues of trust in criminal networks. A large and centralized organized crime network coordinating activities in a more lucrative and higher-risk illicit economy should require more trust and secrecy than a decentralized, nonhierarchical organization operating in an illicit economy of shifting regulation and risk.[33] It is reasonable to assume that trust was more paramount in the Prohibition organized crime network—when the stakes were higher, the laws were irrefutable and more clearly defined, law enforcement was still discretionary but was becoming increasingly more powerful, and more criminals were involved— than in the Progressive Era organized crime network. What do women's romantic relationships and their criminal involvement tell us about trust in this context?

Research on crime, trust, and gender has produced mixed findings. Some research has found that men of the underworld do not trust women and engage stereotypes of women as weak, gossipy, or opportunistic gold-diggers.[34] In this view, women are dispensable and easily manipulated by men to assist with men's criminal tasks that benefit from women's gendered labor. However, other scholars have found that criminally involved men consider women, especially their wives, the most trustworthy people in their lives.[35] For example, when mafia men are incarcerated, their wives fill an essential intermediary role in communication and command because of their access to their incarcerated husbands and the trust between them.[36]

The historical data on men and women in organized crime are often too thin in detail to offer clear or meaningful insights into this question of trust, and historical ambiguities blur possible distinctions among relationships of trust, exploitation, victimization, and just coincidence. For example, if Jack McGurn were a gunman at the St. Valentine's Day Massacre, would he have told Louise Rolfe? Rolfe's providing McGurn's alibi could be indicative of the trust between the couple, or it could be an example of McGurn's manipulation of a beautiful woman who would distract reporters from the massacre.

Prohibition organized crime had fewer women, and the women in organized crime were more likely to be related to, married to, or romantically involved with organized crime men in addition to their criminal connections to these organized crime men. This property of multiple types of relationships existing between two people is a network property known as "multiplexity." Multiplex relationships are often trustworthy because of the layered expectations and obligations within the different types. For organized crime women, a personal, familial, or romantic relationship added depth and complexity to their criminal relationships with organized crime men. Research on multiplexity in Chicago organized crime finds a robust framework of overlapping types of relationships among individuals generating the organized crime network.[37] The argument is that incredible examples of trust between individuals existed within organized crime, but that trust was not spread equally across the entire network.[38] Rather, multiplexity and its trust were dispersed throughout the network to maintain secrecy and efficiency. It is the case that the women of Prohibition era organized crime had more multiplex relationships with men in organized crime than did the women of Progressive Era organized crime. As such, it is entirely possible that these multiplex relationships were more trustworthy connections, and thus it is also possible that the trust between men and women changed between the two eras.

## THE VIOLENCE

The focus on trust and romantic relationships should not ignore the reality of violence in romantic relationships. Some syndicate women were victimized through their romantic relationships to organized crime men when the violence of organized crime spilled into the home. Intimate partners murdered the only two women who died from their connections to the organized crime network. The cases of Rosemary Sanborn and Maybelle Exley were strikingly similar, although they occurred eight years apart. The criminal activities that linked these two women to organized crime were co-offenses that most women would not have engaged in without their gangster boyfriends. Sanborn was a cigarette girl from Chicago and associated with gangster Robert Newberry, also a suspect in the St. Valentine's Day Massacre. In 1932 the couple was wanted in Chicago for defrauding a wealthy man of $25,000. During the search, their bodies were found in a New York apartment. Investigators believed that Newberry had murdered Sanborn before killing himself.[39]

Maybelle Exley was a sex worker in Louisville, Kentucky, when she met John Duffy. Duffy trafficked alcohol and women and had ties to organized crime member Dion O'Banion. Exley left the Louisville brothel with Duffy, and they worked together peddling booze. In 1924 Exley was twenty-one years old when Duffy drunkenly beat and murdered her in their Chicago apartment on Carmen Avenue. Police learned of Exley's murder when, two days later, they found Duffy's corpse dumped on a snowbank with three bullets to the head. Police traced Duffy's residence back to the apartment, where they found Exley. Duffy was last seen alive getting into a car near Capone's Four Deuces on South Wabash Avenue and was presumed to have been Chicago's first instance of a gangster being "taken for a ride," wherein a victim is shot in a car and the body is dumped. Exley's murder was ruled a domestic violence case, and Duffy's murder was assumed to be gangland related, though it was not solved.[40]

The violence against girlfriends and wives by organized crime–involved intimate partners is a theme that has received some attention in contemporary research on women and mafias. Renate Siebert's research on Italian mafias highlights the contradiction between the domestic sphere as a refuge from the violent public space mafia husbands create and the violence that mafia husbands bring into that domestic sphere.[41] Relatedly, contemporary research has thoroughly documented that women involved in the sex economy are at great risk of violence, as well as how the criminalization of their sex work inhibits their calling for help.[42] In the organized crime network context, the publicity of these murders documented women's thin connections to organized crime through their romantic and violent partners.

Illicit markets and violence tend to go hand in hand. Although illicit markets are not inherently violent, violence is often the only resource available to ensure payment, delivery, and security.[43] The Chicago gangland violence of Prohibition received extra news attention—and for good reason. The combination of automobiles and machine guns, rapid and deadly technological innovations, made for good headlines. High-profile shootings such as the murder of Jim Colosimo, the attack on Johnny Torrio, a drive-by machine gun attack on Al Capone while he was having lunch, and fatal attacks on associates of organized crime certainly made Prohibition organized crime feel especially violent. Chicago sociologist of the 1920s John Landesco described the Beer Wars of 1922 to 1926 as the years of gaining "control of the booze and beer business in Cook County"; he estimated that during this period 215 gangsters murdered each other.[44] The first mention of the Beer Wars by the *Chicago Tribune* was in 1922, when Albert Schultz, a saloonkeeper on the North Side, was murdered twenty miles northwest of Chicago. Witnesses claimed they saw a convoy of three beer trucks and two cars stop on the road and men get out of the vehicles and argue, and they heard over fifty shots fired.[45] Schultz's murder, like many of the Beer Wars murders, went unsolved.[46]

Chicago felt more violent under Prohibition because it actually was more violent, but not because of organized crime.[47] The Chicago homicide rate was 10.4 per 100,000 from 1916 to 1920, 13.4 per 100,000 from 1921 to 1925, and 16.4 per 100,000 from 1926 to 1930.[48] As a point of comparison, in the late 1920s when the Chicago homicide rate reached its peak under Prohibition, it was similar to Chicago's homicide rate from 2004 to 2013.[49] The dramatic difference during Prohibition in Chicago was that as the homicide rates increased, so did the violent nature of those deaths. Stranger shootings, armed robberies, and predatory killings redefined Chicago's homicides during the early 1900s and into Prohibition in ways attributed to, but not necessarily connected to, organized crime.[50] Estimates suggest that only 3 percent of homicides during Prohibition were gang related, up from 1.5 percent before Prohibition.[51] However, gang related is a looser criterion for classifying homicides than organized crime related, for which estimates do not exist.

Social science historians have examined multiple demographic factors that contributed to Chicago's increasing homicide rates leading up to and during Prohibition. They have found that increased homicide in the 1920s had less to do with organized crime gangsters equipped with tommy guns than with rapidly growing urban populations, men in their late teens and early twenties increasing as a proportion of the population, urbanization, and the racialized landscape of concentrated disadvantage in Chicago.[52] The rapidly growing African American population forced into Chicago's most disadvantaged, high-crime neighborhoods had a much higher homicide victimization rate than Chicago's ethnic European population.[53] The increase in Chicago's violence during Prohibition was caused by shifting demographics rather than organized crime. Nevertheless, this increase in violence spilled into the illicit economy and organized crime, and Prohibition era organized crime was certainly more violent than Progressive Era organized crime.

Did the increasing violence of Prohibition push women out of organized crime? This question involves several inherent, gendered assumptions that require unpacking before speculating an answer. First, there is the gendered assumption that women flee violent criminal organizations, but men do not. Research certainly indicates that women fear violence more than men and are more likely than men to engage situational avoidance tactics to reduce risk.[54] However, it is difficult to stretch this research finding to interpret gender differences in exiting or entering organized crime in which affiliations and events mattered more than any system of formal membership. The best example of someone fleeing Chicago organized crime because of violence was syndicate boss Johnny Torrio leaving after surviving the gun attack that targeted his wife and him.

Second, inherent in this question is the gendered assumption that organized crime became increasingly committed to women's safety or paternalistic during Prohibition. This is also unlikely, since the women who connected to organized crime were more likely to be family members or romantic partners, arguably the group of women that syndicate men would most want to protect.

Third, and most important, the logic of this question of violence pushing women out of organized crime relies on a causal ordering that is inconsistent with contemporary research on gender, street gangs, and violence. In contemporary street gangs, the gender composition of the group significantly impacts the group's activities. Street gangs with a balance of boys and girls are less involved in violence than street gangs with a majority of boys and a minority of girls—a finding that is not attributed to the gender of individuals in the gang but rather to the group processes and structure of the gang.[55] The causal order garnered from this research insight is that differently gendered organizations lead to different levels of group violence. To relate this insight back to the case at hand (and setting aside for a moment the demographic explanations for Prohibition's increasing homicide rates), it is not impossible that the lower percentage of women and women's involvement in organized crime could have been a factor in the increase in Prohibition era organized crime violence and the lower rates of violence in Progressive Era organized crime. The presence and participation of women in a criminal organization will change the structure and activities of the criminal organization, and this could include violence.

Returning to the question at hand, did the increasing violence of Prohibition push women out of organized crime? I do not believe this to be the case. I base my answer on the gendered assumptions inherent in the question, the recognition that the gender composition of groups influences group activities, and the reality that violence was explained by demographics, not organized crime. Violence was certainly not pushing women out of the city of Chicago any more than it was causing women to flee organized crime.

An important related issue, however, is the role of gender in violence enforcement. Organized crime's increasing need for violence enforcers drew from a pool of eligible gunmen rather than women, which created increased opportunities for men who used violence or had guns. There was at least one case of a violence-dispensing woman defying gender stereotypes near the very end of Prohibition. Pearl Elliot of the Dillinger gang was not romantically involved with men in the gang, and she and Mary Kinder were the first two women in Chicago labeled "public enemies." These two women barely connected to organized crime, because their criminal activities took place during the last month of Prohibition, but Elliot briefly entered the network as a gunwoman for John Dillinger.

The public enemy label has its own history concurrent with Prohibition era organized crime. The Chicago business elite founded the Chicago Crime Commission (CCC) in 1919 with the purpose of protecting the business community from the business of crime, alleging that the Chicago Police Department was too corrupt to be up to the task.[56] The CCC introduced the original public enemies list to Chicago in April 1930, with Al Capone listed as public enemy number 1.[57] The CCC's goal with the public enemy list was to drive the criminal element out of Chicago, or in the words of CCC president Frank Loesch, "to keep the light of publicity on Chicago's most prominent and notorious gangsters to the end that they may be under constant observation by law enforcing authorities."[58] By 1933 the CCC no longer controlled the distribution of and attention to public enemy lists, as police captains and Illinois state's attorney's office began compiling and releasing their own lists.[59] The CCC's public enemies lists never included women, but the state's attorney's list did.

Weeks after the end of Prohibition in December 1933, the state's attorney's office released its public enemy list, with bank robber and jail breaker John Dillinger as public enemy number 1. Among the twenty-one public enemies on this 1933 list were two women—public enemies numbers 8 and 9, Pearl Elliott and Mary Kinder of the Dillinger gang.[60] Less than a month before the end of Prohibition in November 1933, Indiana state police and Chicago detectives set a trap for Dillinger outside a doctor's office following a tip they received regarding Dillinger's appointment there. Dillinger finished his appointment and got in his car, when officers began firing at it. Their gunfire had no effect because the car was armored. The armored car also had a hidden person in the back of the car firing a machine gun in return. To assist with the getaway, Elliott rolled down her window slightly to fire her pistol at police. The police halted their pursuit of Dillinger because of the gunfire.[61] Elliott was described as a friend of the Dillinger gang and not romantically involved with any of the men in it.

Mary Kinder, the other woman on the public enemies list, was a sweetheart of fellow gang member Harry Pierpont. Kinder was indicted for harboring fugitives and helping them elude capture after members of the Dillinger gang escaped from prison.[62] She and some of the other women of the Dillinger gang were in charge of renting new apartments each week while in Chicago so that the gang could remain on the move and in hiding.[63] Kinder was caught and arrested with the Dillinger gang in Tucson, Arizona, but it is unclear what happened to Elliott.[64] There was no mention of her in the *Chicago Tribune* after her name appeared on the public enemies list.

THE BROTHELS

These examples of alibis, victims, and public enemies point to some of the ways women associates became entangled in the organized crime network—and some of the theoretical issues that these cases engage, such as trust and violence. This variety in entrée was quite different than for Progressive Era organized crime, when 89 percent of syndicate women connected to organized crime through the sex economy. During Prohibition, this percentage dropped to a little more than one-third. According to my calculations, fourteen of the thirty-eight women in the Prohibition era organized crime network connected through organized crime's brothels. These women were brothel owners, managers, hostesses, sex workers, and traffickers.

Brothels generated even greater profits under Prohibition, when illegal alcohol complemented sex work and drove up the price of both. As James O'Donnell Bennett wrote for the *Chicago Tribune* in 1929, "There had been money in liquor and girls before prohibition. But there are fortunes in liquor and girls under prohibition."[65] Brothels and cabarets developed a greater relevance because, when paired with good booze, these spaces became the "social center for gangsters."[66] In 1930 the antiprostitution Committee of Fifteen estimated that organized crime controlled 13 percent of all brothels they had investigated.[67] Unnamed police sources alleged that syndicate brothels generated $100,000 a week in revenue (approximately $1.5 million in 2018 dollars), which did not include the additional thousands from alcohol sales in the brothels.[68]

There was nothing particularly special about Prohibition era syndicate brothels except that they provided quality booze. Syndicate brothels paled in comparison to the elite brothels of the former Levee districts, which were costly to maintain and notoriously publicized. Nevertheless, Johnny Torrio's Harlem Inn in the village of Stickney could have up to five hundred men waiting on a Saturday night: "It is known as a $3 place, with the girls getting one-third of the three. It's a typical place—saloon in front, a back room full of women in virtually nothing, and about 50 rooms upstairs. Blonde, brunette, short, tall, fat—all are there."[69]

Al Capone's infamous Four Deuces at 2222 South Wabash Avenue was one of Chicago's bawdiest houses, and it served as a headquarters space for the syndicate.[70] The first floor of the Four Deuces was a saloon, and in the back of the saloon was a corridor to a stairway leading to the brothel on the second floor. Undercover *Chicago Tribune* investigators in 1922 estimated there were thirty sex workers at the Four Deuces:

> The "reception room" is a combination of two rooms in one, with a wide open doorway in between. The place is brilliantly lighted, but otherwise harsh in appearance. There is almost no furniture and the embellishment of the walls is nil. Running practically entirely around the four walls are crude benches. Tribune investigators counted forty-three men—most of them young men—sitting on the benches around the walls, and a dozen more stood or walked about. Four girls—probably the least comely in the house—were among all these men; the remainder of them were said to be "busy." An obese, henna haired "madam" sat in a rocking chair—one of the few pieces of furniture in the big room exhorting the men in a shrill voice: "Come on, boys," she piped again and again: "come on boys; pick a girl."[71]

In this article, the undercover *Chicago Tribune* investigators failed to name the "henna haired madam" and the thirty sex workers. Had these women been identified, I could have included them in the organized crime network as criminal associates involved in the day-to-day labor at the margins of organized crime. This brothel alone would have nearly doubled the number of women in the organized crime network, but these types of oversights in the archives were common during both periods of organized crime, in which there was more investigatory focus on the brothel owners and managers than on the sex workers.

Either women were no longer managers or operators of the organized crime brothels during Prohibition, or they were no longer under the investigative spotlight. Only fourteen women involved in the sex economy had enough information in the archival sources to reveal their organized crime relationships during Prohibition. For example, Emily Marshall was organized crime's only woman persister, and she persisted because of her brothel and single relationship to an organized crime man. The Caldwell women, Audrey, Gladys, and Sara, were brothel owners associated with their relative, Mike Heitler of Progressive Era brothel fame. The family men of brothels were brothers Jack and Harry Guzik; Jack was among Capone's closest associates and the person tied with Johnny Torrio for having sixty-eight criminal relationships in the Prohibition organized crime network. The Guziks were the family men of brothels because they instigated brothel and organized crime connections for several of their relatives: Harry ran a brothel with his wife Alma; Harry purchased a brothel for his sister-in-law Rose to operate; and Jack's sister-in-law, Jeannette Keithly, was deeded the Harlem Inn brothel by one of Jack's associates.

The group of organized crime women involved in the sex economy also included one African American woman, Mary Brown, who worked as a brothel keeper for Abe Weinstein at the Burr Oak Inn. Brown was the only African American woman connected to the Prohibition era organized crime network. Racial exclusion of black Chicagoans in this organized crime network was even more pronounced than the network's gender exclusion. There were only four African American men in the Prohibition era network. Two of them, Joseph Murphy and James Bell, worked as muscle and armed watchmen for Jack Zuta's brothels. From Brown, Murphy, and Bell, we learn that African Americans connected to organized crime only because of their status as laborers. They were at the periphery of the network, with limited access to resources, as indicated by their vulnerability during raids.

The great migration of African Americans from the South to urban centers such as Chicago began around 1916 and lasted until the later years of Prohibition, during which Chicago's African American population grew from

2 to 7 percent of the city's population.[72] There was a separate criminal network of African Americans during Prohibition that concentrated on controlling and exploiting the gambling economy in Chicago's Black Belt; this network did not overlap with the members of the syndicate organized crime network.[73]

The sticky piece of the puzzle of women's dramatic decrease in the Prohibition era organized crime network is that there was a growing sex economy outside of organized crime that did not leave women behind. The superintendent of the Illinois Vigilance Association estimated that there were more than two thousand brothels operating in Chicago in 1922.[74] University of Chicago–trained sociologist Walter Reckless's research on sex work in Chicago showed a large increase in the number of sex work resorts and an increase in sex work–related arrests during Prohibition.[75] In my analysis of the address data, I identified 177 sex work establishments with named proprietors from Prohibition and women's increasing control of the sex economy.

Sex work establishments included brothels, domestic spaces where men and women sold sex, saloons with adjacent rooms for selling sex, and hotels running sex rings. Due to the underground existence of these spaces, I uncovered fewer addresses for sex work establishments with named proprietors during Prohibition (177) than during the Progressive Era (322). The sex work addresses that I recorded from the archives do not show the dramatic increase in sex work locations during Prohibition that Reckless uncovered in his historically concurrent research because my estimates rely heavily on historical documents from the anti-sex work sentiments of the Progressive Era and the *Chicago Tribune's* publication of long lists of brothel addresses, which were more common during the Progressive Era before the formal closing of the Levees. However, even from this smaller sample of sex work establishments than what was available to Walter Reckless, important patterns emerge.

Map 4 plots the sex work establishment addresses (with named and unnamed proprietors) on a map of Chicago's community areas using contemporary mapping software. The left panel shows the geographic distribution of sex work establishments during the Progressive Era (1900–1919), and the right panel shows the geographic distribution during Prohibition (1920–1933). A limitation of map 4 is that it misses the brothels uncovered in the neighboring villages outside the city of Chicago. As I established in chapter 3, the sex work establishments of the Progressive Era were mostly concentrated in the three Levee districts. Map 4 shows that the geographic distribution of sex work did not change dramatically during Prohibition. Even though the Levee districts were formally closed during the Progressive Era, the establishments that were raided and appeared in the papers during

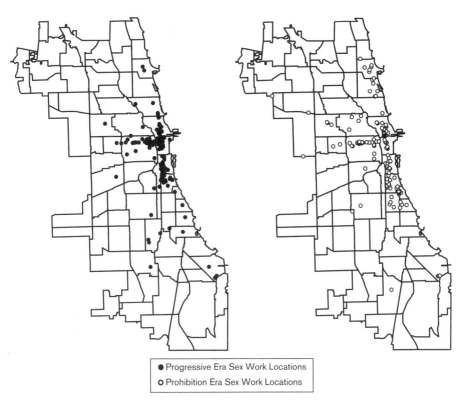

MAP 4. Chicago sex work establishments, 1900–1919 and 1920–1933. *Sources:* Chicago Data Portal, "Boundaries—Community Areas (current)," 2018, https://data.cityofchicago.org/Facilities-Geographic-Boundaries/Boundaries-Community-Areas-current-/cauq-8yn6, accessed June 24, 2018; Andrew Ba Tran, "Mapping with R," 2017, https://andrewbtran.github.io/NICAR/2017/maps/mapping-census-data.html, accessed June 24, 2018.

Prohibition were largely concentrated in the same areas of the city, with some spread farther west and north. The pattern of the large concentration of brothels along Chicago's Black Belt on the south side of the city was consistent during both eras. Historians have documented that the Black Belt was a "dumping ground" for Chicago's sex economy and largely neglected by police.[76] Compared to the geographic analysis of alcohol establishments between the Progressive and Prohibition eras (map 3 in chapter 5), there was a resiliency to the geography of Chicago's sex economy.

The line graph in figure 10 shows the change in proportion of sex work addresses that named women and organized crime individuals as

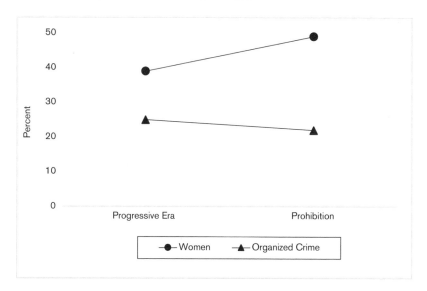

FIGURE 10.   Women-involved and organized crime–involved percent of sex work establishments in Chicago, 1900–1919 and 1920–1933.

proprietors, coproprietors, operators, or managers from the Progressive Era to Prohibition. Compared to the alcohol establishments analyzed in chapter 5, the counts of sex work establishments were much higher during both eras for women and organized crime. Women's names were listed as being involved at 125 sex work establishments during the Progressive Era and 86 establishments during Prohibition. Names confirmed in the organized crime network were listed as being involved at 80 sex work establishments during the Progressive Era and 39 establishments during Prohibition. Of the total uncovered sex work establishments with named proprietors, women's percentage of involvement increased from 39 percent of establishments to 49 percent, whereas organized crime's percentage of involvement stayed about the same, from 25 percent to 22 percent.

Women's involvement in the management and proprietorship of the illicit economy of sex work was greater during Prohibition even though brothels and sex work had faced more legal ambiguity during the Progressive Era days of the segregated red-light districts. Much like the uncovering of women's alcohol establishments, this higher percentage for women likely indicates a lack of legal protection and increased surveillance of the domestic sphere. However, it may also indicate a small increase in women's ownership and management of their gendered labor in the sex economy. Moreover, even though women's proportion of sex work establishments was increasing in Chicago, for the most part these locations were not connected to the larger and more powerful organized crime network of Chicago. Similar to women's domestic distilling and brewing, most women's brothels operated in isolation and separate from organized crime.

Organized crime's involvement in the sex economy was quite stable between the Progressive Era and Prohibition. This stability reinforces the historical research presented here regarding the importance of brothels to the illicit alcohol market. Rather than selling protection to include women's brothels in the organized crime network, the men of organized crime syndicated their own brothels, with a few exceptions. Reckless described organized crime brothels as having poor working conditions, long hours, and low pay compared to women's independent brothels outside the central city.[77] There was no mention of women's being managers or operators of these organized crime brothels generating $100,000 a week.[78] The takeaway from this piece of the puzzle is that women were not pushed out of the sex economy during Prohibition; rather, they were pushed out of management and ownership positions in organized crime's portion of the sex economy. I argue that this occurred because of organizational restructuring and inequality-producing relational processes of this network.

## THE END OF PROHIBITION

Mabel Walker Willebrandt, the second woman to serve as assistant attorney general of the United States, handled federal Prohibition cases. She was often asked to comment on women's universal attitudes toward Prohibition, and she included her perspective in her 1929 book, *The Inside of Prohibition*: "The modern girl, who makes no protest when her escort to dinner produces a pocket flask and shares its contents with her, has no stake in prohibition enforcement. But the moment that girl marries, she probably will, whether consciously or not, become a supporter of prohibition, because she always will be unwilling to share any part of her husband's income with either a bootlegger or a saloon-keeper operating legally. I am convinced that as far as the women of the country are concerned, prohibition has come to stay."[79] Willebrandt's universal declarations for women under Prohibition, as well as her predictions, were wrong, as the Prohibition law had not "come to stay." Women's political organizing was as responsible for the repeal of Prohibition as it had been for its introduction.

Chaired by Pauline Morton Sabine of the Morton Salt family, the Women's Organization for Prohibition Reform (WOPR) was a national organization and a powerful group of women. Many WOPR members had originally supported Prohibition but came to recognize that the law had failed on all four of its major promises: eradicating the saloon, stopping drinking, reducing crime, and saving children from alcohol.[80] WOPR gained political momentum by appealing to moral concerns and Prohibition's failures, as well as the classist implications of the Prohibition law: "If the head of a corporation is free to drink intoxicants in his leisure hours, as and when he sees fit, what right has he to determine what his employee shall do in his leisure hours for his own enjoyment?"[81] Ione Nicoll, secretary for WOPR, wrote an article titled "Should Women Vote Wet?" in 1930 for the literary magazine *The North American Review*, in which she asserted: "A heavy responsibility rests today on American women. The time has come when they must face conditions as they are and not as a few fanatics would have us believe they are. . . . Women have had suffrage for ten years; what more magnificent opportunity will ever present itself for an intelligent, constructive and patriotic use of this power?"[82] More than 1.3 million racially and socioeconomically diverse members of WOPR defined the repeal of Prohibition as women's first major political issue since gaining suffrage.[83]

During the 1932 presidential election, democratic candidate Franklin Delano Roosevelt focused his campaign on the economy and recovery from the Great Depression. However, the social issue of repealing Prohibition was dominating the democratic political conversation, and Roosevelt had wavered as a moderate dry.[84] He finally took an ardent stand against Prohibition minutes before the Democratic National Convention began, to secure the party's nomination.[85] In the end, Roosevelt won by a landslide. Days after his inauguration, he called a special session of Congress to legalize beer and wine as part of his New Deal strategy. On December 5, 1933, Utah became the thirty-sixth and final state to ratify the Twenty-first Amendment, which repealed the Eighteenth Amendment.

At 4:32 p.m. on December 5, 1933, Chicago Loop hotels and the old favorite bars began serving alcohol legally for the first time in fourteen years.[86] Responding to talk of repeal, the Palmer House Hotel had built a new bar, which the workmen did not finish until 4:00 p.m. Hundreds of men and women lined up outside the Palmer House in anticipation of the new bar's opening. Palmer House officials estimated that by midnight "guests in the bar and the hotel dining room had consumed 50 cases of bourbon and rye, 25 of Scotch, 50 of gin, 75 of wine, including a sizable quantity of champagne, 10 of cordials, and 20 barrels of beer."[87] Hotels and bars around Chicago happily reported similar booms in the evening's business. Within two weeks following repeal, more than fifteen hundred applications for

FIGURE 11.    Patrons drinking after the repeal of Prohibition at Hotel Brevoort's world-famous Crystal Bar, Chicago, Illinois, 1933. *Source:* DN-A-4954, *Chicago Daily News* negatives collection, Chicago History Museum.

liquor licenses along with the $250 application fee had been filed with the city of Chicago.[88] Prohibition was over.

Some of the consequences of Prohibition and its repeal were for the better. Alcohol quality went up and costs went down, although it was not as cheap as pre-Prohibition alcohol.[89] Prohibition did actually cut down alcohol consumption in the United States, which did not return to pre-Prohibition levels until the 1970s.[90] Perhaps one of the most interesting unintended consequences of Prohibition was that it made women regular patrons and workers in public drinking spaces. The days of the men-only or working-man's saloon were over; women could serve cocktails or enjoy public drinking leisure without its being assumed they were sex workers.[91] On the night of repeal, women lined up at the bars and ordered their own drinks as pictured in figure 11 at the Crystal Bar; such an action was inconceivable before Prohibition.[92] The new bar at the Palmer House was intended to be a men's oyster bar, but 30 percent of the patrons on opening night were women.[93]

Organized crime still faced pending Prohibition cases upon repeal. One judge resolved the pending alcohol violation cases against organized crime individuals by charging them a total of $500 in fines, even though these cases had cost the government $100,000 to prepare.[94] The IRS, however, continued attacking organized crime members and their Prohibition profits for years afterward.[95] Chicago organized crime did not disappear. The network had already claimed its share of the labor racketeering market—an illicit economy that would continue to exclude women.[96]

SUMMARY

The Chicago organized crime network changed dramatically during Prohibition, multiplying in size, becoming sparser and centralized, and spreading into territories outside of the Levee districts. These network changes increased gender inequality in organized crime: men's relationships fueled growth in organized crime, men comprised the powerful core of organized crime bosses, and there were few relationships between women. Women's participation in organized crime dropped to 4 percent over a short period of time, during which women's broader criminal participation did not decrease.

The major change for syndicate women during Prohibition was their entrée into organized crime, which came from the private sphere through their relationships to male relatives, boyfriends, and husbands. Gone were the days of syndicate women mostly entering organized crime through the public sphere of the Levees where they, as illicit economy entrepreneurs, paid into the protection markets. Even though the sex economy had steady importance to Prohibition era organized crime, and women's proportion of sex work establishments increased, organized crime's control of the sex economy largely excluded women from management and ownership.

# 7. The Case for Syndicate Women

Vic Shaw, vice queen of Chicago's underworld before Prohibition and Chicago's faded queen during that period, lived until her eighty-ninth year. She died in 1951 in her brownstone mansion at 2906 Prairie Avenue—a house that had once served as one of her brothels and later as a cheap hotel for transients.[1] Vic Shaw's biography suggests that her fall in Chicago organized crime was a consequence of her failed marriages, her narcotics habit, and her trouble with the law.[2] This book argues that her underworld career coincided with a dramatic shift in the structure of Chicago organized crime from a small, flat, decentralized, and clustered network that was more inclusive of women to a large, sparse, and centralized network that mostly excluded them.

In this book I have presented the intriguing puzzle I uncovered in this research. Women composed a substantial 18 percent of organized crime in Chicago in the early 1900s before Prohibition, but during Prohibition, when criminal opportunities increased for both men and women, women composed only 4 percent of the network and were mostly excluded from organized crime. The gender gap in offending and arrests is historical, persistent, and as some scholars have argued, universal. So how did the gender composition of a single historical criminal organization change so rapidly? What were the criteria of inclusion during the Progressive Era and the criteria of exclusion during Prohibition that had such dramatic effects on women's participation?

This puzzle required examining Chicago's illicit economies of sex and alcohol during the Progressive Era and Prohibition to see if women's broader criminal participation changed outside of organized crime. The sex economy's heavy reliance on women's gendered labor made it one of the few profitable options available to working women at the turn of the twentieth century—which remains the case for many women today. Progressive Era brothel owners and sex workers navigated shifting regulations, legal ambiguity, and dramatic, overnight changes in law enforcement. When Chicago's red-light districts formally closed in 1912 and the most infamous Levee brothels were boarded up, brothels and sex work were pushed underground. Sex work increased in Chicago following the closing of the red-light districts and into Prohibition, as did women's participation in the proprietorship of Chicago's brothel establishments. In contrast to the pattern of women's near exclusion from organized crime, women's participation in the sex economy increased during Prohibition.

Producing, selling, and distributing illicit alcohol is differently gendered than sex work. Before Prohibition, saloons were predominantly male-only or workingmen's spaces. Women who wanted to enter saloons were required to be escorted by a man and to sit in rooms separate from men. Progressive Era moralizing assumed that any woman alone in a saloon was a sex worker looking for clients. During Prohibition, the illicit alcohol economy generated massive profits for men, who purchased brewing equipment, had access to storage facilities, drove beer trucks, and connected Chicago's thirsty patrons to their favorite beverages. Although alcohol production and distribution were largely men's work during Prohibition, women and families converted the domestic sphere into small moonshine and bootlegging operations. Women brothel owners increased profits by complementing the sale of sex with the sale of alcohol, as the clients and workers were already in a position of trust and secrecy in their exchange. The narrative that organized crime controlled all of the alcohol poured in Chicago ignores the profitable opportunities for domestic labor that Prohibition provided to poor, working-class, and immigrant women and families. The scale of production and distribution was much smaller, but women increasingly participated in the illicit alcohol economy even when they were mostly excluded from organized crime.

My investigation of Chicago's illicit economies of sex and alcohol shows that women's participation in crime did not dramatically decrease in the short twenty years from the beginning of the Progressive Era to the start of Prohibition. Rather, women's participation actually increased as the illicit economies shifted in response to changing regulations and the exogenous shock of Prohibition. Progressive Era activists succeeded in pushing Chicago's illicit entertainment landscape underground, and I found fewer sex and alcohol establishments mentioned in the archives and increasing criminalization of women in these spaces. While women faced barriers in Chicago's illicit economies, the illicit economies themselves did not exclude them.

Enough men of organized crime in Chicago understood early on the profitability of coordinating a protection market for the brothels, gambling dens, saloons, and other illicit entertainment in the Levee districts. The demand for a protection market increased as city and state regulations changed, morals courts and investigations opened, and police chiefs developed new, Progressive Era convictions. During the Progressive Era, the illicit entertainment economy was spatially concentrated in Chicago's three Levee districts. Clever brokers with important connections could collect payments from the illicit business owners to pay off police, judges, and politicians. Out of the Levees grew the Progressive Era organized crime network, which was small, clustered, and decentralized, with no clear leadership structure or bosses.

The US prohibition on the production, transportation, and sale of intoxicating beverages from 1920 to 1933 was an exogenous legal shock to Chicago's illicit economies. The Progressive Era organized crime network was the market-oriented actor in the best position to respond to and exploit the new market opportunities. The persisters in organized crime during both eras had the illicit entertainment establishments, the political connections, and the protection market. Some rapidly ascended to become the bosses of Chicago organized crime. The restructuring of the Chicago organized crime network saw a tripling in size and a more centralized organization with a powerful core. Organized crime expanded its profit-generating schemes beyond gambling, brothels, and alcohol and extended their protection to include legitimate businesses, labor racketeering, and political donations. Organized crime spread geographically from the three Levee districts into Chicago's neighboring villages. The organization was more powerful, profitable, and violent than ever before.

Women made up 18 percent of the organized crime network during the Progressive Era from 1900 to 1919, when organized crime in Chicago was small, flat, decentralized, and clustered. Nearly all of these women were madams or proprietors in the sex economy who had increased opportunities in organized crime's territorial and localized protection market. Women's criminal connections to organized crime were through male brokers or male co-offenders. Brokerage and co-offending are relational processes in which preferences, opportunity, experience, trust, and cooperation shape who chooses whom. Relational processes in criminal networks are inherently shaped by gender through preferences for masculinity and the greater pool of eligible men. However, Progressive Era organized crime included some equal-opportunity male brokers, who collected bribes, fines, and graft payments from men and women alike in the Levees and passed those payments on to the Levee district protectors. Brokers may have selected women as co-offenders through gender-neutral decisions based on cooperation and trust, but it is more likely that brokers' co-offending decisions were advantageous (and possibly exploitative) and driven by access to women's gendered labor in the sex economy.

Women were only 4 percent of Chicago's organized crime network during Prohibition from 1920 to 1933, when the network was large, sparse, and centralized with a powerful core of bosses. Women's criminal connections to Prohibition era organized crime mostly co-occurred with familial and romantic connections to men in organized crime. This was a dramatic shift from the public sphere—in which women ran illicit businesses and bought into the protection market—to the private sphere, where wives and girlfriends were arrested and criminally involved through small schemes, guilt by association, or being in the wrong place at the wrong time. Some of the cases from the private sphere revealed the increasing trust between men and women of organized crime. Instead of providing advantageous or exploitative access to women's gendered labor in the sex economy, many women's organized crime relationships existed on top of what appear to have been loving and trusting personal relationships with men. These deeper relationships provided a different type of gendered labor, such as a woman serving as a flawless alibi or an unencumbered property holder. The change in the quality of women's relationships to men in organized crime, plus the higher risk and higher profit of organized crime markets, demonstrate the increased need for trust in organized crime during Prohibition, which was less necessary during the Progressive Era.

Organized crime maintained its financial interests in the sex economy during Prohibition. Brothels were social meeting places for gangsters and brought in incredible profits with the additional sale of quality booze. Entrée to organized crime for some of the syndicate women (37 percent) was still through the sex economy, which often overlapped with familial and romantic relationships. But these syndicate women who were part of the organized crime network were largely in contrast to women's increasing proprietorship of sex work establishments during Prohibition outside of the organized crime network. Organized crime was controlling and expanding its own brothel establishments for distributing its booze, continuing to exploit sex workers' gendered labor (but not the gendered labor of madams), and not providing the same protection market to women entrepreneurs that it had during the Progressive Era.

Conventional theories of the gender gap in crime fall short of explaining such a dramatic change in the gender composition of a criminal organization. Women's entrepreneurial spirit and economic need did not dramatically change between the Progressive and Prohibition eras. Rather, the structural barriers of access and prosperity changed in ways that limited opportunities for women. Access to organizations, even criminal organizations, requires social capital, which is the resources contained within relationships with other people. But social capital is unequally distributed and thus is a source of inequality. Who gets meaningful relationships containing social capital is determined by status, preferences, organizational structure, and, consequently, gender.

The dramatic decrease in women in this criminal organization was due to the interaction of gender with the relational processes that generated organized crime during Prohibition. The interaction between gender and relational processes occurred in a variety of consequential ways. For example, the core of organized crime was more centralized and powerful, but the core only included men. The hierarchical, restructured organization did not incorporate localized brokerage opportunities with equal-opportunity brokers. The illicit alcohol economy increased criminal opportunities for both men and women, but men's and women's preferences for male co-offenders shaped the network. During the Progressive Era, some of the relational processes shaping organized crime in Chicago were gender neutral or were accessing women's gendered labor in the sex economy. During Prohibition, the relational processes accessed women's gendered labor in the sex economy through men rather than through women directly. Finally, women's participation in the alcohol economy went ignored and unprotected by organized crime. Across these examples, I have identified the actors and their relationships—or lack of relationships—to solve the puzzle of women's decreasing participation in the Prohibition era organized crime network.

## THEORETICAL CONTRIBUTIONS

The theoretical goal of *Syndicate Women* is to showcase how relational approaches can generate new insights for stale criminological debates. Gender socialization and cultural conceptions of masculinity and femininity have changed dramatically in the past century, even though the gender gap in crime has persisted as one of the largest gaps between men and women in the twenty-first century. Gender theory has challenged the binary construction of the categories of men and women, which poses questions about nonbinary gender inequalities in crime that the traditional focus on the gender gap in crime misses. A relational theoretical approach to the study of the gender gap and crime requires a new starting place other than categorical differences in offending and instead begins with how gender interacts with social processes that generate or limit relationships that in turn produce unequal outcomes.

Gender is not the only attribute interacting with social processes that produce inequality in crime. Relational approaches should consider other attributes of consequence (such as race and class) or intersections of attributes of even greater consequence (such as black masculinity) to see how these (and their intersections) interact with relational processes leading to other inequalities in crime, victimization, and incarceration. Relational approaches do not replace theories of categorical difference, but rather add depth to prior theories by focusing on the processes that generate unequal outcomes. Instead of big, structural explanations of inequality, such as racism or patriarchy, a relational approach focuses on specific actors and their actions or inactions that produce inequality.[3] These actors, actions, and inactions can be described as racist or patriarchal, but the relational approach shows us where and how macro structures persist in everyday interactions.

Theoretically, relational approaches allow criminologists to think more critically about social capital as it relates to crime and co-offending. Social capital is the resources that can be accessed through relationships.[4] Resources accessed through social capital may include information, recommendations, trust, and opportunity. Social capital can be hoarded and exclusive, which is how it contributes to inequality.[5] Social capital theory often focuses on legitimate organizations or personal connections, but social capital is also incredibly useful for thinking about who succeeds in crime and how inequality emerges in crime. For example, sociologists Bill McCarthy and John Hagan's concept of criminal capital as the accumulation of criminal experience and access to potential co-offenders engages the importance of relational resources in the criminal context.[6] Their focus on criminal capital as a social resource explains how certain people are chosen and given more criminal opportunities, but also how inequality can occur in co-offending decisions when the resources are not equally distributed.

Trust is a meaningful social capital resource in many relationships. People trust others to watch their children or to put in a good word for them at a potential job. Trust is paramount in the criminal context. The resource of trust in criminal relationships means knowing that the other people will be able to complete their part of the scheme, they will not divulge the scheme, and they will not snitch on the other co-offenders. Even the more exploitative criminal relationships, such as between a pimp and a sex worker, still require trust.[7] Co-occurring multiplex relationships, such as two people involved in a romantic relationship and also involved in crime together, reveal the potential depths and complexity of trust. This project has only been able to scratch the surface of what trust means between men and women co-offenders, and this issue of gender and trust in crime is largely unresolved in the research. On the other hand, the dissolving of romantic or personal relationships generates additional risks to the co-offenders. Ex-romantic partners who are angry at each other have incriminating information from their co-offenses that they could potentially use against each other. A social capital approach can be attentive to how relational resources change, for example, from trust to threat. The amount of trust required in criminal relationships exceeds the level of trust in most day-to-day relationships. Understanding how this relational resource generates inclusion and exclusion can potentially speak to broader topics of crime and inequality.

Social capital converts gendered labor in crime into a resource available to others. For example, women's access to feminine gendered labor in the sex economy is a social capital resource, and so is men's access to masculine violence enforcement. When women sex workers need protection from violent clients and men need a way to convert violence (or the threat of violence) into money, the cooperative criminal relationship between them converts the gendered labor of each into shared social capital resources. This collaboration and pooling of resources cannot be done in isolation; it requires criminal relationships. These relationships increase opportunities and chances of success for groups establishing them.

Methodologically, relational approaches to crime are essential to mapping out and measuring the structure of criminal networks. As I have established throughout this book, network structures have consequences for inequality. Networks and organizations reproduce categorical differences through the unequal distribution of relationships. Organizational structures generate equality or inequality when the structure determines who can form relationships with whom. A dense and decentralized network is more equitable because it is possible for individuals to make connections across ranks and positions in the network and access the social capital of those relationships. Large, sparse, and hierarchical organizational structures generate the greatest inequality because people at the margins are farther from the powerful center and have fewer opportunities to connect with those in the center who control and hoard the networked resources. Women are not likely to enter criminal organizations in the first place because of relational processes of exclusion, but the structure of some criminal organizations can increase or decrease women's opportunities within them.

## BROADER IMPLICATIONS

The case of *Syndicate Women* is a fascinating history from one hundred years ago, but this case and some of its unresolved pieces have important implications related to crime, gender, power, and networks in the twenty-first century. First, women continue to have a precarious foothold in criminal economies and criminal organizations. The relational processes of inclusion and exclusion are still at play and still gendered. Organized crime has gone global and continues to keep women at the margins. Research on international organized crime groups involved in drug trafficking, human trafficking, and sex trafficking shows that women were suspects in 68 percent of cases in the Dutch Organized Crime Monitor, but that women made up only 11 percent of the total suspects.[8] In other words, women's gendered labor is still critical to organized crime networks, but women's participation remains marginal.

One global crime that provides ample criminal opportunities for women is human trafficking and smuggling operations. Chinese human smuggling chains, Nigerian human trafficking networks, and small Dutch sex trafficking operations rely on women's gendered labor to procure women, house them, create assumptions of safety, communicate in multiple languages, and provide knowledge of the destination and the work.[9] Global trafficking networks have unique organizational structures consisting of decentralized chains, dense networks in which all people have many connections, or decentralized networks with multiple clusters linked together through brokers (such as the structural pattern from Chicago's Progressive Era organized crime).[10] Multiple studies show no evidence of large, hierarchical, centralized, global mafia groups for this global crime that tends to include many women offenders.

Contemporary research finds a clearer picture of violence against women in organized crime that was not as clear in Chicago a hundred years ago. Women in relationships with men in Italian mafia organizations are victims of misogyny and violence from their male partners.[11] Research on global trafficking networks shows that men and women who traffic other women use violence against these women to maintain power and control.[12] Violence and victimization, especially violence against women, tend to be analyzed through a lens of power and dominance. However, research by sociologist Andrew Papachristos and colleagues shows how gun violence spreads like a contagious disease through high-risk networks of co-offenders.[13] Power and dominance are still at play in these high-risk networks, but the social proximity to violence is a new and important insight into thinking about women's exposure to violence in organized crime.

Sex work is still criminalized in the United States, with the exception of some rural Nevada counties. A little over one hundred years ago, brothels in Chicago and across the United States operated in the open, with some risk of raids and arrests, but for the most part law enforcement and politicians avoided talking about the issue and sided with arguments that containing sex work was better than letting it go underground. Today the debate around legalizing sex work persists and echoes some of the same concerns from the Progressive Era in Chicago. Some scholars argue that the legalization and decriminalization of sex work in parts of Europe have increased sex trafficking and organized crime.[14] Other scholars point to the success of legalization at providing the safest working conditions for sex workers.[15] The sex workers themselves are organizing for labor protections and workplace regulations and still trying to move past one hundred years of moralizing and conservative bulwarks.

One of the consequences of forcing and keeping sex work underground for over a century in the United States is the persistence of substantial inequality in wages, experiences, and violence among sex workers. Women continue to experience inequality, sexual harassment, and degradation in legitimate and official workplaces, and this is especially true for black and Latina women. For women from disadvantaged circumstances, sex work provides a constrained choice for those trying to care for their children, have some autonomy over their schedules, and/or support their drug habits or addictions.[16] Sex work provides a solution to periods of unemployment or times in which immediate off-the-books income is desperately needed.[17] Much like the stratification of brothels and sex workers' earnings from the early 1900s, sex work continues to be stratified at the intersections of race, class, and migration status. White women sex workers who are not financially desperate, have some college education, and are technologically savvy have the lowest risk of violence and arrest and have the highest rate of earnings.[18] Sex work remains the one crime for which police arrest more women than men, but increasing attention is being paid to the arrests, harassment, and incarceration of transgender women and gay youth participating in the illicit sex economy.

The most remarkable exogenous legal shock to illicit markets in the twenty-first century has been the legalization of recreational marijuana. To date, nine states have ended a long-standing prohibition in the United States. Marijuana's prohibition history lasted much longer than alcohol's fourteen years and had massive consequences during the war on drugs and mass incarceration. Under new state regulations, California growers have moved their plants indoors, the Colorado cannabis industry has opened accounts at credit unions and small banks willing to risk violating Federal

Deposit Insurance Corporation (FDIC) laws, and Alaska has updated its driving under the influence laws. Much like sex work in the segregated Levee districts of Chicago, recreational marijuana regulations are changing at the local and state levels, resulting in conflicting federal regulations and discretionary law enforcement.

Men have dominated the illicit marijuana economy, with women occupying only peripheral roles in the industry.[19] Yet the criminalization of marijuana has been largely on the backs of black adults and juveniles in the United States.[20] The exogenous legal shock to the newly licit economy could create new opportunities for women and marginalized racial groups, but publications on the cannabis industry present an entrepreneurial start-up culture in which "tech bros" are the best-positioned market actors. In response, people of color, including women, entrepreneurs, and activists, are organizing around and calling out the past injustices in arrests with the current barriers to entrance. State licit marijuana economies are an important space to watch who gets opportunities, how they get opportunities, and who is excluded.

The case of *Syndicate Women* suggests that scholarship should be attentive to how contemporary criminal economies and criminal organizations can abruptly change in response to exogenous shocks or organizational or market restructuring. How stable is the gender gap in criminal markets and criminal organizations when police arrest high-status men, leaving holes in the leadership structure; when residential instability aggravates gang turf boundaries, such as the demolition of a housing project, forcing gang-involved residents to relocate; when illicit products are decriminalized, such as certain states legalizing recreational marijuana; when new competitors enter a criminal market, such as a new trafficking ring in the Netherlands; or when technology moves criminal market transactions from the streets to the Internet, such as the dark web's role in selling drugs and sex?[21] Answers to these questions require longitudinal studies of criminal markets and criminal organizations, and research in this vein could clarify the durability or instability of gender segregation among criminals. Similarly, do these shocks and shifts create conditions in which the criminally powerful consolidate their power and the criminally powerless fall further into the margins? My hope is that scholars see the unique case of *Syndicate Women* as a meaningful, theoretical insight into broader and contemporary cases of inequality and crime.

CONCLUDING REMARKS

To be clear, *Syndicate Women* is not advocating for gender equality in some of society's most violent institutions (e.g., organized crime, the military, police departments, terrorist organizations, street gangs). Rather, this book argues for the more sociologically relevant approach to understanding the processes of why and how violent and masculine institutions are so successful at excluding women. Understanding who is excluded and why provides nuance and a better understanding of these organizations. Unregulated and unequal-opportunity networks shed light on the most consequential relationship processes for gender inequality during exogenous shocks— processes that certainly exist in legitimate organizations, albeit in more subtle forms. Similar attention should be paid to legitimate organizations when they respond to dramatic changes, such as in immigration or trade policy, decreased market competition, or weakening federal regulations.

Social networks are abstractions—images of dots and lines that can be reduced to a table of statistical properties. Yet the bird's-eye perspective illuminates networks beyond the local and reveals patterns that otherwise might have been hidden—even to the members of the networks themselves.[22] Organized crime associates are no longer hidden in boxes and folders full of crumbling pages when information on their relationships to others can be organized in a networked way. Social network analysis provides a means to organize historical data and the tools to analyze the data statistically. Most important, from the Capone Database of 3,321 individuals and their 15,861 relationships, I could filter out the noise that existed within some of the archival sources to reveal the structure of organized crime at two points in time. Not every individual mentioned in the archives was connected to organized crime, but when the connection to organized crime was not clear in the source, it became clear in the extraction of the networks.

Social network analysis requires a level of abstraction that limits explanation beyond the processes of the network. Interpreting the social network results through historical narrative methods contextualizes the networks and brings the power of temporal ordering and causality back to the analysis. It was only by zooming in on small sections of the network and investigating the historical detail of women's connections to organized crime that I was able to discover the importance of the location of establishments and of location-based relationships for women in the first time period and their near absence in the second time period. Identifying the various processes behind women's criminal relationships to organized crime required historical methods. The narratives are often not flattering, but they reconstruct a historical moment to correct misconceptions about women's locations in history and render women, even criminal women, visible and relevant.

# Notes

## 1. GENDER AND ORGANIZED CRIME

1. "'Vic' Shaw's Flat Raided: 'Doctor' and Drugs Taken," *Chicago Daily Tribune*, December 18, 1915, 5.

2. Norma Lee Browning, "Oldest Vice Queen Finds Reform at 70," *Chicago Daily Tribune*, March 14, 1949, 1, 6.

3. Norma Lee Browning, "Grandeur Turns to Squalor for Ex-Levee Queen," *Chicago Daily Tribune*, March 15, 1949, 4.

4. Browning, "Grandeur Turns to Squalor for Ex-Levee Queen," 4.

5. Blair (2010, 132); Browning, "Grandeur Turns to Squalor for Ex-Levee Queen," 4.

6. "'Vic' Shaw's Flat Raided," 5; "'Vic' Shaw, Vice 'Queen,' Deported from Canada," *Chicago Daily Tribune*, March 13, 1916, 13.

7. Browning, "Oldest Vice Queen Finds Reform at 70," 1, 6.

8. "Vic Shaw, Queen of Vice on the Old Levee, Dies," *Chicago Daily Tribune*, November 13, 1951, 20.

9. James Janega, "Norma Lee Browning, 86," *Chicago Tribune*, June 14, 2001, http://articles.chicagotribune.com/2001-06-14/news/0106140288_1_ms -browning-norma-lee-browning-hollywood-columnist.

10. Browning, "Oldest Vice Queen Finds Reform at 70," 1, 6 (ellipses in original).

11. Browning, "Oldest Vice Queen Finds Reform at 70," 1, 6; Browning, "Grandeur Turns to Squalor for Ex-Levee Queen," 4.

12. Browning, "Grandeur Turns to Squalor for Ex-Levee Queen," 4.

13. Browning, "Oldest Vice Queen Finds Reform at 70," 1, 6.

14. "Vice Sleuths Raid Flat of Roy Jones," *Chicago Daily Tribune*, November 16, 1914, 1; Landesco ([1929] 1968, 27–31).

15. Asbury (1940, 300).

16. "Wayman Men Raid Resorts: Levee in Panic," *Chicago Daily Tribune*, October 5, 1912, 1.

17. "Wayman Men Raid Resorts," 1.

18. Asbury (1940, 300).

19. Browning, "Grandeur Turns to Squalor for Ex-Levee Queen," 4; "Vice Sleuths Raid Flat of Roy Jones," 1.

20. "Vice Sleuths Raid Flat of Roy Jones," 1.

21. "'Vic' Shaw's Flat Raided," 5.

22. Willrich (2003).

23. "Inside Story of Vice's Grip on Chicago," *Chicago Daily Tribune*, July 18, 1914, 1, 3; "'Vic' Shaw's Flat Raided," 5.

24. "Sift Jones Raid Data for Mann Act Violations," *Chicago Daily* Tribune, November 17, 1914, 13; "Vice Sleuths Raid Flat of Roy Jones," 1.

25. "Sift Jones Raid Data for Mann Act Violations," 13; "Vice Sleuths Raid Flat of Roy Jones," 1.

26. "Inmates of 'Jones' Flat Face New Prosecution," *Chicago Daily Tribune*, November 18, 1914, 13; "Vice Sleuths Raid Flat of Roy Jones," 1.

27. Norma Lee Browning, "Dope and Death Doomed Levee, 'Queen' Recalls," *Chicago Daily Tribune*, March 16, 1949, 12.

28. "'Vic Shaw,' 60, Fined $500 for Possessing Liquor," *Chicago Daily Tribune*, January 28, 1928, 1.

29. "'Vic' Shaw Reports Big Gem Theft at Her 'House Party,'" *Chicago Daily Tribune*, December 17, 1921, 2; "'Vic Shaw,' 60, Fined $500 for Possessing Liquor," 1.

30. Reckless (1933, 105).

31. Joseph U. Dugan, "Gang Women of Dry Era Bid for Spurious Fame," *Chicago Daily Tribune*, December 31, 1933, G3.

32. See also Haller (1990).

33. Belknap (2015); Cullen et al. (2015); Lauritsen, Heimer, and Lynch (2009).

34. Bureau of Justice Statistics (2018); Federal Bureau of Prisons (2018). These percentages reflect the most recent years available at the time of this writing.

35. Britton (2000); De Coster, Heimer, and Cumley (2013, 313); Steffensmeier and Allan (1996).

36. Feeley and Little (1991).

37. Gambetta (1993); Siebert (1996).

38. Giancana and Renner (1984); Ianni and Reuss-Ianni (1972).

39. Block (1977).

40. Holub (2007).

41. Ingrasci (2007); Massari and Motta (2007); Pizzini-Gambetta (2014); Siebert (1996).

42. Daly and Chesney-Lind (1988); Miller (2014); Steffensmeier and Allan (1996).

43. Katz (1990); Messerschmidt (1993); West and Zimmerman (1987).

44. Britton (2011); Miller (1998, 2014).

45. Contreras (2009); Jacobs and Miller (1998); Maher (1997); Miller (1998); Steffensmeier, Schwartz, and Roche (2013).

46. Burgess and Akers (1966); Sutherland (1947).

47. Haynie (2001); Haynie et al. (2005); Haynie and Kreager (2013); Kreager, Rulison, and Moody (2011); Young (2011); Young et al. (2014).

48. Haynie, Doogan, and Soller (2014); Zimmerman and Messner (2010).

49. Adler (1985); Giordano, Deines, and Cernkovich (2006); Haynie et al. (2005); Leverentz (2006, 2014); Mullins and Wright (2003); Steffensmeier, Schwartz, and Roche (2013); Zhang, Chin, and Miller (2007).

50. Faris and Felmlee (2011); McCarthy and Casey (2008); McCarthy, Felmlee, and Hagan (2004); Peterson, Miller, and Esbensen (2001).

51. De Coster, Heimer, and Cumley (2013).

52. Black (2009); Bourgois (1996); Contreras (2013); Venkatesh (2006).

53. McPherson, Smith-Lovin, and Cook (2001).

54. Abadinsky (2017); Steffensmeier (1983).

55. Kadushin (2012); Marsden (1990); Scott (2017); Wasserman and Faust (1994); Wellman (1983).

56. Tomaskovic-Devey (2014).

57. Felson (2003); Nguyen and McGloin (2013); Reiss (1988).

58. Tremblay (1993).

59. McCarthy and Hagan (1995); McCarthy, Hagan, and Cohen (1998).

60. Charette and Papachristos (2017); McCarthy and Hagan (1995); McCarthy, Hagan, and Cohen (1998); McGloin and Nguyen (2012); Nguyen and McGloin (2013).

61. Becker and McCorkel (2011); Koons-Witt and Schram (2003); Schwartz, Conover-Williams, and Clemons (2015); Steffensmeier (1983); Steffensmeier and Terry (1986).

62. Black (2009); Decker and Van Winkle (1996); Ianni and Reuss-Ianni (1972); Morselli, Tremblay, and McCarthy (2006); Mullins and Wright (2003); Shaw (1938).

63. Adler (1985); Giordano, Deines, and Cernkovich (2006); Haynie et al. (2005); Leverentz (2006, 2014); Mullins and Wright (2003); Steffensmeier, Schwartz, and Roche (2013); Zhang, Chin, and Miller (2007).

64. Baker and Faulkner (1993).

65. Adler (1985); Gambetta (1993); Goffman (2009).

66. Adler (1985); Gambetta (1993).

67. Dino (2007); Pizzini-Gambetta (2014).

68. Pizzini-Gambetta (2014).

69. Adler (1985).

70. Adler (1985).

71. Maher (1997).

72. Maher (1997).

73. Maher (1997). See also Clement (2006) on the increasing violence and exploitation of sex work during Prohibition, when organized crime controlled the alcohol market.

74. Zhang (2014).

75. Zhang, Chin, and Miller (2007).

76. Bourdieu (1986); Burt (2005); Coleman (1988); Lin (2001); Small (2009).

77. Burt (1998).
78. Reckless (1933); Rosen (1982).
79. Rosen (1982).
80. Rosen (1982); Weitzer (2009).

## 2. MAPPING CHICAGO'S ORGANIZED CRIME AND ILLICIT ECONOMIES

1. Howell and Prevenier (2001); Nora (1989); Schwartz and Cook (2002).
2. Moseley (1973); Voss-Hubbard (1995).
3. Chicago Crime Commission Archives, Capone File 1, August 1930; Chicago Crime Commission, Capone Public Enemy Timeline, Capone File 1, 13190.
4. "Capone Man Absolves Editor," *Sarasota Herald*, August 28, 1930, 1–2; "Capone's Name Is Brought into Governor 'Plot,'" *Chicago Daily Tribune*, August 19, 1930, 2.
5. "Capone's Name Is Brought into Governor 'Plot,'" 2.
6. "Capone's Name Is Brought into Governor 'Plot,'" 2.
7. "Capone's Name Is Brought into Governor 'Plot,'" 2.
8. Organized crime constitutes a hidden population. Hidden populations are hidden because their total population is unknown to the public, and the activities of the group are largely unknown (Heckathorn 1997). Hidden populations can include drug users, people infected with HIV, or affiliates of organized crime. They are difficult to study because entering institutions (e.g., a hospital or a research center) as members of a hidden population, whether for medical treatment or filling out a survey, unveils individuals' previously hidden activities and identities. One acceptable strategy to sample hidden populations is snowball sampling (Watters and Biernacki 1989). A snowball sample is a chain of referrals that begins with an informant or initial seed. By asking the informant for referrals to other members of the hidden population, the sample of people in the research multiplies, and eventually the researcher is talking with referees far removed from the initial informant (Wright et al. 1992). Because there is no master list of organized crime members from which I could draw a truly random sample, this project employed two snowball sampling approaches, using Al Capone as the historical seed from which to grow his network of affiliations. The first snowball sample was through sources and the second was through associates.

As a source-based seed, I used "Al Capone" (and spelling variations) as a search term to locate primary sources in archives and historical secondary sources at libraries. When I coded these sources, I expanded my coding beyond each source's sections on Al Capone to generate the snowball effect that started with him but moved further from his historical events. This is how I came across, for example, John Landesco's *Illinois Crime Survey of 1929* ([1929] 1968). While searching for archival sources pertaining to Al Capone, I located a reference to the *Illinois Crime Survey*, which was eventually published in 1968 and renamed *Organized Crime in Chicago*. I ended up coding this historical book in its entirety even though Capone appeared on only 40 of the 146 coded pages. This source-based snowball began with one seed, Al Capone, but in this source I located 660 individuals mentioned in connection to organized crime beyond Al Capone.

The origin of this project was also a source-based sample. The Chicago Crime Commission (CCC) is a watchdog organization founded in 1919 by business leaders concerned with corruption in Chicago. The organization still exists today and houses a large card catalog linking organized crime individuals through archival folders. Requesting a random selection of its files on organized crime created a random seed from which to start building the database. The CCC's random selection of files included many folders pertaining to Al Capone, but also included consolidation folders on a variety of major crime activities from the early 1900s, as well as the CCC's original public enemy reports. The CCC folders contained mostly newspaper clippings, but there were also some investigator notes, legal documents, letters to CCC members, arrest records, and reports. This source-based snowball approach expanded the network beyond Al Capone without having to manually locate and code every document from Prohibition era Chicago.

The second type of snowball sampling was through associates. For an associate-based snowball, I used the list of names generated from Capone's archives as a starting point for new searches. Online access to the *Chicago Tribune* provided a search function for some of these names. Due to time constraints, I could not exhaust the list of Al Capone's associates. However, I strategically targeted certain associates on the list (e.g., public enemies and women) and reached saturation around prominent historical events and the individuals involved. Overall, this project required creative approaches to snowball sampling a hidden population, because I could not ask informants for a list of referrals. Instead, I snowballed within the archives, chasing leads and digging through boxes.

The major criticism of snowball sampling is that the final sample is biased by the initial seed or informant. In this case, it means that had I started with an informant other than Al Capone, I might have generated a very different view of Chicago organized crime. Al Capone was by no means normal in terms of his social position in Chicago. In fact, what makes Capone a useful informant is that he had hundreds of discrete, documented relationships. From Capone's not-so-normal point of view, we get a picture of the largest organized crime network in Chicago during this period. I agree with critics that using Capone as the informant introduces bias to the sample, but I argue that it is that very bias that is of interest in social network research. The Capone bias in the data captures the reality that friends and bootlegging partners were not random events. In traditional statistical linear modeling, Al Capone would be an elephant-sized sampling challenge; however, social network tools are designed for exploring nonrandom and clustered aspects of social life.

9. Felson (2006); Paoli (2002); von Lampe (2014).

10. See von Lampe (2001, 104, 2016, 19). However, there are some alternative discussions about the origins of the term "organized crime." See also Paoli and Vander Beken (2014).

11. For item 1, see Abadinsky (2017); Albanese (1989); Gambetta (1993); Paoli (2002); Paoli and Vander Beken (2014); Reuter (1983); von Lampe (2016). For item 2, see Collins (2011); Haller (1990); Landesco ([1929] 1968); Papachristos and Smith (2014); Smith and Papachristos (2016). For item 3, see Albanese (1989); Collins (2011); Gambetta (1993); von Lampe (2016). For item 4, see Abadinsky (2017); Albanese (1989).

12. Tomaskovic-Devey (2014).

13. Small (2009); Tomaskovic-Devey (2014).

14. The technical definition of a component of a graph is "a maximal connected subgraph . . . a component is a subgraph in which there is a path between all pairs of nodes in the subgraph (all pairs of nodes in a component are reachable), and (since it is maximal) there is no path between a node in the component and any node not in the component" (Wasserman and Faust 1994, 110).

15. Scott (2017); Wasserman and Faust (1994).

16. I dropped criminal relationships with missing dates from the networks when I could not approximate a year or time period based on the context of the documents. This step resulted in thirteen nodes, all men, being dropped entirely from the organized crime networks. There were fifty-one dyads with no date information; however, according to different sources, one of these fifty-one dyads had a criminal tie in the Progressive Era, and thirteen of them had a criminal tie in the Prohibition era. It is possible that the missing date information from one source was captured by different sources that included dates on these criminal relationships, in which case only thirty-seven criminal relationships were lost entirely due to missing time information.

17. See Kadushin (2012) and Scott (2017) for introductions to social network analysis. See Wasserman and Faust (1994) for the comprehensive reference on social network analysis.

18. Density equals the number of edges present in a network divided by the total possible edges of a network. Total possible edges means the maximum number of edges that could exist between a given set of nodes if every single node were connected to every other node. In other words, network density is the proportion or percent of all possible edges that exist within the network.

19. Kadushin (2012, 205). The geodesic distance is the shortest possible path between two nodes in the same component. It is measured by the number of links along the shortest possible path. Every node in a network has a geodesic to every other node in the network, but the geodesic between nodes of different components is undefined. Betweenness is measured as the sum of geodesics on which a node of interest lies (Wasserman and Faust 1994). Betweenness can range from zero (a node is not an intermediary on any of the paths between pairs of nodes) to the maximum of all the geodesics in a network, excluding a node's own geodesics.

20. Yang, Keller, and Zheng (2017).

21. Wasserman and Faust (1994).

22. Social networks—even social networks of unique cases and historical relationships—follow mathematical rules. For example, as networks get larger, they are more sparsely connected and have a greater diameter (Scott 2017; Wasserman and Faust 1994). For this reason, it is inappropriate to make direct comparisons of network measures for networks of different sizes. Reading down the columns in table 2 (rather than across the rows) shows how organized crime grew in size during Prohibition and how the increase in the size of the network produced a sparser, more centralized network.

23. McDonald and Benton (2017).

24. "O'Banion Gang Like Pirates of Olden Days," *Chicago Daily Tribune*, November 11, 1924, 3.

25. My Al Capone Museum, "The Four Deuces," 2009, www.myalcapone-museum.com/id152.htm, accessed June 5, 2015.

26. "Silver's Palace Denied License," *Chicago Daily Tribune*, May 28, 1903, 3.

27. "Gentleman's Killing Bares Wide Gambling," *Chicago Daily Tribune*, September 2, 1919, 1; Landesco ([1929] 1968).

28. "Gentleman's Killing Bares Wide Gambling," 1.

29. The row total in table 3 does not add up to the total of 480 sex work–related addresses with named proprietors because some of these addresses persisted across the two eras and are counted in both columns.

30. The row total in table 3 does not add up to the total of 480 alcohol-related addresses with named proprietors because some of these addresses persisted across the two eras and are counted in both columns.

31. "Dr. Bundesen Denies Drive Condones Vice," *Chicago Daily Tribune*, August 18, 1922, 1.

32. Donovan (1920).

33. Le Sueur ([1978] 2006).

34. Siebert (1996).

35. Brunson and Miller (2006); Feeley and Little (1991); Klein (1973).

36. Andreas (2013, xii).

## 3. CHICAGO, CRIME, AND THE PROGRESSIVE ERA

1. Addams ([1909] 1972, 5–6).

2. See Jennifer Fronc's (2009) discussion of the importance of the term "activists" in contrast to "reformers" when referring to the social movements of the Progressive Era (4).

3. Cohen (2003).

4. Blair (2010); Clement (2006); Fronc (2006, 2009); Heap (2009); McGirr (2016); Mitrani (2013).

5. Fronc (2009); Willrich (2003).

6. Fronc (2009, 4–5).

7. Fronc (2009, 5).

8. Lombroso and Ferrero ([1893] 2004); Willrich (2003).

9. D'Emilio and Freedman ([1988] 1997); Willrich (2003).

10. Keire (2001).

11. Grattet and Jenness (2005).

12. Starr and Curtis (1885); Stead (1894, 452).

13. Joslyn (1920, 817–18).

14. Gilfoyle (1992).

15. Cynthia Blair (2010) utilized 1880–1910 Census data in the study of black women sex workers in Chicago and detailed the occupational and address information on sex work collected by Census workers (248–49).

16. Common Council (1837).

17. Jamieson and Adams (1881).

18. See also Linehan (2017).

19. Tolman (1905, 405).

20. Tolman (1905, 396, 401).

21. Joslyn (1920, 37).

22. Grattet and Jenness (2005).

23. Mitrani (2013).

24. Mitrani (2013, 32).

25. John Callan O'Laughlin, "Vice Is Flaunted in Chicago's Face," *Chicago Daily Tribune*, October 10, 1909, 1, 4.

26. Reckless (1933, 1–2).

27. "Steward's Order Throttles Levee," *Chicago Daily Tribune*, October 11, 1909, 1.

28. "Police Seize Men in Levee Raids," *Chicago Daily Tribune*, October 13, 1909, 1.

29. "Vice Regulation Methods Opposed," *Chicago Daily Tribune*. October 17, 1909, 3.

30. "Police Close Limits Hotel," *Chicago Daily Tribune*, October 29, 1909, 3; "Mann Act Case Bares Vice Ring," *Chicago Daily Tribune*, October 19, 1913, 3.

31. "Graft or a Plot? M'Cann Fight On," *Chicago Daily Tribune*, July 25, 1909, 1.

32. "Vice Loses Pomp in Levee Penance," *Chicago Daily Tribune*, October 12, 1909, 1.

33. "Vice Regulation Methods Opposed," *Chicago Daily Tribune*, October 17, 1909, 3.

34. "Vice Regulation Methods Opposed," 3.

35. "Find 'Dago Frank' Levee Insurgent," *Chicago Daily Tribune*, May 1, 1911, 3.

36. Reckless (1933, 238).

37. "The Vice Report," *Chicago Daily Tribune*, April 7, 1911, 8; Reckless (1933, 239).

38. Reckless (1933, 1–2).

39. Reckless (1933, 243).

40. Reckless (1933, 60, 243).

41. Reckless (1933, 243).

42. "'Blind to Vice': 35 Lieutenants," *Chicago Daily Tribune*, October 26, 1911, 3.

43. "'Vag' Warrants for Women," *Chicago Daily Tribune*, December 19, 1913, 3.

44. Brady, Biradavolu, and Blankenship (2015) have a similar discussion of legal ambiguity creating risk for sex workers in Andhra Pradesh, India.

45. "Morals Chief Traps Briber for Vice Ring," *Chicago Daily Tribune*, February 26, 1914, 1.

46. Meyerowitz (1988).

47. Donovan (1920); Meyerowitz (1988).

48. Bureau of Labor Statistics (2018).

49. Blair (2010).

50. Stead (1894, 249–50).

51. Stead (1894, 251).

52. Bureau of Labor Statistics (2018); "What the Vice Commission Found; How It Would Correct Evil," *Chicago Daily Tribune*, April 6, 1911, 6.

53. Abbott (2007, 24–27); Bureau of Labor Statistics (2018).

54. Abbott (2007).

55. Landesco (1936, 896).

56. Bureau of Labor Statistics (2018); Landesco (1936).

57. "Gipsy's Marchers Storm Sin's Front," *Chicago Daily Tribune*, October 19, 1090, 1.

58. "Gipsy's Marchers Storm Sin's Front," 1.

59. Norma Lee Browning, "Oldest Vice Queen Finds Reform at 70," *Chicago Daily Tribune*, March 14, 1949, 1, 6; Norma Lee Browning, "Grandeur Turns to Squalor for Ex-Levee Queen," *Chicago Daily Tribune*, March 15, 1949, 4.

60. "Franks Confess Graft in Detail," *Chicago Daily Tribune*, July 25, 1909, 2.

61. "West Side Levee Hears Its Knell," *Chicago Daily Tribune*, November 5, 1903, 1.

62. Blair (2010, 45).

63. Blair (2010, 28).

64. Blair (2010, 46, 143).

65. Blair (2010, 141); Fronc (2009, 100–102). See also Cressey (1932); Reckless (1933).

66. Blair (2010, 143).

67. Diffee (2005); Gleeson (1915); Harland (1912); Turner-Zimmerman (1911).

68. Keire (2001, 8).

69. Blair (2010); "Steward's Order Throttles Levee," *Chicago Daily Tribune*, October 11, 1909, 1; "Police Seize Men in Levee Raids," *Chicago Daily Tribune*, October 13, 1909, 1.

70. "Steward's Order Throttles Levee," 1.

71. "Steward's Order Throttles Levee," 1; "Find 'Dago Frank' Levee Insurgent," 3.

72. "Steward's Order Throttles Levee," 1.

73. "Find 'Dago Frank' Levee Insurgent," 3.

74. "Vice Loses Pomp in Levee Penance," 1.

75. "Steward's Order Throttles Levee," 1.

76. "Vice Loses Pomp in Levee Penance," 1.

77. Reckless (1933, 15–16).

78. Blair (2010, 82).

79. Acker (1990); Tomaskovic-Devey and Skaggs (2002).

80. Linehan (2017).

81. Zhang, Chin, and Miller (2007).

82. Contreras (2009).

83. Steffensmeier, Schwartz, and Roche (2013).

84. Contreras (2009); Steffensmeier, Schwartz, and Roche (2013).

85. Dank and Johnson (2014); Zhang (2011).

86. Morselli and Savoie-Gargiso (2014).

87. Pizzini-Gambetta (2014).

88. Landesco ([1929] 1968, 846).

89. Mitrani (2013).

90. Blair (2010, 27, 51).

91. O'Laughlin, "Vice Is Flaunted in Chicago's Face," 1, 4.

92. Reckless (1933, 101).

93. "Charges of Graft Pile up on Police," *Chicago Daily Tribune*, October 3, 1907, 2; "Nootbaar Goes Back to Levee in New Shakeup," *Chicago Daily Tribune*, October 8, 1916, 3; Reckless (1933).

94. "West Side Hotels Raided: Eight Houses Visited and Only Fifteen Arrests Made," *Chicago Daily Tribune*, September 5, 1906, 5.

95. O'Laughlin, "Vice Is Flaunted in Chicago's Face," 1, 4.

96. "Levee Is Resuming Activity," *Chicago Daily Tribune*, April 14, 1900, 5.

97. Reckless (1933, 54).

98. "Defends Honor of Yale," *Chicago Daily Tribune*, May 25, 1907, 2.

99. "Defends Honor of Yale," 2.

100. "What the Vice Commission Found," 6.

101. Stead (1894).

102. Bureau of Labor Statistics (2018); "Chott Is Shifted; Will Have Trial," *Chicago Daily Tribune*, October 9, 1906, 4.

103. "Federal Vicenet Entangles Eight," *Chicago Daily Tribune*, November 8, 1911, 7.

104. "Silver's Palace Denied License," *Chicago Daily Tribune*, May 28, 1903, 3; "Quits the Levee Crusade," *Chicago Daily Tribune*, July 2, 1903, 7.

105. "Silver's Palace Denied License," 3.

106. Blair (2010, 51, 128).

107. Officer 666, "Vice Trust Tactics Bared by Insider," *Chicago Daily Tribune*, July 20, 1914, 1–2.

108. Blair (2010, 127); Harrison (1935, 311).

109. Blair (2010, 51, 126).

110. Black (2013).

111. "Wheelock Gives Police Officers Lesson on Vice," *Chicago Daily Tribune*, November 2, 1911, 1, 4.

112. "Lawyers Visit Vice Center," *Chicago Daily Tribune*, July 10, 1907, 2; O'Laughlin, "Vice Is Flaunted in Chicago's Face," *Chicago Daily Tribune*, October 10, 1909, 1, 4.

113. "Raid on Woodruff Hotel," *Chicago Daily Tribune*, February 11, 1901, 3; "Man Patron Slain Mysteriously in Roy Jones' Dive," *Chicago Daily Tribune*, April 9, 1914, 1–2; "Mayor Queries about Shooting," *Chicago Daily Tribune*, April 10, 1914, 3; "Gentleman's Killing Bares Wide Gambling," 1; "O'Banion Gang Like Pirates of Olden Days," *Chicago Daily Tribune*, November 11, 1924, 3.

114. Eig (2010).

115. "Divorced Wife's Brother Tells of Family Rows," *Chicago Daily Tribune*, May 12, 1920, 3.

116. "Drinks for Soldiers and Sailors," *Chicago Daily Tribune*, September 2, 1918, 13; "Tilting of Lid Brings Big Jim Second Arrest," *Chicago Daily Tribune*, May 21, 1919, 14.

117. "Colosimo Gives Realty to Wife," *Chicago Daily Tribune*, August 27, 1914, 13.

118. "Divorced Wife's Brother Tells of Family Rows," 3.

119. Landesco ([1929] 1968).

120. Burgess ([1929] 1968, 1091).

121. "Inside Story of Vice's Grip on Chicago," *Chicago Daily Tribune*, July 18, 1914, 1, 3.

122. Keire (2001).

123. "Mann Act Case Bares Vice Ring," *Chicago Daily Tribune*, October 19, 1913, 3; "Police Fail to Close Up Levee Capitol," *Chicago Daily Tribune*, July 24, 1914, 1.

124. Abbott (2007).

125. "Brolaski's Story Imperils Police in the 'Vice Trust,'" November 19, 1911, 1.

126. "Mrs. Nation in Tour of Levee," *Chicago Daily Tribune*, February 13, 1901, 1.

127. "First Ward in Annual Orgy," *Chicago Daily Tribune*, December 10, 1907, 5.

128. "Levee's Hordes Storm Coliseum," *Chicago Daily Tribune*, December 15, 1908, 1.

129. "Calls Ward Orgy Boon to Charity," *Chicago Daily Tribune*, December 12, 1906, 4.

130. "Levee's Hordes Storm Coliseum," 1.

131. "Calls Ward Orgy Boon to Charity," 4.

132. Bureau of Labor Statistics (2018); "Calls Ward Orgy Boon to Charity," 4.

133. "Levee's Hordes Storm Coliseum," 1.

134. "First-Warders at Ball," *Chicago Daily Tribune*, January 16, 1902, 9.

135. "Big Dance Is a 'Sizzler,'" *Chicago Daily Tribune*, January 7, 1903, 3.

136. Abbott (2007); "Immune to Law at Craig's Tivoli," *Chicago Daily Tribune*, December 26, 1906, 8.

137. "Huge Vice Trust Thwarted Here," *Chicago Daily Tribune*, August 19, 1912, 5.

138. Erenberg (1981, 73, 154–56); Heap (2009, 56, 130–31).

139. Officer 666, "Vice Trust Tactics Bared by Insider," 1–2.

## 4. SYNDICATE WOMEN, 1900–1919

1. Landesco (1936, 892).

2. "Immune to Law at Craig's Tivoli," *Chicago Daily Tribune*, December 26, 1906, 8.

3. Blair (2010); Haller (1971, 1990); Harrison (1935); Landesco ([1929] 1968); Reckless (1933).

4. "Effort to Close Vicious Saloons," *Chicago Daily Tribune*, September 29, 1907, 2; "Steward's Order Throttles Levee," *Chicago Daily Tribune*, October 11, 1909, 1; "Gambling Rife; Vice Trust Bold," *Chicago Daily Tribune*, October 7, 1911, 3; "Morals Chief Traps Briber for Vice Ring," *Chicago Daily Tribune*, February 26, 1914, 1; "Healey Trial Bares Rivals to Vice Ring," *Chicago Daily Tribune*, November 20, 1917, 7; Landesco ([1929] 1968); Reckless (1933).

5. Keire (2001).

6. "Inside Story of Vice's Grip on Chicago," *Chicago Daily Tribune*, July 18, 1914, 1, 3; "Quiz Levee Police at Secret Advance Trial," *Chicago Daily Tribune*, July 23, 1914, 1.

7. "Brolaski's Story Imperils Police in the 'Vice Trust,'" *Chicago Daily Tribune*, November 19, 1911, 1; "Inside Story of Vice's Grip on Chicago," 1, 3; Officer 666, "Vice Trust Tactics Bared by Insider," *Chicago Daily Tribune*, July 20, 1914, 1–2; "Hoyne Arrests Healey," *Chicago Daily Tribune*, January 9, 1917, 1.

8. "Inside Story of Vice's Grip on Chicago," 1, 3.

9. "Ask City to Call Nation's Experts on Vice Problem," *Chicago Daily Tribune*, October 30, 1912, 1.

10. "Steward's Order Throttles Levee," 1; "M'Weeny to File Charges against Bonfield Today," *Chicago Daily Tribune*, June 9, 1911, 1; "Brolaski's Story Imperils Police in the 'Vice Trust,'" 1; "Ask City to Call Nation's Experts on Vice Problem," 1; Officer 666, "Vice Trust Tactics Bared by Insider," 1–2.

11. Elsewhere I define the criminal elite as the individuals in a network who have the top 10 percent of degree scores (Smith and Papachristos 2016).

12. "Frank on Stand Accuses M'Cann," *Chicago Daily Tribune*, September 11, 1909, 1.

13. Becker and McCorkel (2011); Koons-Witt and Schram (2003); Schwartz, Conover-Williams, and Clemons (2015).

14. Charette and Papachristos (2017); McCarthy and Hagan (1995); McCarthy, Hagan, and Cohen (1998); McGloin and Nguyen (2012); Nguyen and McGloin (2013); Steffensmeier (1983); Steffensmeier and Terry (1986).

15. Contreras (2009); Steffensmeier, Schwartz, and Roche (2013).

16. Contreras (2009, 2013).

17. "Detectives Seize M'Cann's Relative," *Chicago Daily Tribune*, September 12, 1909, 1.

18. Gilfoyle (1992).

19. "Returns Woman for Vice Inquiry," *Chicago Daily Tribune*, December 4, 1911, 3.

20. "Returns Woman for Vice Inquiry," 3.

21. Pizzini-Gambetta (2014).

22. Haynie et al. (2005); Leverentz (2006, 2014); Mullins and Wright (2003).

23. The co-occurrence of two or more different types of relationships between a pair of individuals is a network property called "multiplexity." Elsewhere I have examined the role of multiplexity in Chicago's historical organized crime network and found rare, but strong, dependencies between familial relationships and criminal relationships in these networks (Smith and Papachristos 2016).

24. Abbott (2007).

25. Abbott (2007).

26. "Levee's Hordes Storm Coliseum," *Chicago Daily Tribune*, December 15, 1908, 1.

27. Bureau of Labor Statistics (2018); Landesco ([1929] 1968, 850).

28. "'Blind to Vice': 35 Lieutenants," *Chicago Daily Tribune*, October 26, 1911, 3.

29. "Starts Vice War," *Chicago Daily Tribune*, October 25, 1911, 1.

30. "Wheelock Gives Police Officers Lesson on Vice," *Chicago Daily Tribune*, November 2, 1911, 1, 4.

31. "Photo Standalone 3," *Chicago Daily Tribune*, February 19, 1925, 32; "Wreckers Begin Tearing Down Everleigh Club," *Chicago Daily Tribune*, July 25, 1933, 3.

32. Blair (2010).

33. Asbury (1940, 300).

34. Asbury (1940, 300).

35. Mancuso (2014); Morselli and Roy (2008).

36. Brady, Biradavolu, and Blankenship (2015); Kleemans, Kruisbergen, and Kouwenberg (2014); Morselli and Roy (2008).

37. Brady, Biradavolu, and Blankenship (2015).

38. Burt (2005); Padgett and Ansell (1993); Stovel and Shaw (2012).

39. "Graft or a Plot? M'Cann Fight On," *Chicago Daily Tribune*, July 25, 1909, 1.

40. "Franks Confess Graft in Detail," *Chicago Daily Tribune*, July 25, 1909, 2.

41. "Detectives Seize M'Cann's Relative," 1.

42. "Jury Debate Long, but Calm," *Chicago Daily Tribune*, September 24, 1909, 2; "High Court Gives a Stay to M'Cann," *Chicago Daily Tribune*, February 1, 1910, 9.

43. "Franks Confess Graft in Detail," 2.

44. "Would Keep Vice in One District," *Chicago Daily Tribune*, October 28, 1903, 2; "Ask City to Call Nation's Experts on Vice Problem," 1.

45. "Would Keep Vice in One District," 2.

46. "Ask City to Call Nation's Experts on Vice Problem," 1.

47. "Ask City to Call Nation's Experts on Vice Problem," 1.

48. "Ask City to Call Nation's Experts on Vice Problem," 1.

49. Drake and Cayton ([1945] 1962). The quotation is from "Ask City to Call Nation's Experts on Vice Problem," 1.

50. "Vice Regulation Methods Opposed," *Chicago Daily Tribune*, October 17, 1909, 3.

51. "Wayman Men Raid Resorts; Levee in Panic," *Chicago Daily Tribune*, October 5, 1912, 1.

52. Drake and Cayton ([1945] 1962); Reckless (1933, vii).

53. Langum (2006).

54. "Ask City to Call Nation's Experts on Vice Problem," 1; "Inside Story of Vice's Grip on Chicago," 1, 3; Henry M. Hyde, "Zone of Vice Affords Cloak to Crook Ring," *Chicago Daily Tribune*, January 13, 1916, 17.

55. "Duel in Levee Gangster Job; Ended Wrong," *Chicago Daily Tribune*, July 19, 1914, 1.

56. Henry M. Hyde, "Old Red Light District Like Earthquake City," *Chicago Daily Tribune*, January 11, 1916, 13.

57. Blair (2010); Reckless (1933).

58. "Maj. Funkhouser to Resist Ouster," *Chicago Daily Tribune*, January 19, 1914, 3.

59. "Morals Chief Traps Briber for Vice Ring," *Chicago Daily Tribune*, February 26, 1914, 1; "Second Bribery Plot of Vice Ring." *Chicago Daily Tribune*, February 27, 1914, 3.

60. Bureau of Labor Statistics (2018); "Morals Chief Traps Briber for Vice Ring," 1; "Second Bribery Plot of Vice Ring," 3.

61. Officer 666, "Vice Trust Tactics Bared by Insider," 1–2.

62. "Hoyne Arrests Healey," 1.

63. "Mr. Hoyne's Conference; One of the 'Big Three'; The Accused Chief; An Arrested Lieutenant; Page from Vice 'Red Book,'" *Chicago Daily Tribune*, January 9, 1917, 3.

64. "Hoyne Arrests Healey," 1.

65. Bureau of Labor Statistics (2018); "Hoyne Arrests Healey," 1.

66. "$13,900 Chief's Share in Graft, Costello Says," *Chicago Daily Tribune*, December 19, 1917, 1, 10.

67. "$13,900 Chief's Share in Graft, Costello Says," 1, 10.

68. "Maj. Funkhouser to Resist Ouster," 3; "Inside Story of Vice's Grip on Chicago," 1, 3.

69. "Colosimo Gives Realty to Wife," *Chicago Daily Tribune*, August 27, 1914, 13; Harrison (1935, 304).

70. "Sift Jones Raid Data for Mann Act Violations," *Chicago Daily Tribune*, November 17, 1914, 13; "Mike De Pike Convicted as 'White Slaver,'" *Chicago Daily Tribune*, June 2, 1916, 17; Linehan (2017).

71. "Vice Women Held Vagrants," *Chicago Daily Tribune*, January 11, 1914, 1.

## 5. CHICAGO, CRIME, AND PROHIBITION

1. Lerner (2007, 2).
2. "Council Acts on Licenses as Booze Dies," *Chicago Daily Tribune*, July 1, 1919, 1.
3. "J. Barleycorn Moves from Loop to Homes," *Chicago Daily Tribune*, January 17, 1920, 1.
4. "J. Barleycorn Moves from Loop to Homes," 1.
5. Andreas (2013); Fronc (2009, 4–5).
6. Lerner (2007, 13).
7. Lerner (2007, 174).
8. Griswold (1993).
9. Lerner (2007, 174).
10. McCammon et al. (2001).
11. Flanagan (2002); Trout (1920).
12. Lerner (2007, 13, 29–31, 96–97).
13. Lerner (2007, 2); McGirr (2016).
14. "Names Found on Vice Ring Books Are Kept Secret," *Chicago Daily Tribune*, April 8, 1925, 5; McGirr (2016).
15. Arthur Evans, "Home Stillers Flood Chicago with Moonshine," *Chicago Daily Tribune*, November 24, 1923, 5.
16. Avent-Holt (2012); Fligstein (1996); Radaev (2017); Rao, Monin, and Durand (2003).
17. Spilerman and Stecklov (2009).
18. Avent-Holt (2012); Fligstein (1996).
19. Leinenkugel's, "Our Story," 2018, www.leinie.com/our-story.
20. "Mayor, Clyne, Decree Booze Cheaters' Doom," *Chicago Daily Tribune*, November 5, 1920, 1.
21. Fligstein (1996, 665).
22. Landesco (1932).
23. Decker et al. (2009); Lewis et al. (2012).
24. Bureau of Labor Statistics (2018); "What You Can Do, and What You Cannot Do," *Chicago Daily Tribune*, January 17, 1920, 2; "Chief Orders Army of Police to Throttle Vice," *Chicago Daily Tribune*, March 6, 1923, 1; McGirr (2016).
25. "Take 12 Pts. Rum and a New York Bad Man in Raid," *Chicago Daily Tribune*, October 1, 1920, 3; McGirr (2016, 208–9).
26. Haller (1970, 1976).
27. McGirr (2016, 94).
28. "Mayor, Clyne, Decree Booze Cheaters' Doom," 1; Schmidt (2013, 89).
29. Schmidt (2013).
30. Beckert and Dewey (2017).
31. Haller (1976).
32. "Vice and Graft at High Tide, City Hall Told," *Chicago Daily Tribune*, July 21, 1922, 5; McGirr (2016, 54–56).

33. "'Count' Yaselli, Dry Ace, Sought Bribe, Is Charge," *Chicago Daily Tribune*, July 19, 1922, 4; "'Count' Yaselli Is Here Again for Rum Raid Trials," *Chicago Daily Tribune*, August 14, 1922, 6.

34. "Yaselli 'Bulls' Compel U.S. to Drop Rum Cases," *Chicago Daily Tribune*, March 9, 1923, 5; Newberry Library, Waller & Beckwith Realty Co. Records Collection, Legal Prohibition Violations 1922–1928, Box 18, Folder 238.

35. "Attorney Punches 'Count' Yaselli on Nose in Court Row," *Chicago Daily Tribune*, February 20, 1923, 7.

36. "Arrest Yaselli, Dry Ace, Under State Rum Law," *Chicago Daily Tribune*, February 7, 1923, 3.

37. "Yaselli 'Bulls' Compel U.S. to Drop Rum Cases," 5; "Count May Sell Forty Disguises; Also Whiskers," *Chicago Daily Tribune*, March 21, 1923, 13; Newberry Library, Waller & Beckwith Records Collection, Box 18, Folder 238.

38. McGirr (2016).

39. Chicago History Museum, Institute for Juvenile Research Life Histories Collection, 1910s–1940s (mainly 1929–1933), Box 50, 131 G 3,874, Folder 1, IJR Life History 9-1. I have replaced all names from the Institute of Juvenile Research archival sources with pseudonyms as required by the researcher confidentiality agreement. Direct quotations from this material come from my typed notes and may contain minor transcription errors or minor grammatical and spelling corrections.

40. "His Overcoat Betrays Him as Walking Saloon," *Chicago Daily Tribune*, May 11, 1928, 19; Evans, "Home Stillers Flood Chicago with Moonshine," 5.

41. Chicago History Museum, Institute for Juvenile Research Life Histories Collection, Box 50, 131 G 3,874, Folder 1, IJR Life History 9-1.

42. Bennett (1996).

43. Meacham (2009).

44. Miller (1991).

45. Miller (1991).

46. Murphy (1994).

47. Willrich (2003).

48. Sidney Sutherland, "Dry Hootch Fills City Cells, Graham Asserts," *Chicago Daily Tribune*, December 30, 1925, 3.

49. "'Hootch Cases' Gain, Humane Society Finds," *Chicago Daily Tribune*, February 3, 1922, 17.

50. "City's Toughest District Is Made Dry for Once," *Chicago Daily Tribune*, October 8, 1923, 2.

51. Chicago History Museum, Institute for Juvenile Research Life Histories Collection, Box 44, 131 F 3,867, Folder 8, IJR Life History 3-8.

52. Chicago History Museum, Institute for Juvenile Research Life Histories Collection, Box 44, 131 F 3,867, Folder 8, IJR Life History 3-8.

53. Chicago History Museum, Institute for Juvenile Research Life Histories Collection, Box 44, 131 F 3,867, Folder 13, IJR Life History 3-13.

54. Chicago History Museum, Institute for Juvenile Research Life Histories Collection, Box 44, 131 F 3,867, Folder 13, IJR Life History 3-13.

55. Chicago History Museum, Institute for Juvenile Research Life Histories Collection, Box 44, 131 F 3,867, Folder 13,. IJR Life History 3-13.

56. Venkatesh (2006).

57. Chicago History Museum, Institute for Juvenile Research Life Histories Collection, Box 44, 131 F 3,867, Folder 2, IJR Life History 3-2.

58. "Woman Goes on Trial for Death by Poison Rum," *Chicago Daily Tribune*, March 12, 1924, 12; "Her Rum Fatal; Woman Begins 'Year to Life,'" *Chicago Daily Tribune*, February 5, 1925, 12.

59. Lisa McGirr's (2016) research on Prohibition shows that this pattern of women bootleggers not having access to organized protection occurred in locations across the United States.

60. McGirr (2016, 71).

61. Chicago History Museum, Institute for Juvenile Research Life Histories Collection, Box 46, 131 F 3,870, Folder 5, IJR Life History 5-5.

62. "17,000 Barrels of Real Beer Seized in Raid," *Chicago Daily Tribune*, June 3, 1924, 4; "Cops Land in Jail; Freed on Bail," *Chicago Daily Tribune*, May 20, 1924, 1, 6; "O'Banion Beer Factory Locked by Court's Order," *Chicago Daily Tribune*, October 7, 1924, 2; "O'Banion Quiz, Leads Way to Cicero Dives," *Chicago Daily Tribune*, November 20, 1924, 1, 3; Landesco ([1929] 1968, 910, 912).

63. "Drys Find 41,400 Gallons of Beer in Brewery Raid," *Chicago Daily Tribune*, June 2, 1929, 6.

64. "Jury to Report on Capone Rum Inquiry Sept. 10," *Chicago Daily Tribune*, September 5, 1931, 3; "$100,000 Beer Case Ends in $500 in Fines," *Chicago Daily* Tribune, December 9, 1933, 16.

65. Chicago Crime Commission Archives, Public Enemies File 21700, Public Enemies 4, June 26, 1930; Chicago Crime Commission Archives, Public Enemies File 21700, Public Enemies 5, May 1930–June 1930; "Giant Brewery of Capone Gang Seized by U.S.," *Chicago Daily Tribune*, June 13, 1930, 5.

66. "Torrio Is Shot; Police Hunt for O'Banion Men," *Chicago Daily Tribune*, January 25, 1925, 5.

## 6. SYNDICATE WOMEN, 1920–1933

1. Degree centralization is a score that ranges from 0 (when ties are equally distributed across the individuals) to 1 (when all ties concentrate on a single individual). Degree centralization for Prohibition era organized crime was 0.33, which suggests some concentrating of ties.

2. McDonald and Benton (2017).

3. Bill McCarthy and John Hagan (1995) conceptualize criminal capital as the accumulation of criminal experience and access to potential co-offenders.

4. "$13,900 Chief's Share in Graft, Costello Says," *Chicago Daily Tribune*, December 19, 1917, 1, 10; "Court Rebukes Schoemaker for 'Third Degree,'" *Chicago Daily Tribune*, August 29, 1920, 6.

5. Oscar Hewitt, "Figures Reveal Big Increase in White Slavery," *Chicago Daily Tribune*, February 1, 1931, 22.

6. "U.S. Raiders Put End to Resort Long Immune," *Chicago Daily Tribune*, February 20, 1918, 5; "Court Rebukes Schoemaker for 'Third Degree,'" *Chicago Daily Tribune*, August 29, 1920, 6; "Robbers Bind Woman in Flat; Loot Is $6,200," *Chicago Daily Tribune*, February 2, 1926, 5.

7. "Colosimo Slain; Seek Ex-Wife, Just Returned," *Chicago Daily Tribune*, May 12, 1920, 1; Charles Collins, "Who Killed Big Jim Colosimo?," *Chicago Daily Tribune*, February 7, 1954, C19, C38.

8. "Burnham Fire No Mystery," *Chicago Daily Tribune*, February 10, 1916, 13; "Gunmen Brought from New York, Levee Rumor," *Chicago Daily Tribune*, November 26, 1916, 6; "'Wop Tommy' Now Sought as Enright Killer," *Chicago Daily Tribune*, February 6, 1920, 1.

9. Regarding the argument about Colisomo's death: Asbury (1940, 317–22); Eig (2010); Landesco ([1929] 1968, 909); Russo (2001). Regarding Torrio's relentless pursuit: "O'Banion Quiz, Leads Way to Cicero Dives," *Chicago Daily Tribune*, November 20, 1924, 1, 3; Landesco ([1929] 1968, 909).

10. "O'Banion Quiz, Leads Way to Cicero Dives," 1, 3.

11. Bureau of Labor Statistics (2018); Landesco ([1929] 1968, 910).

12. Bureau of Labor Statistics (2018); Landesco ([1929] 1968, 912).

13. Chicago Crime Commission Archives, Public Enemies Miscellaneous 2, June 1931; Internal Revenue Service Archives, Letter, July 8, 1931, www.irs.gov/pub/irs-utl/file-1-letter-dated-07081931-in-re-alphonse-capone.pdf.

14. "Torrio Is Shot; Police Hunt for O'Banion Men," *Chicago Daily Tribune*, January 25, 1925, 5.

15. Guy Murchie, "Capone's Decade of Death," *Chicago Daily Tribune*, February 9, 1936, D1.

16. Chicago Crime Commission Archives, "Yarrow Drive Stirs Hughes," Newspaper clipping, December 7, 1929.

17. Papachristos and Smith (2014).

18. Haller (1990).

19. McPherson and Smith-Lovin (1987).

20. Kalev (2009); Smith-Doerr (2004).

21. Adler (1985); Maher (1997); Maher and Hudson (2007); Pizzini-Gambetta (2014); Zhang, Chin, and Miller (2007).

22. Siebert (1996, 2007).

23. Chicago Crime Commission. Capone Public Enemy Timeline, Capone File 1, 13190.

24. Internal Revenue Service Archives, Letter, July 8, 1931; National Archives Regional Archives–Great Lakes, IRS non-record, Box 4, Witness Transcripts, Part I, June 16, 1931.

25. "Capone's Miami, Fla., Home Saved, U.S. Lien and Taxes Are Paid," *Chicago Daily Tribune*, November 8, 1936, 12; National Archives Regional Archives–Great Lakes, Box 4, Witness Transcripts, Part I, June 16, 1931.

26. "Capone's Miami, Fla., Home Saved," 12.

27. Pizzini-Gambetta (2014).

28. "Captured Gangster's Girl Friend Revealed a Divorcee and Mother of 5-Year Old Child," *Chicago Daily Tribune*, March 1, 1929, 5.

29. "Jack McGurn and His Alibi Seized Under Mann Act," *Chicago Daily Tribune*, June 26, 1929, 13.

30. "Jack McGurn and His Alibi Seized Under Mann Act," 13.

31. Chicago Crime Commission Archives, Folder Public Enemies, File 21700-8, 1931–1933; "Gunner M'Gurn Weds Girl Who Gave Him Alibi," *Chicago Daily Tribune*, May 7, 1931, 5; "M'Gurn and Wife Sentenced in Mann Act Case," *Chicago Daily Tribune*, July 22, 1931, 9; "M'Gurn Mann Act Sentence Is Set Aside," *Chicago Daily Tribune*, November 8, 1932, 11.

32. Langum (2006); Pliley (2014).

33. Baker and Faulkner (1993).

34. Adler (1985); Contreras (2009); Gambetta (1993); Goffman (2009).

35. Dino (2007); Pizzini-Gambetta (2014).

36. Massari and Motta (2007); Pizzini-Gambetta (2014).

37. Smith and Papachristos (2016).

38. Smith and Papachristos (2016).

39. Chicago Crime Commission Archives, Consolidation Folder, File Number 28562, 8-2-32, Re. Sanborn, Rosemary, deceased.

40. Chicago Crime Commission Archives, Consolidation Folder, File Number 6486: Exley, Leah Belle, Duffy, Leah Exley; Northwestern History of Homicide Records, Record Number 5981.

41. Siebert (1996, 2007).

42. Oselin (2014); Rosen and Venkatesh (2008); Weitzer (2009).

43. Beckert and Dewey (2017, 20–21).

44. Landesco ([1929] 1968, 923–24).

45. "Quiz 13 in Vain Effort to Solve Beer War Death," *Chicago Daily Tribune*, September 2, 1922, 8; "Slayers in Rum War Named," *Chicago Daily Tribune*, September 1, 1922, 1.

46. "Many Mystery Murders of 1922 Still Unsolved," *Chicago Daily Tribune*, January 1, 1923, A1.

47. Asbridge and Weerasinghe (2009); Owens (2011).

48. Bowman and Altman (2003, 759); Monkkonen (2003).

49. Papachristos (2013).

50. Adler (2006).

51. Owens (2014). See also Adler (2006).

52. Adler (2015); Asbridge and Weerasinghe (2009); Bowman and Altman (2003); Owens (2011, 2014).

53. Adler (2006, 2015); Bowman and Altman (2003); Drake and Cayton ([1945] 1962).

54. May, Rader, and Goodrum (2010).

55. Peterson, Miller, and Esbensen (2001).

56. Ruth (1996).

57. Chicago Crime Commission Archives, Folder Public Enemies, File 21700, April 23, 1930; "List 28 as 'Public Enemies,'" *Chicago Daily Tribune*, April 24, 1930, 1.

58. "List 28 as 'Public Enemies,'" 1.

59. "39 Hoodlums on New 'Public Enemy' Roster," *Chicago Daily Tribune*, January 10, 1933, 1.

60. "Dillinger Gang Named as Chief Public Enemies," *Chicago Daily Tribune*, December 29, 1933, 1.

61. "City to Shut Up Gang Bars," *Chicago Daily Tribune*, December 26, 1933, 1; "Fight 16 Police; Elude Trap," *Chicago Daily Tribune*, November 16, 1933, 1.

62. "Arizona Rules Indiana Gets Dillingers; Tucson Wants Gang Pending Rewards," *Chicago Daily Tribune*, January 28, 1934, 3.

63. "City to Shut Up Gang Bars," *Chicago Daily Tribune*, December 26, 1933, 1.

64. "Arizona Rules Indiana Gets Dillingers," 3.

65. James O'Donnell Bennett, "Chicago Gangland: The True Story of Its Murders, Its Vices, and Its Reprisals," *Chicago Daily Tribune*, February 24, 1929, G1, 9.

66. Reckless (1933, 103, 137).

67. Chicago Crime Commission Archives, Folder on the Committee of Fifteen, File Number 4525-4. Clement (2006) found that organized crime in New York City took over the sex economy during Prohibition and pushed women out of ownership and into managerial positions.

68. Bureau of Labor Statistics (2018); "Cicero's Hiding Apaches Wait Caponi Return," *Chicago Daily Tribune*, July 4, 1926, 1.

69. "O'Banion Quiz Leads Way to Cicero Dives," *Chicago Daily Tribune*, November 20, 1924, 1, 3.

70. "O'Banion Gang Like Pirates of Olden Days," 3.

71. "Dr. Bundesen Denies Drive Condones Vice," *Chicago Daily Tribune*, August 18, 1922, 1.

72. Blair (2010); Drake and Cayton ([1945] 1962).

73. Drake and Cayton ([1945] 1962); Lombardo (2013).

74. "Rev. Williamson Tires Vigilantes, Insist City Act," *Chicago Daily Tribune*, July 10, 1922, 7.

75. Reckless (1933, 10, 21).

76. Willrich (2003, 569).

77. Reckless (1933, 145). See also Clement's (2006) discussion on the increasing corruption among police officers during Prohibition in New York City, which generated greater violence against and exploitation of sex workers.

78. "Cicero's Hiding Apaches Wait Caponi Return," 1.

79. Willebrandt (1929, 278).

80. Lerner (2007, 192); Nicoll (1930, 561).

81. Nicoll (1930, 565).

82. Nicoll (1930, 565).

83. Lerner (2007, 195, 197).

84. Lerner (2007, 295–305).

85. Lerner (2007).

86. "Liquor Flows Again; Chicago Gaily Responds," *Chicago Daily Tribune*, December 6, 1933, 1.

87. "Liquor Flows Again," 1.

88. "Allman Pushes Drive on Liquor Law Violators," *Chicago Daily Tribune*, December 15, 1933, 10.

89. "14-Year Dry Era Ends Today," *Chicago Daily Tribune*, December 5, 1933, 1.

90. Andreas (2013, 235); McGirr (2016).

91. McGirr (2016).

92. "Liquor Flows Again," 1.

93. "14-Year Dry Era Ends Today," 1; "Liquor Flows Again," 1.

94. "$100,000 Beer Case Ends in $500 in Fines," *Chicago Daily Tribune*, December 9, 1933, 16.

95. "Torrio Indicted with Three Aids as Tax Evaders," *Chicago Daily Tribune*, September 5, 1937, 4.

96. "Terror Killing Traced to Gang Rule of Strike," *Chicago Daily Tribune*, February 16, 1938, 1; James Doherty, "Charge Gang Rule over 15 Unions in City," *Chicago Daily Tribune*, June 3, 1940, 1; Lloyd Wendt, "The Men Who Prey on Labor," *Chicago Daily Tribune*, August 10, 1941, F2.

## 7. THE CASE FOR SYNDICATE WOMEN

1. "Vic Shaw, Queen of Vice on the Old Levee, Dies," *Chicago Daily Tribune*, November 13, 1951, 20.

2. "Vic Shaw, Queen of Vice on the Old Levee, Dies," 20.

3. Tomaskovic-Devey and Avent-Holt (2019).

4. Bourdieu (1986); Burt (2005); Coleman (1988); Lin (2001); Small (2009).

5. Tilly (1998).

6. McCarthy and Hagan (1995); McCarthy, Hagan, and Cohen (1998).

7. Morselli and Savoie-Gargiso (2014).

8. Kleemans, Kruisbergen, and Kouwenberg (2014).

9. Mancuso (2014); Siegel and de Blank (2010); Zhang, Chin, and Miller (2007).

10. Campana (2016); Mancuso (2014); Zhang (2014).

11. Dino (2007); Ingrasci (2007); Siebert (1996).

12. Hughes (2000); Siegel and de Blank (2010).

13. Papachristos, Hureau, and Braga (2013); Papachristos and Wildeman (2014).

14. Hughes (2000); Raymond (2004).

15. Weitzer (2009).

16. Oselin (2014); Rosen and Venkatesh (2008); Venkatesh (2006).

17. Rosen and Venkatesh (2008); Venkatesh (2006).

18. Murphy and Venkatesh (2006); Venkatesh (2013); Weitzer (2009).

19. August (2013).

20. Nguyen and Reuter (2012).

21. Morselli, Paquet-Clouston, and Provost (2017); Murphy and Venkatesh (2006).

22. Kadushin (2005, 149).

# References

Abadinsky, Howard. 2017. *Organized Crime.* 11th ed. Boston: Cengage Learning.

Abbott, Karen. 2007. *Sin in the Second City: Madams, Ministers, Playboys, and the Battle for America's Soul.* New York: Random House.

Acker, Joan. 1990. "Hierarchies, Jobs, Bodies: A Theory of Gendered Organizations." *Gender & Society* 4(2):139–58.

Addams, Jane. (1909) 1972. *The Spirit of Youth and the City Streets.* Champaign: University of Illinois Press.

Adler, Jeffrey S. 2006. *First in Violence, Deepest in Dirt: Homicide in Chicago, 1875–1920.* Cambridge, MA: Harvard University Press.

———. 2015. "Less Crime, More Punishment: Violence, Race, and Criminal Justice in Early Twentieth-Century America." *Journal of American History* 102(1):34–46.

Adler, Patricia A. 1985. *Wheeling and Dealing: An Ethnography of an Upper-Level Drug Dealing and Smuggling Community.* New York: Columbia University Press.

Albanese, Jay. 1989. *Organized Crime in America.* 2nd ed. Cincinnati, OH: Anderson Publishing Co.

Andreas, Peter. 2013. *Smuggler Nation: How Illicit Trade Made America.* New York: Oxford University Press.

Asbridge, Mark, and Swarna Weerasinghe. 2009. "Homicide in Chicago from 1890 to 1930: Prohibition and Its Impact on Alcohol- and Non-Alcohol-Related Homicides." *Addiction* 104(3):355–64.

Asbury, Herbert. 1940. *Gem of the Prairie: An Informal History of the Chicago Underworld.* New York: Alfred A. Knopf.

August, Karen. 2013. "Women in the Marijuana Industry." *Humboldt Journal of Social Relations* 35:89–103.

Avent-Holt, Dustin. 2012. "The Political Dynamics of Market Organization: Cultural Framing, Neoliberalism, and the Case of Airline Deregulation." *Sociological Theory* 30(4):283–302.

Baker, Wayne E., and Robert R. Faulkner. 1993. "The Social Organization of Conspiracy: Illegal Networks in the Heavy Electric Equipment Industry." *American Sociological Review* 58(6):837–60.

Becker, Sarah, and Jill A. McCorkel. 2011. "The Gender of Criminal Opportunity: The Impact of Male Co-Offenders on Women's Crime." *Feminist Criminology* 6(2):79–110.

Beckert, Jens, and Matias Dewey, eds. 2017. *The Architecture of Illegal Markets: Towards an Economic Sociology of Illegality in the Economy*. New York: Oxford University Press.

Belknap, Joanne. 2015. *The Invisible Woman: Gender, Crime, and Justice*. 4th ed. Belmont, CA: Cengage Learning.

Bennett, Judith M. 1996. *Ale, Beer, and Brewsters in England: Women's Work in a Changing World, 1300–1600*. New York: Oxford University Press.

Black, Joel E. 2013. "Space and Status in Chicago's Legal Landscapes." *Journal of Planning History* 12(3):227–44.

Black, Timothy. 2009. *When a Heart Turns Rock Solid: The Lives of Three Puerto Rican Brothers on and off the Streets*. New York: Vintage Books.

Blair, Cynthia M. 2010. *I've Got to Make My Livin': Black Women's Sex Work in Turn-of-the-Century Chicago*. Chicago: University of Chicago Press.

Block, Alan. 1977. "Aw! Your Mother's in the Mafia: Women Criminals in Progressive New York." *Contemporary Crises* 1(1):5–22.

Bourdieu, Pierre. 1986. "The Forms of Capital." Pp. 241–58 in *Handbook of Theory and Research for the Sociology of Education*, edited by J.G. Richardson. New York: Greenwood.

Bourgois, Philippe. 1996. *In Search of Respect: Selling Crack in El Barrio*. 2nd ed. New York: Cambridge University Press.

Bowman, Cynthia Grant, and Ben Altman. 2003. "Wife Murder in Chicago: 1910–1930." *Journal of Criminal Law and Criminology* 92(3/4):739–90.

Brady, David, Monica Biradavolu, and Kim M. Blankenship. 2015. "Brokers and the Earnings of Female Sex Workers in India." *American Sociological Review* 80(6):1123–49.

Britton, Dana M. 2000. "Feminism in Criminology: Engendering the Outlaw." *Annals of the American Academy of Political and Social Science* 571(1):57–76.

———. 2011. *The Gender of Crime*. Lanham, MD: Rowan & Littlefield Publishers.

Brunson, Rod K., and Jody Miller. 2006. "Gender, Race, and Urban Policing: The Experience of African American Youths." *Gender & Society* 20(4):531–52.

Bureau of Justice Statistics. 2018. "Arrest Data Analysis Tool." Washington, DC: US Department of Justice. www.bjs.gov/index.cfm?ty=datool&surl=/arrests/index.cfm#.

Bureau of Labor Statistics. 2018. "Consumer Price Index Inflation Calculator." Washington, DC: US Department of Labor. http://data.bls.gov/cgi-bin/cpicalc.pl.

Burgess, Ernest W. (1929) 1968. "Summary and Recommendations." Pp. 1091–1100 in *Organized Crime in Chicago*. Chicago: University of Chicago Press.

Burgess, Robert L., and Ronald L. Akers. 1966. "A Differential Association-Reinforcement Theory of Criminal Behavior." *Social Problems* 14(2):128–47.

Burt, Ronald S. 1998. "The Gender of Social Capital." *Rationality and Society* 10(1):5–46.

———. 2005. *Brokerage and Closure: An Introduction to Social Capital*. New York: Oxford University Press.

Campana, Paulo. 2016. "The Structure of Human Trafficking: Lifting the Bonnet on a Nigerian Transnational Network." *British Journal of Criminology* 56(1):68–86.

Charette, Yanick, and Andrew V. Papachristos. 2017. "The Network Dynamics of Co-Offending Careers." *Social Networks* 51:3–13.

Clement, Elizabeth Alice. 2006. *Love for Sale: Courting, Treating, and Prostitution in New York City, 1900–1945*. Chapel Hill: University of North Carolina Press.

Cohen, Andrew W. 2003. "The Racketeer's Progress: Commerce, Crime, and the Law in Chicago, 1900–1940." *Journal of Urban History* 29(5):575–96.

Coleman, James S. 1988. "Social Capital in the Creation of Human Capital." *American Journal of Sociology* 94:S95–S120.

Collins, Randall. 2011. "Patrimonial Alliances and Failures of State Penetration: A Historical Dynamic of Crime, Corruption, Gangs, and Mafias." *Annals of the American Academy of Political and Social Science* 636(1):16–31.

Common Council. 1837. *The Laws and Ordinances of the City of Chicago: Passed in Common Council*. Chicago: Office of the Chicago Democrat. https://babel.hathitrust.org/cgi/pt?id=uiuo.ark:/13960/t63498t9k;view =image;seq=11.

Contreras, Randol. 2009. "'Damn, Yo—Who's That Girl?': An Ethnographic Analysis of Masculinity in Drug Robberies." *Journal of Contemporary Ethnography* 38(4):465–92.

———. 2013. *The Stickup Kids: Race, Drugs, Violence, and the American Dream*. Berkeley: University of California Press.

Cressey, Paul G. 1932. *The Taxi-Dance Hall: A Sociological Study in Commercialized Recreation and City Life*. Chicago: University of Chicago Press.

Cullen, Francis T., Pamela Wilcox, Jennifer L. Lux, and Cheryl Lero Jonson, eds. 2015. *Sisters in Crime Revisited: Bringing Gender into Criminology in Honor of Freda Adler*. New York: Oxford University Press.

Daly, Kathleen, and Meda Chesney-Lind. 1988. "Feminism and Criminology." *Justice Quarterly* 5(4):497–538.

Dank, Meredith, and Matthew Johnson. 2014. *The Hustle: Economics of the Underground Commercial Sex Industry*. Washington, DC: Urban Institute.

De Coster, Stacy, Karen Heimer, and Samantha R. Cumley. 2013. "Gender and Theories of Delinquency." Pp. 313–30 in *The Oxford Handbook of Criminological Theory*, edited by F.T. Cullen, and P. Wilcox. New York: Oxford University Press.

Decker, Scott H., Paul G. Lewis, Doris M. Provine, and Monica W. Varsanyi. 2009. "On the Frontier of Local Law Enforcement: Local Police and Federal Immigration Law." Pp. 261–76 in *Immigration, Crime and Justice*, vol. 13, edited by W. F. McDonald. Bingley, UK: Emerald Group Publishing Limited.

Decker, Scott H., and Barrik Van Winkle. 1996. *Life in the Gang: Family, Friends, and Violence*. New York: Cambridge University Press.

D'Emilio, John, and Estelle B. Freedman. (1988) 1997. *Intimate Matters: A History of Sexuality in America*. 2nd ed. Chicago: University of Chicago Press.

Diffee, Christopher. 2005. "Sex and the City: The White Slavery Scare and Social Governance in the Progressive Era." *American Quarterly* 57(2):411–37.

Dino, Alessandra. 2007. "Symbolic Domination and Active Power: Female Roles in Criminal Organizations." Pp. 67–86 in *Women and the Mafia: Female Roles in Organized Crime Structures*, edited by G. Fiandaca. New York: Springer.

Donovan, Frances. 1920. *The Woman Who Waits*. Boston: Gorham Press.

Drake, St. Clair, and Horace R. Cayton. (1945) 1962. *Black Metropolis: A Study of Negro Life in a Northern City*. New York: Harcourt, Brace & World.

Eig, Jonathan. 2010. *Get Capone: The Secret Plot That Captured America's Most Wanted Gangster*. New York: Simon & Schuster.

Erenberg, Lewis A. 1981. *Stepping' Out: New York Nightlife and the Transformation of American Culture, 1890–1930*. Chicago: University of Chicago Press.

Faris, Robert, and Diane Felmlee. 2011. "Status Struggles: Network Centrality and Gender Segregation in Same- and Cross-Gender Aggression." *American Sociological Review* 76(1):48–73.

Federal Bureau of Prisons. 2018. "Inmate Statistics: Inmate Gender." Washington, DC: US Department of Justice. www.bop.gov/about/statistics /statistics_inmate_gender.jsp.

Feeley, Malcolm M., and Deborah L. Little. 1991. "The Vanishing Female: The Decline of Women in the Criminal Process, 1687–1912." *Law & Society Review* 25(4):719–58.

Felson, Marcus. 2003. "The Process of Co-Offending." Pp. 149–67 in *Theory for Practice in Situational Crime Prevention*, vol. 16, edited by M. J. Smith and D. B. Cornish. Monsey, NY: Criminal Justice Press.

———. 2006. "The Ecosystem for Organized Crime." Paper presented at the HEUNI 25th Anniversary Lecture, Helsinki, Finland. www.heuni.fi /material/attachments/heuni/papers/6Ktmwqur9/HEUNI_papers_26.pdf.

Flanagan, Maureen A. 2002. *Seeing with Their Hearts: The Vision of the Good City, 1871–1933*. Princeton, NJ: Princeton University Press.

Fligstein, Neil. 1996. "Markets as Politics: A Political-Cultural Approach to Market Institutions." *American Sociological Review* 61(4):656–73.

Fronc, Jennifer. 2006. "The Horns of the Dilemma: Race Mixing and the Enforcement of Jim Crow in New York City." *Journal of Urban History* 33(1):3–25.

—. 2009. *New York Undercover: Private Surveillance in the Progressive Era.* Chicago: University of Chicago Press.

Gambetta, Diego. 1993. *The Sicilian Mafia: The Business of Private Protection.* Cambridge, MA: Harvard University Press.

Giancana, Antoinette, and Thomas C. Renner. 1984. *Mafia Princess: Growing up in Sam Giancana's Family.* New York: William Morrow and Company.

Gilfoyle, Timothy J. 1992. *City of Eros: New York City, Prostitution, and the Commercialization of Sex, 1790–1920.* New York: W. W. Norton & Company.

Giordano, Peggy C., Jill A. Deines, and Stephen A. Cernkovich. 2006. "In and Out of Crime: A Life Course Perspective on Girls' Delinquency." Pp. 17–40 in *Gender and Crime: Patterns in Victimization and Offending,* edited by K. Heimer, and C. Kruttschnitt. New York: New York University Press.

Gleeson, William. 1915. *Can Such Things Be? A Story of a White Slave.* Chicago: Holland Press.

Goffman, Alice. 2009. "On the Run: Wanted Men in a Philadelphia Ghetto." *American Sociological Review* 74(3):339–57.

Grattet, Ryken, and Valerie Jenness. 2005. "The Reconstitution of Law in Local Settings: Agency Discretion, Ambiguity, and a Surplus of Law in the Policing of Hate Crime." *Law & Society Review* 39(4):893–941.

Griswold, Robert L. 1993. *Fatherhood in America: A History.* New York: Basic Books.

Haller, Mark H. 1970. "Urban Crime and Criminal Justice: The Chicago Case." *Journal of American History* 57(3):619–35.

—. 1971. "Organized Crime in Urban History: Chicago in the Twentieth Century." *Journal of Social History* 5(2):210–34.

—. 1976. "Historical Roots of Police Behavior: Chicago, 1890–1925." *Law & Society Review* 10(2):303–23.

—. 1990. "Illegal Enterprise: A Theoretical and Historical Interpretation." *Criminology* 28(2):207–35.

Harland, Robert O. 1912. *The Vice Bondage of a Great City.* Chicago: Young People's Civic League.

Harrison, Carter H. 1935. *Stormy Years: The Autobiography of Carter H. Harrison, Five Times Mayor of Chicago.* New York: Bobbs-Merrill Company.

Haynie, Dana L. 2001. "Delinquent Peers Revisited: Does Network Structure Matter?" *American Journal of Sociology* 106(4):1013–57.

Haynie, Dana L., Nathan J. Doogan, and Brian Soller. 2014. "Gender, Friendship Networks, and Delinquency: A Dynamic Network Approach." *Criminology* 52(4):688–722.

Haynie, Dana L., Peggy C. Giordano, Wendy D. Manning, and Monica A. Longmore. 2005. "Adolescent Romantic Relationships and Delinquency Involvement." *Criminology* 43(1):177–210.

Haynie, Dana L., and Derek A. Kreager. 2013. "Peer Networks and Crime." Pp. 257–73 in *Oxford Handbook of Criminological Theory,* edited by F. T. Cullen, and P. Wilcox. New York: Oxford University Press.

Heap, Chad. 2009. *Slumming: Sexual and Racial Encounters in American Nightlife, 1885–1940*. Chicago: University of Chicago Press.

Heckathorn, Douglas D. 1997. "Respondent-Driven Sampling: A New Approach to the Study of Hidden Populations." *Social Problems* 44(2):174–99.

Holub, Rona L. 2007. "Fredericka 'Marm' Mandelbaum, 'Queen of Fences': The Rise and Fall of a Female Immigrant Criminal Entrepreneur in Nineteenth-Century New York City." PhD diss., Department of History, Columbia University.

Howell, Martha, and Walter Prevenier. 2001. *From Reliable Sources: An Introduction to Historical Methods*. Ithaca, NY: Cornell University Press.

Hughes, Donna M. 2000. "The 'Natasha' Trade: The Transnational Shadow Market of Trafficking in Women." *Journal of International Affairs* 53(2):625–51.

Ianni, Francis A. J., and Elizabeth Reuss-Ianni. 1972. *A Family Business: Kinship and Social Control in Organized Crime*. New York: Russell Sage Foundation.

Ingrasci, Ombretta. 2007. "Women in the 'Ndrangheta: The Serraino-Di Giovine Case." Pp. 47–52 in *Women and the Mafia: Female Roles in Organized Crime Structures*, edited by G. Fiandaca. New York: Springer.

Jacobs, Bruce A., and Jody Miller. 1998. "Crack Dealing, Gender, and Arrest Avoidance." *Social Problems* 45(4):550–69.

Jamieson, Egbert, and Francis Adams. 1881. *The Municipal Code of Chicago: Comprising the Laws of Illinois Relating to the City of Chicago, and the Ordinances of the City Council; Codified and Revised*. Chicago: Beach, Barnard & Co., Legal Printers. https://babel.hathitrust.org/cgi/pt?id=uc2 .ark:/13960/t1sf3060h;view=1up;seq=5.

Joslyn, Waite R. 1920. *Criminal Law and Statutory Penalties of Illinois: A Compilation of the Statutes and Decisions as to Crimes and Offenses, in the State of Illinois*. Chicago: T. H. Flood & Co.

Kadushin, Charles. 2005. "Who Benefits from Network Analysis: Ethics of Social Network Research." *Social Networks* 27(2):139–53.

———. 2012. *Understanding Social Networks: Theories, Concepts, and Findings*. New York: Oxford University Press.

Kalev, Alexandra. 2009. "Cracking the Glass Cages? Restructuring and Ascriptive Inequality at Work." *American Journal of Sociology* 114(6):1591–1643.

Katz, Jack. 1990. *Seductions of Crime: Moral and Sensual Attractions in Doing Evil*. New York: Basic Books.

Keire, Mara L. 2001. "The Vice Trust: A Reinterpretation of the White Slavery Scare in the United States, 1907–1917." *Journal of Social History* 35(1):5–41.

Kleemans, Edward R., Edwin W. Kruisbergen, and Ruud F. Kouwenberg. 2014. "Women, Brokerage and Transnational Organized Crime. Empirical Results from the Dutch Organized Crime Monitor." *Trends in Organized Crime* 17(1–2):16–30.

Klein, Dorie. 1973. "The Etiology of Female Crime: A Review of the Literature." *Issues in Criminology* 8(2):3–30.

Koons-Witt, Barbara A., and Pamela J. Schram. 2003. "The Prevalence and Nature of Violent Offending by Females." *Journal of Criminal Justice* 31(4):361–71.

Kreager, Derek A., Kelly Rulison, and James Moody. 2011. "Delinquency and the Structure of Adolescent Peer Groups." *Criminology* 49(1):95–127.

Landesco, John. (1929) 1968. *Organized Crime in Chicago*. Chicago: University of Chicago Press.

———. 1932. "Crime and the Failure of Institutions in Chicago's Immigrant Areas." *Journal of Criminal Law and Criminology* 23(2):238–48.

———. 1936. "The Woman and the Underworld." *Journal of Criminal Law and Criminology* 26:891–902.

Langum, David J. 2006. *Crossing over the Line: Legislating Morality and the Mann Act*. Chicago: University of Chicago Press.

Lauritsen, Janet L., Karen Heimer, and James P. Lynch. 2009. "Trends in the Gender Gap in Violent Offending: New Evidence from the National Crime Victimization Survey." *Criminology* 47(2):361–99.

Le Sueur, Meridel. (1978) 2006. *The Girl*. 2nd ed. Albuquerque, NM: West End Press.

Lerner, Michael A. 2007. *Dry Manhattan: Prohibition in New York City*. Cambridge, MA: Harvard University Press.

Leverentz, Andrea M. 2006. "The Love of a Good Man? Romantic Relationships as a Source of Support or Hindrance for Female Ex-Offenders." *Journal of Research in Crime and Delinquency* 43(4):459–88.

———. 2014. *The Ex-Prisoner's Dilemma: How Women Negotiate Competing Narratives of Reentry and Desistance*. New Brunswick, NJ: Rutgers University Press.

Lewis, Paul G., Doris Marie Provine, Monica W. Varsanyi, and Scott H. Decker. 2012. "Why Do (Some) City Police Departments Enforce Federal Immigration Law? Political, Demographic, and Organizational Influences on Local Choices." *Journal of Public Administration Research and Theory* 23(1):1–25.

Lin, Nan. 2001. *Social Capital: A Theory of Social Structure and Action*. New York: Cambridge University Press.

Linehan, Mary. 2017. "Prostitution in the US: Chicago." Pp. 386–413 in *Selling Sex in the City: A Global History of Prostitution, 1600s–2000s*, edited by M. Rodriguez Garcia, L. Heerma van Voss, and E. van Nederveen Meerkerk. Leiden, The Netherlands: Brill.

Lombardo, Robert M. 2013. *Organized Crime in Chicago: Beyond the Mafia*. Champaign: University of Illinois Press.

Lombroso, Cesare, and Guglielmo Ferrero. (1893) 2004. *Criminal Woman, the Prostitute, and the Normal Woman*. Translated by N.H. Rafter and M. Gibson. Durham, NC: Duke University Press.

Maher, Lisa. 1997. *Sexed Work: Gender, Race, and Resistance in a Brooklyn Drug Market*. New York: Oxford University Press.

Maher, Lisa, and Susan L. Hudson. 2007. "Women in the Drug Economy: A Metasynthesis of the Qualitative Literature." *Journal of Drug Issues* 37(4):805–26.

Mancuso, Marina. 2014. "Not All Madams Have a Central Role: Analysis of a Nigerian Sex Trafficking Network." *Trends in Organized Crime* 17(1):66–88.

Marsden, Peter V. 1990. "Network Data and Measurement." *Annual Review of Sociology* 16:435–63.

Massari, Monica, and Cataldo Motta. 2007. "Women in the Sacra Corona Unita." Pp. 53–66 in *Women and the Mafia: Female Roles in Organized Crime Structures*, edited by G. Fiandaca. New York: Springer.

May, David C., Nicole E. Rader, and Sarah Goodrum. 2010. "A Gendered Assessment of the 'Threat of Victimization': Examining Gender Differences in Fear of Crime, Perceived Risk, Avoidance, and Defensive Behaviors." *Criminal Justice Review* 35(2):159–82.

McCammon, Holly J., Karen E. Campbell, Ellen M. Granberg, and Christine Mowery. 2001. "How Movements Win: Gendered Opportunity Structures and U.S. Women's Suffrage Movements, 1866 to 1919." *American Sociological Review* 66(1):49–70.

McCarthy, Bill, and Teresa Casey. 2008. "Love, Sex, and Crime: Adolescent Romantic Relationships and Offending." *American Sociological Review* 73(6):944–69.

McCarthy, Bill, Diane Felmlee, and John Hagan. 2004. "Girl Friends Are Better: Gender, Friends, and Crime among School and Street Youth." *Criminology* 42(4):805–36.

McCarthy, Bill, and John Hagan. 1995. "Getting into Street Crime: The Structure and Process of Criminal Embeddedness." *Social Science Research* 24(1):63–95.

McCarthy, Bill, John Hagan, and Lawrence E. Cohen. 1998. "Uncertainty, Cooperation, and Crime: Understanding the Decision to Co-Offend." *Social Forces* 77(1):155–84.

McDonald, Steve, and Richard A. Benton. 2017. "The Structure of Internal Job Mobility and Organizational Wage Inequality." *Research in Social Stratification and Mobility* 47:21–31.

McGirr, Lisa. 2016. *The War on Alcohol: Prohibition and the Rise of the American State*. New York: W.W. Norton & Company.

McGloin, Jean Marie, and Holly Nguyen. 2012. "It Was My Idea: Considering the Instigation of Co-Offending." *Criminology* 50(2):463–94.

McPherson, Miller, and Lynn Smith-Lovin. 1987. "Homophily in Voluntary Organizations: Status Distance and the Composition of Face-to-Face Groups." *American Sociological Review* 52(3):370–79.

McPherson, Miller, Lynn Smith-Lovin, and James M. Cook. 2001. "Birds of a Feather: Homophily in Social Networks." *Annual Review of Sociology* 27(1):415–44.

Meacham, Sarah Hand. 2009. *Every Home a Distillery: Alcohol, Gender, and Technology in the Colonial Chesapeake*. Baltimore, MD: Johns Hopkins University Press.

Messerschmidt, James W. 1993. *Masculinities and Crime: Critique and Reconceptualization of Theory*. Lanham, MD: Rowman & Littlefield Publishers.

Meyerowitz, Joanne J. 1988. *Women Adrift: Independent Wage Earners in Chicago, 1880–1930*. Chicago: University of Chicago Press.

Miller, Jody. 1998. "Up It Up: Gender and the Accomplishment of Street Robbery." *Criminology* 36(1):37–66.

———. 2014. "Doing Crime as Doing Gender? Masculinities, Femininities, and Crime." Pp. 19–39 in *The Oxford Handbook of Gender, Sex, and Crime*, edited by R. Gartner, and B. McCarthy. New York: Oxford University Press.

Miller, Wilbur R. 1991. *Revenuers and Moonshiners: Enforcing Federal Liquor Law in the Mountain South, 1865–1900*. Chapel Hill: University of North Carolina Press.

Mitrani, Sam. 2013. *The Rise of the Chicago Police Department: Class and Conflict, 1850–1894*. Urbana: University of Illinois Press.

Monkkonen, Eric H. 2003. "Homicide in New York, Los Angeles, and Chicago." *Journal of Criminal Law and Criminology* 92(3–4):809–42.

Morselli, Carlo, Masarah Paquet-Clouston, and Chloe Provost. 2017. "The Independent's Edge in an Illegal Drug Distribution Setting: Levitt and Venkatesh Revisited." *Social Networks* 51:118–26.

Morselli, Carlo, and Julie Roy. 2008. "Brokerage Qualifications in Ringing Operations." *Criminology* 46(1):71–98.

Morselli, Carlo, and Isa Savoie-Gargiso. 2014. "Coercion, Control, and Cooperation in a Prostitution Ring." *Annals of the American Academy of Political and Social Science* 653:247–65.

Morselli, Carlo, Pierre Tremblay, and Bill McCarthy. 2006. "Mentors and Criminal Achievement." *Criminology* 44(1):17–43.

Moseley, Eva. 1973. "Women in Archives: Documenting the History of Women in America." *American Archivist* 36(2):215–22.

Mullins, Christopher W., and Richard T. Wright. 2003. "Gender, Social Networks, and Residential Burglary." *Criminology* 41(3):813–40.

Murphy, Alexandra K., and Sudhir Alladi Venkatesh. 2006. "Vice Careers: The Changing Contours of Sex Work in New York City." *Qualitative Sociology* 29(2):129–54.

Murphy, Mary. 1994. "Bootlegging Mothers and Drinking Daughters: Gender and Prohibition in Butte, Montana." *American Quarterly* 46(2):174–94.

Nguyen, Holly, and Jean Marie McGloin. 2013. "Does Economic Adversity Breed Criminal Cooperation? Considering the Motivation Behind Group Crime." *Criminology* 51(4):833–70.

Nguyen, Holly, and Peter Reuter. 2012. "How Risky Is Marijuana Possession? Considering the Role of Age, Race, and Gender." *Crime & Delinquency* 58(6):879–910.

Nicoll, Ione. 1930. "Should Women Vote Wet?" *North American Review* 229(5):561–65.

Nora, Pierre. 1989. "Between Memory and History: Les Lieux De Memoire." *Representations* 26:7–24.

Oselin, Sharon S. 2014. *Leaving Prostitution: Getting out and Staying out of Sex Work*. New York: New York University Press.

Owens, Emily G. 2011. "Are Underground Markets Really More Violent? Evidence from Early 20th Century America." *American Law and Economics Review* 13(1):1–44.

———. 2014. "The American Temperance Movement and Market-Based Violence." *American Law and Economics Review* 16(2):433–72.

Padgett, John F., and Christopher K. Ansell. 1993. "Robust Action and the Rise of the Medici, 1400–1434." *American Journal of Sociology* 98(6):1259–1319.

Paoli, Letizia. 2002. "The Paradoxes of Organized Crime." *Crime, Law & Social Change* 37(1):51–97.

Paoli, Letizia, and Tom Vander Beken. 2014. "Organized Crime: A Contested Concept." Pp. 13–31 in *Oxford Handbook of Organized Crime*, edited by L. Paoli. New York: Oxford University Press.

Papachristos, Andrew V. 2013. "48 Years of Crime in Chicago: A Descriptive Analysis of Serious Crime Trends from 1965 to 2013." ISPS Working Paper. Institution for Social and Policy Studies, Yale University.

Papachristos, Andrew V., David M. Hureau, and Anthony A. Braga. 2013. "The Corner and the Crew: The Influence of Geography and Social Networks on Gang Violence." *American Sociological Review* 78(3):417–47.

Papachristos, Andrew V., and Chris M. Smith. 2014. "The Embedded and Multiplex Nature of Al Capone." Pp. 97–115 in *Crime and Networks*, edited by C. Morselli. New York: Routledge.

Papachristos, Andrew V., and Christopher Wildeman. 2014. "Network Exposure and Homicide Victimization in an African American Community." *American Journal of Public Health* 104(1):143–50.

Peterson, Dana, Jody Miller, and Finn-Aage Esbensen. 2001. "The Impact of Sex Composition on Gangs and Gang Member Delinquency." *Criminology* 39(2):411–39.

Pizzini-Gambetta, Valeria. 2014. "Organised Crime: The Gender Constraints of Illegal Markets." Pp. 448–67 in *The Oxford Handbook of Sex, Gender and Crime*, edited by R. Gartner, and B. McCarthy. Oxford: Oxford University Press.

Pliley, Jessica R. 2014. *Policing Sexuality: The Mann Act and the Making of the FBI*. Cambridge, MA: Harvard University Press.

Radaev, Vadim. 2017. "A Crooked Mirror: The Evolution of Illegal Alcohol Markets in Russia since the Late Socialist Period." Pp. 218–41 in *The Architecture of Illegal Markets: Towards an Economic Sociology of Illegality in the Economy*, edited by J. Beckert, and M. Dewey. New York: Oxford University Press.

Rao, Hayagreeva, Philippe Monin, and Rodolphe Durand. 2003. "Institutional Change in Toque Ville: Nouvelle Cuisine as an Identity Movement in French Gastronomy." *American Journal of Sociology* 108(4):795–843.

Raymond, Janice G. 2004. "Ten Reasons for Not Legalizing Prostitution and a Legal Response to the Demand for Prostitution." *Journal of Trauma Practice* 2(3–4):315–32.

Reckless, Walter C. 1933. *Vice in Chicago*. Chicago: University of Chicago Press.

Reiss, Albert J. 1988. "Co-Offending and Criminal Careers." Pp. 117–70 in *Crime and Justice: A Review of Research*, vol. 10, edited by M. Tonry, and N. Morris. Chicago: University of Chicago Press.

Reuter, Peter. 1983. *Disorganized Crime: The Economics of the Visible Hand*. Cambridge: Massachusetts Institute of Technology Press.

Rosen, Eva, and Sudhir Alladi Venkatesh. 2008. "A 'Perversion' of Choice: Sex Work Offers Just Enough in Chicago's Urban Ghetto." *Journal of Contemporary Ethnography* 37(4):417–41.

Rosen, Ruth. 1982. *The Lost Sisterhood: Prostitution in America, 1900–1918*. Baltimore, MD: Johns Hopkins University Press.

Russo, Gus. 2001. *The Outfit: The Role of Chicago's Underworld in the Shaping of Modern America*. New York: Bloomsbury.

Ruth, David E. 1996. *Inventing the Public Enemy: The Gangster in American Culture, 1918–1934*. Chicago: University of Chicago Press.

Schmidt, John R. 2013. "William E. Dever: A Chicago Political Fable." Pp. 82–98 in *The Mayors: The Chicago Political Tradition*. 4th ed. Edited by P. M. Green and M. G. Holli. Carbondale: Southern Illinois University Press.

Schwartz, Jennifer, Meredith Conover-Williams, and Katie Clemons. 2015. "Thirty Years of Sex Stratification in Violent Crime Partnerships and Groups." *Feminist Criminology* 10(1):60–91.

Schwartz, Joan M., and Terry Cook. 2002. "Archives, Records, and Power: The Making of Modern Memory." *Archival Science* 2(1–2):1–19.

Scott, John. 2017. *Social Network Analysis*. 4th ed. Thousand Oaks, CA: Sage.

Shaw, Clifford R. 1938. *Brothers in Crime*. Chicago: University of Chicago Press.

Siebert, Renate. 1996. *Secrets of Life and Death: Women and the Mafia*. Translated by L. Heron. New York: Verso.

———. 2007. "Mafia Women: The Affirmation of a Female Pseudo-Subject; The Case of the 'Ndrangheta." Pp. 19–45 in *Women and the Mafia: Female Roles in Organized Crime Structures*, edited by G. Fiandaca. New York: Springer.

Siegel, Dina, and Sylvia de Blank. 2010. "Women Who Traffic Women: The Role of Women in Human Trafficking Networks—Dutch Cases." *Global Crime* 11(4):436–47.

Small, Mario Luis. 2009. *Unanticipated Gains: Origins of Network Inequality in Everyday Life*. New York: Oxford University Press.

Smith, Chris M., and Andrew V. Papachristos. 2016. "Trust Thy Crooked Neighbor: Multiplexity in Chicago Organized Crime Networks." *American Sociological Review* 81(4):644–67.

Smith-Doerr, Laurel. 2004. *Women's Work: Gender Equality vs. Hierarchy in the Life Sciences*. Boulder, CO: Lynne Rienner Publishers.

Spilerman, Seymour, and Guy Stecklov. 2009. "Societal Responses to Terrorist Attacks." *Annual Review of Sociology* 35:167–89.

Starr, Merritt, and Russell Hurd Curtis. 1885. *Annotated Statutes of the State of Illinois in Force January 1, 1885*. Chicago: Callaghan and Company.

Stead, William T. 1894. *If Christ Came to Chicago!* Chicago: Laird & Lee Publishers.

Steffensmeier, Darrell J. 1983. "Organization Properties and Sex-Segregation in the Underworld: Building a Sociological Theory of Sex Differences in Crime." *Social Forces* 61(4):1010–32.

Steffensmeier, Darrell J., and Emilie Allan. 1996. "Gender and Crime: Toward a Gendered Theory of Female Offending." *Annual Review of Sociology* 22:459–87.

Steffensmeier, Darrell J., Jennifer Schwartz, and Michael Roche. 2013. "Gender and Twenty-First-Century Corporate Crime: Female Involvement and the Gender Gap in Enron-Era Corporate Frauds." *American Sociological Review* 78(3):448–76.

Steffensmeier, Darrell J., and Robert M. Terry. 1986. "Institutional Sexism in the Underworld: A View from the Inside." *Sociological Inquiry* 56(3):304–23.

Stovel, Katherine, and Lynette Shaw. 2012. "Brokerage." *Annual Review of Sociology* 38:139–58.

Sutherland, Edwin H. 1947. *Principles of Criminology.* 4th ed. Chicago: J. B. Lippincott.

Tilly, Charles. 1998. *Durable Inequality.* Berkeley: University of California Press.

Tolman, Edgar Bronson. 1905. *The Revised Municipal Code of Chicago of 1905.* Chicago: The Lawyers' Co-operative Publishing Company.

Tomaskovic-Devey, Donald. 2014. "The Relational Generation of Workplace Inequalities." *Social Currents* 1(1):51–73.

Tomaskovic-Devey, Donald, and Dustin Avent-Holt. 2019. *Relational Inequalities: An Organizational Approach.* New York: Oxford University Press.

Tomaskovic-Devey, Donald, and Sheryl Skaggs. 2002. "Sex Segregation, Labor Process Organization, and Gender Earnings Inequality." *American Journal of Sociology* 108(1):102–28.

Tremblay, Pierre. 1993. "Searching for Suitable Co-Offenders." Pp. 17–36 in *Routine Activity and Rational Choice: Advances in Criminological Theory,* vol. 5, edited by R. V. Clarke and M. Felson. New Brunswick, NJ: Transaction Publishers.

Trout, Grace Wilbur. 1920. "Side Lights on Illinois Suffrage History." *Journal of the Illinois State Historical Society* 13(2):145–79.

Turner-Zimmerman, Jean. 1911. *Chicago's Black Traffic in White Girls.* Chicago: Chicago Rescue Mission.

Venkatesh, Sudhir Alladi. 2006. *Off the Books: The Underground Economy of the Urban Poor.* Cambridge, MA: Harvard University Press.

———. 2013. *Floating City: A Rogue Sociologist Lost and Found in New York's Underground Economy.* New York: The Penguin Press.

von Lampe, Klaus. 2001. "Not a Process of Enlightenment: The Conceptual History of Organized Crime in Germany and the United States of America." *Forum on Crime and Society* 1(2):99–116.

———. 2014. "Definitions of Organized Crime." www.organized-crime.de /organizedcrimedefinitions.htm.

———. 2016. *Organized Crime: Analyzing Illegal Activities, Criminal Structures, and Extra-Legal Governance*. Thousand Oaks, CA: Sage.

Voss-Hubbard, Anke. 1995. "'No Document—No History': Marry Ritter Beard and the Early History of Women's Archives." *American Archivist* 58(1):16–30.

Wasserman, Stanley, and Katherine Faust. 1994. *Social Network Analysis: Methods and Applications*. New York: Cambridge University Press.

Watters, John K., and Patrick Biernacki. 1989. "Targeted Sampling: Options for the Study of Hidden Populations." *Social Problems* 36(4):416–30.

Weitzer, Ronald. 2009. "Sociology of Sex Work." *Annual Review of Sociology* 35:213–34.

Wellman, Barry. 1983. "Network Analysis: Some Basic Principles." *Sociological Theory* 1:155–200.

West, Candace, and Don H. Zimmerman. 1987. "Doing Gender." *Gender & Society* 1(2):125–51.

Willebrandt, Mabel Walker. 1929. *The Inside of Prohibition*. Indianapolis, IN: Bobbs-Merrill Company.

Willrich, Michael. 2003. "'Close That Place of Hell': Poor Women and the Cultural Politics of Prohibition." *Journal of Urban History* 29(5):555–74.

Wright, Richard T., Scott H. Decker, Allison K. Redfern, and Dietrich L. Smith. 1992. "A Snowball's Chance in Hell: Doing Field Research with Residential Burglars." *Journal of Research in Crime and Delinquency* 29(2):148–61.

Yang, Song, Franziska B. Keller, and Lu Zheng. 2017. *Social Network Analysis: Methods and Examples*. Thousand Oaks, CA: Sage.

Young, Jacob T. N. 2011. "How Do They 'End Up Together'? A Social Network Analysis of Self-Control, Homophily, and Adolescent Relationships." *Journal of Quantitative Criminology* 27(3):251–73.

Young, Jacob T. N., Cesar J. Rebellon, J. C. Barnes, and Frank M. Weerman. 2014. "Unpacking the Black Box of Peer Similarity in Deviance: Understanding the Mechanisms Linking Personal Behavior, Peer Behavior, and Perceptions." *Criminology* 52(1):60–86.

Zhang, Sheldon X. 2011. "Woman Pullers: Pimping and Sex Trafficking in a Mexican Border City." *Crime, Law and Social Change* 56(5):509–28.

———. 2014. "Snakeheads and the Cartwheel Network: Functional Fluidity as Opposed to Structural Flexibility." Pp. 116–30 in *Crime and Networks*, edited by C. Morselli. New York: Routledge.

Zhang, Sheldon X., Ko-lin Chin, and Jody Miller. 2007. "Women's Participation in Chinese Transnational Human Smuggling: A Gendered Market Perspective." *Criminology* 45(3):699–733.

Zimmerman, Gregory M., and Steven F. Messner. 2010. "Neighborhood Context and the Gender Gap in Adolescent Violent Crime." *American Sociological Review* 75(6):958–80.

# Index